First World War
and Army of Occupation
War Diary
France, Belgium and Germany

7 DIVISION
20 Infantry Brigade
Headquarters
3 March 1914 - 30 April 1915

WO95/1650

The Naval & Military Press Ltd
www.nmarchive.com
Published in association with The National Archives

Published by

The Naval & Military Press Ltd

Unit 10 Ridgewood Industrial Park,

Uckfield, East Sussex,

TN22 5QE England

Tel: +44 (0) 1825 749494

www.naval-military-press.com

www.nmarchive.com

This diary has been reprinted in facsimile from the original. Any imperfections are inevitably reproduced and the quality may fall short of modern type and cartographic standards.

© **Crown Copyright**
Images reproduced by permission of The National Archives, London, England, 2015.

Contents

Document type	Place/Title	Date From	Date To
Heading	7th Division 20th Infy Bde Bde Headquarters. 1914 Oct-1915 Apr		
Heading	7th Division. Brigade Landed At Zeebrugge 7th October 1914. B.H.Q. 20th Infantry Brigade October 1914		
War Diary	Zeebrugge	07/10/1914	07/10/1914
War Diary	Bruges	07/10/1914	07/10/1914
War Diary	Zeebrugge	08/10/1914	08/10/1914
War Diary	Westkerke	08/10/1914	08/10/1914
War Diary	Steene	09/10/1914	09/10/1914
War Diary	Ostend	09/10/1914	09/10/1914
War Diary	Ghent	10/10/1914	10/10/1914
War Diary	Environs Of Ghent.	10/10/1914	11/10/1914
War Diary	Somergem	12/10/1914	12/10/1914
War Diary	Thielt.	12/10/1914	13/10/1914
War Diary	Pithem	13/10/1914	13/10/1914
War Diary	Roulers	13/10/1914	13/10/1914
War Diary	Ypres	14/10/1914	15/10/1914
War Diary	Zandvoorde	16/10/1914	17/10/1914
War Diary	Kruiseik	18/10/1914	26/10/1914
War Diary	Basseville	27/10/1914	28/10/1914
War Diary	Gheluvelt	28/10/1914	28/10/1914
War Diary	Veldhoek	29/10/1914	29/10/1914
War Diary	Zandvoorde	30/10/1914	31/10/1914
War Diary	Chateau-Heronthal	31/10/1914	31/10/1914
Miscellaneous	The 20th Infantry Brigade (Guards) Of The 7th Division.		
Heading	B.H.Q. 20th Infantry Brigade November 1914		
War Diary	Chateau Heronthal	01/11/1914	29/11/1914
War Diary		30/11/1914	30/11/1914
Miscellaneous	Report By Capt E.L. Speirs.	30/11/1914	30/11/1914
Heading	B.H.Q. 20th Infantry Brigade December 1914		
War Diary	Headquarters, 20th Infantry Brigade.	01/12/1914	31/12/1914
Miscellaneous	20th Infy Bde.	12/12/1914	12/12/1914
Miscellaneous	20th Infantry Brigade.		
Miscellaneous	W20th Infantry Brigade 1st Battalion Grenadier Guards.		
Miscellaneous	2nd Battalion Border Regiment.		
Miscellaneous	2nd Battalion Cordon Highlanders		
Miscellaneous	Addendum "B." French Attack Near St. Menehould.		
Map	Note. Front of Division about S Kilometers		
Miscellaneous	(Translation Of A Gorman Document) VII Corps H.Q., Phalempin. 25-12-14.	25/12/1914	25/12/1914
Map			
Miscellaneous	Notes On Recent German Methods Of Attack.		
Heading	Headquarters. 20th Infantry Brigade. (7th Division) January 1915		
Miscellaneous	On His Majesty's Service		
War Diary		01/01/1915	31/01/1915
Miscellaneous	Appendix		
Miscellaneous	20th Inf. Brigade.	04/01/1915	04/01/1915

Miscellaneous	Notes On the effect of French Artillery Fire, issued by staff of the French 4th Army, January, 2nd, 1915.		
Heading	Headquarters. 20th Infantry Brigade. (7th Division) February 1915		
Miscellaneous	On His Majesty's Service.		
War Diary	Headquarters, 20th Infantry Brigade.	01/02/1915	28/02/1915
Miscellaneous	Appendices.		
Miscellaneous	20th Infantry Brigade.	04/02/1915	04/02/1915
Miscellaneous	The Brigade Major	04/02/1915	04/02/1915
Miscellaneous	The Brigade Major 20th Bde	05/02/1915	05/02/1915
Miscellaneous	2nd Bn Border Regt.		
Miscellaneous	Present Position of Grenade Co and Grenades	04/02/1915	04/02/1915
Miscellaneous	7th Division.	05/02/1915	05/02/1915
Miscellaneous	Some Notes on the French System of Defence in Second and Third Line.	01/02/1915	01/02/1915
Miscellaneous	20th Infantry Brigade.	07/02/1915	07/02/1915
Miscellaneous	20th Infantry Brigade.	10/02/1915	10/02/1915
Miscellaneous	20th Infantry Brigade.	16/02/1915	16/02/1915
Miscellaneous	20th Infantry Brigade 34	19/02/1915	19/02/1915
Miscellaneous	20th Infantry Brigade Tramway Regulations		
Miscellaneous	20th Infantry Brigade. 40	23/02/1915	23/02/1915
Miscellaneous	20th Inf. Brigadier 42	24/02/1915	24/02/1915
Miscellaneous			
Heading	War Diary B.H.Q. 20th Infantry Brigade March 1915		
Miscellaneous	Reports on Operations At Neuve Chapelle		
Heading	20th Infantry Brigade		
Map			
Miscellaneous	Report on the attack of 10th to 14th March, 1915.	10/03/1915	10/03/1915
Miscellaneous	7th Division.	20/03/1915	20/03/1915
Miscellaneous	Amendments to Report on Operations of 20th Brigade 10th-14th instant.	20/03/1915	20/03/1915
Miscellaneous	1st Grenadier Guards		
Miscellaneous	Headquarters IVth Corps.	24/03/1915	24/03/1915
Miscellaneous	Headquarters, 20th Brigade.	21/03/1915	21/03/1915
Miscellaneous	O.C. 1st Bn. Grenadier Guards.	21/03/1915	21/03/1915
Miscellaneous	2nd Scots Guards		
Miscellaneous	Account of recent operations. 2nd Battalion Scots Guards.		
Miscellaneous	2nd Gordon Highlanders		
Miscellaneous	Account of the operations 10th to 14th March, 1915	10/03/1915	10/03/1915
Miscellaneous	6th Gordon Highlanders		
Miscellaneous	Report as to the part taken by 1/6th Gordon Highlanders in Operations from 10th-14th March, 1915.	10/03/1915	10/03/1915
Miscellaneous	2nd Border Regiment		
Miscellaneous	To Headquarters, XXth Brigade.	21/03/1915	21/03/1915
Miscellaneous	Account of Operations 10th to 14th March, 1915	21/03/1915	21/03/1915
Miscellaneous	Headquarters, XXth Brigade.		
Miscellaneous	2nd Bn. Border Regiment.		
Miscellaneous	Reports on Battalions		
Miscellaneous	7th Division. 1st Battalion Grenadier Guards.	19/03/1915	19/03/1915
Miscellaneous	2nd Battalion Gordon Highlanders.		
Miscellaneous	20th Inf. Bde	30/03/1915	30/03/1915
Miscellaneous	Circular Memorandum No. 14	24/03/1915	24/03/1915
Map			
War Diary		03/03/1914	31/03/1914
Miscellaneous	Operation Orders		

Type	Description	Date	Date
Map			
Miscellaneous	Divisional Orders. Sketch of Trenches Common Lane.		
Miscellaneous	20th Infantry Brigade		
Miscellaneous	Operation Orders are to be thoroughly studied, and memorized. Copies are not to be taken into the field. 7th Division Operation Order No. 46	08/03/1915	08/03/1915
Miscellaneous	Officer Commanding	09/03/1915	09/03/1915
Miscellaneous	A Form. Messages And Signals.		
Operation(al) Order(s)	Operation Orders by Brigadier-General F.J. Heyworth. D.S.O. Commanding 20th Infantry Brigade.	09/03/1915	09/03/1915
Miscellaneous	March Table.	09/03/1915	09/03/1915
Operation(al) Order(s)	Supplementary to 7th. Division Operation Order No. 46	08/03/1915	08/03/1915
Miscellaneous	20th Infantry Brigade.		
Miscellaneous	Notes on ground between Neuve chapelle and Lille-La Bassee road from experience gained during fighting in October 1914.		
Miscellaneous	Reconnaisance of County Positions of Artillery		
Miscellaneous	General		
Miscellaneous	20th Infantry Brigade.	08/03/1915	08/03/1915
Miscellaneous	Headquarters. 7th Division.	31/03/1915	31/03/1915
Miscellaneous	20th Infantry Brigade.	22/03/1915	22/03/1915
Miscellaneous	2nd Echelon 4th Corps.	12/03/1915	12/03/1915
Miscellaneous	Head Quarters. 7th Division.	24/03/1915	24/03/1915
Miscellaneous	Circular Memorandum No. 10.		
Miscellaneous	Instructions For Cavalry Officers Who Are Making A Reconnaissance of the German Line.		
Miscellaneous	Memorandum No. 11.		
Miscellaneous	20th Infantry Brigade.	04/03/1915	04/03/1915
Miscellaneous	Not To Be Taken Into The Trenches. Area Occupied By VII German Corps.		
Miscellaneous	Appendix IV.		
Miscellaneous	Appendix V		
Miscellaneous	Appendix VI.		
Miscellaneous	Explanation of Panorama		
Miscellaneous	Intelligence G. 474.	09/03/1915	09/03/1915
Miscellaneous	Information given by a resident of Neuve Chapelle.	09/03/1915	09/03/1915
Miscellaneous	20th Infantry Brigade.	01/03/1915	01/03/1915
Miscellaneous	Instructions for handing over to Canadian Division.	01/03/1915	01/03/1915
Miscellaneous			
War Diary	20th Inf. Bde		
Miscellaneous	Officer Commanding	09/03/1915	09/03/1915
Miscellaneous	Brigade Orders by Brigadier-General F.J. Heyworth. D.S.O. Commanding, 20th Infantry Brigade.	18/03/1915	18/03/1915
Miscellaneous	March Table.	18/03/1915	18/03/1915
Miscellaneous	Hd. Qrs. IV Army No.480 (G).	22/03/1915	22/03/1915
Miscellaneous	Brigade Major	24/03/1915	24/03/1915
Map			
Miscellaneous	Officer Commanding	25/03/1915	25/03/1915
Miscellaneous	Instructions for Artillery support of the defence	28/03/1915	28/03/1915
Miscellaneous	O.C. 5th Group.	29/03/1915	29/03/1915
Miscellaneous	1st Canadian Division.	30/03/1915	30/03/1915
Miscellaneous	Circular Memorandum No. 15.		
Miscellaneous	Circular Memorandum No. 15 T.C. 131.	31/03/1915	31/03/1915
Miscellaneous	20th Infantry Brigade.	30/03/1915	30/03/1915
Miscellaneous	Panorama No. 49		
Miscellaneous	Fauquissart Church		

Miscellaneous			
Miscellaneous	G.O.C. 7 Div.	30/01/1915	30/01/1915
Heading	Headquarters. 20th Infantry Brigade. (7th Division) April 1915		
War Diary		01/04/1915	30/04/1915
Miscellaneous	Divisional Operation Orders.		
Operation(al) Order(s)	7th Division Operation Order No. 1.	20/04/1915	20/04/1915
Operation(al) Order(s)	Operation Order No. 2	20/04/1915	20/04/1915
Operation(al) Order(s)	7th. Division Operation Order No. 3	28/04/1915	28/04/1915
Miscellaneous	Brigade Operation Orders.		
Miscellaneous	Brigade Orders by Brigadier-General F.J. Heyworth. D.S.O.	07/04/1915	07/04/1915
Operation(al) Order(s)	Brigade Orders by Lieutenant-Colonel L.I. Wood. Commanding 20th Infantry Brigade.	10/04/1915	10/04/1915
Operation(al) Order(s)	Brigade Orders By Brigadier-General F.J. Heyworth. D.S.O.	20/04/1915	20/04/1915
Operation(al) Order(s)	Brigade Orders By Brigadier-General F.J. Heyworth. D.S.O.	23/04/1915	23/04/1915
Operation(al) Order(s)	Brigade Orders By Brigadier-General F.J. Heyworth. D.S.O.	27/04/1915	27/04/1915
Map			
Miscellaneous	Brigade Orders by Brigadier-General F.J. Heyworth. D.S.O.	28/04/1915	28/04/1915
Miscellaneous	Brigade Orders By Brigadier-General F.J. Heyworth. D.S.O.	29/04/1915	29/04/1915
Miscellaneous	Brigade Orders by Brigadier-General F.J. Heyworth. D.S.O. Commanding 20th Infantry Brigade.	30/04/1915	30/04/1915
Miscellaneous	Brigade Orders By Brigadier-General F.J. Heyworth. D.S.O. Commanding 20th Infantry Brigade.	01/05/1915	01/05/1915
Miscellaneous	Brigade Orders By Brigadier-General F.J. Heyworth. D.S.O. Commanding 20th Infantry Brigade.	04/05/1915	04/05/1915
Miscellaneous	Appendices.		
Miscellaneous	G.S.		
Map			
Miscellaneous	Circular Memorandum No. 16	24/03/1915	24/03/1915
Miscellaneous	Programme of Training.	08/04/1915	08/04/1915
Miscellaneous	20th Infantry Brigade.	08/04/1915	08/04/1915
Miscellaneous	Headquarters, 7th Division.	08/04/1915	08/04/1915
Miscellaneous	Formation of a Machine Gun Company in an Infantry Brigade.		
Miscellaneous	Brigade Machine Gun Company. War Establishment.		
Miscellaneous	1st Bn Grenadier Guard	09/04/1915	09/04/1915
Miscellaneous	20th. Infantry Brigade.	09/04/1915	09/04/1915
Miscellaneous	Headquarters. 7th Division.	10/04/1915	10/04/1915
Miscellaneous	Headquarters. VIIth Division.	12/04/1915	12/04/1915
Miscellaneous	Projecting Written Messages From A Very Pistol	11/04/1915	11/04/1915
Miscellaneous	Reference 7th Div. Div. No. 7/D/500		
Miscellaneous	Instruction For Escort of Bombers.	12/04/1915	12/04/1915
Miscellaneous	Officer Commanding. 1st Battalion Grenadier Guards.	14/04/1915	14/04/1915
Miscellaneous	Headquarters. 7th Division.	15/04/1915	15/04/1915
Miscellaneous	General Staff 7th Div. 504/G.	11/04/1915	11/04/1915
Miscellaneous	121/Stores/955 (F.W.40.)		
Miscellaneous	7th Division.	10/04/1915	10/04/1915
Miscellaneous	Q.M.G., G.M.Q.No.Q/1606 IVth Corps No. 491.	07/04/1915	07/04/1915
Miscellaneous	General Officer Commanding. 7th Division.	14/04/1915	14/04/1915
Miscellaneous	121/Stores/955. (F.W.40).		

Miscellaneous	Officer's Commanding,	15/04/1915	15/04/1915
Miscellaneous	20th Infantry Brigade.	15/04/1915	15/04/1915
Miscellaneous	1st Army G.S. 137 (G).	08/04/1915	08/04/1915
Miscellaneous	20th Brigade No. 20/271	16/04/1915	16/04/1915
Miscellaneous	G.O.C., 7th Division.	05/04/1915	05/04/1915
Miscellaneous	Use of Rabbit Wire in Crossing Wire entanglements.		
Miscellaneous	Use of Rabbit netting for crossing wire entanglements.	16/04/1915	16/04/1915
Miscellaneous	Officer Commanding, All Battalions.	18/04/1915	18/04/1915
Miscellaneous	Officer Commanding Battalions.	18/04/1915	18/04/1915
Miscellaneous	H.Q. 4th Corps No. 553 (G).	13/04/1915	13/04/1915
Miscellaneous	Programme of Inspections by Commander-in-Chief.		
Miscellaneous	Headquarters. Officers	15/04/1915	15/04/1915
Miscellaneous	Hd. Qrs. 4th. Corps No. 553 (G).	10/04/1915	10/04/1915
Miscellaneous	Inspection of Infantry Brigades of The IVth Corps By The Field-Marshal Commanding-In-Chief.		
Miscellaneous	20th Infantry Brigade.	20/04/1915	20/04/1915
Miscellaneous	Headquarters, Meerut Divn. 19th April, 1915.	19/04/1915	19/04/1915
Miscellaneous	20th Infantry Brigade. 7th Division.	21/04/1915	21/04/1915
Miscellaneous			
Miscellaneous	Special Instructions for the Infantry.		
Miscellaneous	20th. Infantry Brigade.	22/04/1915	22/04/1915
Miscellaneous		22/04/1915	22/04/1915
Miscellaneous	G.O.C. 20th Brigade	10/04/1915	10/04/1915
Miscellaneous	G.O.C. 20th Guards Brigade		
Miscellaneous	To Fire		
Miscellaneous	XXth Brigade	10/04/1915	10/04/1915
Miscellaneous	Headquarters 20th Infantry Brigade.	10/04/1915	10/04/1915
Miscellaneous	Quarters 20th Brigade	11/04/1915	11/04/1915
Miscellaneous	Headquarters 20th Brigade.	13/04/1915	13/04/1915
Miscellaneous			
Miscellaneous	Organisation of Artillery For Defence 7th Division	24/04/1915	24/04/1915
Miscellaneous	Instructions For The Artillery Support Of the Defence.	24/04/1915	24/04/1915
Miscellaneous	Officer Commanding All Battalions.	25/04/1915	25/04/1915
Miscellaneous	Headquarters 20th Infantry Brigade		
Miscellaneous	20th Infantry Brigade.	27/04/1915	27/04/1915
Miscellaneous	20th Infantry Brigade.	29/04/1916	29/04/1916
Miscellaneous	20th Infantry Brigade.	28/04/1915	28/04/1915
Miscellaneous	Officer Commanding All Battalions.	29/04/1915	29/04/1915
Miscellaneous	Works Being Done.		
Miscellaneous	Subject.		

7TH DIVISION
20TH INFY BDE

BDE HEADQUARTERS.
~~OCT 1914 - MAY 1915~~

1914 OCT - 1915 APR

7th Division.

Brigade landed at ZEEBRUGGE 7th October 1914.

B. H. Q.

20th INFANTRY BRIGADE

OCTOBER 1 9 1 4

Army Form C. 2118.

20th Brigade } Page 1.
7th Division

WAR DIARY
or
INTELLIGENCE SUMMARY.
(Erase heading not required.)

Instructions regarding War Diaries and Intelligence Summaries are contained in F. S. Regs., Part II. and the Staff Manual respectively. Title pages will be prepared in manuscript.

Hour, Date, Place 1914.	Summary of Events and Information	Remarks and references to Appendices
3.30 a.m., 7th October. ZEEBRUGGE.	After steaming all night from DOVER the 20th Infantry Brigade arrived off ZEEBRUGGE at 3.30 a.m. apparently. The Germans had made some sort of attempt to attack the transports with submarines, as the cloud destroyers who had been escorting us reported their presence, one claiming to have sunk a German submarine, lying outside the harbour at daybreak one could hear the guns booming round ANTWERP.	Arrival in the country.
6 a.m.	At 6 a.m. the transports were ordered to come alongside the Quay and disembark. Orders came in that the Infantry proceed at once by road for BRUGES, some eight miles away, guns and transport to proceed there by road, leaving parties behind to unload the wagons and baggage. The whole of the 20th Brigade arrived in BRUGES by 3 p.m. The population seemed very pleased to see the British, and the troops were welcomed everywhere. ANTWERP is apparently on its last legs, and the rôle of the 7th Division is	Antwerp.
BRUGES, 3 p.m.		Objective.

Army Form C. 2118.

20th Brigade } Page 2.
7th Division }

WAR DIARY
or
INTELLIGENCE SUMMARY.
(Erase heading not required.)

Instructions regarding War Diaries and Intelligence Summaries are contained in F.S. Regs., Part II. and the Staff Manual respectively. Title pages will be prepared in manuscript.

Hour, Date, Place	Summary of Events and Information	Remarks and references to Appendices
7th October 1914. cont?	to draw off the German Army at present besieging the town, and thus enable the Belgian Army to leave ANTWERP without being molested.	
8th October, ZEEBRUGGE	The day began by a nct jumble. Division ordered to march to neighbourhood of OSTEND, each Brigade by a different road. The start was ordered for 7 a.m. but orders were only received at 6.30 a.m., and it was impossible to collect units from their widely scattered areas in time	Division moves to Ostend.
8.30 a.m.	to make a punctual start. Eventually at 8.30 a.m. all units were on the move, more or less in their proper order. The object of the march was for the Division to take up a defensive line on the BRUGES - NIEUPORT canal striving	Chaotic orders.
" — WESTKERKE	at WESTKERKE the dispositions of the troops were altered. After much marching and countermarching the Division	
10 p.m.	occupied its position by 10 p.m., after a long and fatiguing day for the troops, much of which could have been avoided	

Army Form C. 2118.

20th Brigade } Page 3
7th Division }

WAR DIARY
or
INTELLIGENCE SUMMARY.
(Erase heading not required.)

Instructions regarding War Diaries and Intelligence Summaries are contained in F.S. Regs., Part II. and the Staff Manual respectively. Title pages will be prepared in manuscript.

Hour, Date, Place	Summary of Events and Information	Remarks and references to Appendices
8th October, continued	avoided by the receipt of orders earlier, and not altering the dispositions of troops in the middle of the march. Owing to the alteration many of the troops did not get their rations. The 20th Brigade took up headquarters at	
STEENE	STEENE, three miles outside OSTEND. Disposition of the Brigade as follows:- Border Regiment on the right at LELLINGHE; Gordon Highlanders at SNAESKERKE; Grenadier Guards at GHISTELLES; Scots Guards in reserve at STEENE, the line being prolonged to the East by the 21st and 22nd Brigades. Our right was covered by the Northumberland Hussars (Territorials) at RAVERSYDE. So far we have not come into actual touch with the Germans. A Taube aeroplane was however flying over us the greater part of the afternoon, only disappearing upon the arrival of a British aeroplane from OSTEND. On the road today we passed many hundreds of Belgian refugees, all looking exceptionally miserable and frightened, with them were	Disposition near Ostend

Taube aeroplane.

Belgian refugees. |

(9 29 6) W 4141—463 100,000 9/14 H W V Forms/C. 2118/10

Army Form C. 2118.

20th Brigade } Page 4.
7th Division }

WAR DIARY
or
INTELLIGENCE SUMMARY.
(Erase heading not required.)

Instructions regarding War Diaries and Intelligence Summaries are contained in F. S. Regs., Part II. and the Staff Manual respectively. Title pages will be prepared in manuscript.

Hour, Date, Place	Summary of Events and Information	Remarks and references to Appendices
8th October, continued	disorganised parties of the Belgian Army. The Belgians in these parts have prepared several entrenched positions, but from what one could see their positions were all very disjointed, no organised line of resistance being made. All railway and canal bridges however were guarded.	Belgian entrenchments.
9th October 1914, STEENE 7 a.m.	Orders were received during the night for the Division to entrain at OSTEND, commencing with the 20th Infantry Brigade at 7 a.m.; only first line transport to be taken and two days rations carried on each man. Battalions to entrain at intervals of a quarter of an hour, for GHENT. It all sounded very simple and seemed to be plain sailing, but words cannot describe the chaos which we found in OSTEND, ANTWERP having fallen or being just about to fall. In addition to 2000 wounded Belgians in OSTEND (who had arrived from ANTWERP	Entraining at Ostend.
" OSTEND		

Army Form C. 2118.

WAR DIARY
or
INTELLIGENCE SUMMARY.
(Erase heading not required.)

20th Brigade } Page 5.
7th Division }

Hour, Date, Place	Summary of Events and Information	Remarks and references to Appendices
9th October 1914 cont'd. OSTEND	ANTWERP) were many thousands of refugees, all town-stricken, wandering aimlessly about, making the streets almost impassable. The OSTEND railway staff were quite unable to cope with this abnormal irregular traffic, in addition to which they had demands made upon them to entrain and despatch our 7th Division to GHENT. As for our Battalions departing at intervals of fifteen minutes, we thought ourselves very fortunate to send away Divisional	Entraining at Ostend cont?
10.30a Headquarters and half a Battalion at 10.30 a.m., their scheduled time for leaving being originally 8 a.m.! OSTEND railway station is badly adapted for entraining troops, there being no ramps for loading vehicles and horses. One ramp however was improvised in the Goods Yard outside the station. After another long and weary day, by dint of much badgering in		
10th October 1914. GHENT. (1 A.M.)	GHENT had French, the last man of our Brigade arrived in GHENT at 1 a.m. on the 10th October. The remainder of the Division followed	Arrival in Ghent

Army Form C. 2118.

20th Brigade } Page 6.
7th Division }

WAR DIARY
or
INTELLIGENCE SUMMARY.
(Erase heading not required.)

Instructions regarding War Diaries and Intelligence Summaries are contained in F.S. Regs., Part II. and the Staff Manual respectively. Title pages will be prepared in manuscript.

Hour, Date, Place	Summary of Events and Information	Remarks and references to Appendices
10th October 1914. GHENT. cont.	followed throughout the night and the following day. All day we saw an endless flow of refugees and Belgian troops, the latter utterly disorganised and undisciplined, with no officers. The 21st Brigade was left behind at BRUGES. Strong German patrols were seen at intervals during the day. Our dispositions were above a division of French cavalry held a line about EVERGEM, covering the North and North East of GHENT. They were joined up by our Divisional Cyclist Company, under Captain Pell, the Yorkshire Regiment. The 20th Brigade continued the line covering the East of the town MONT ST AMAND – DESTELBERGCH – GENT- BRUGGE, hence the line was	21st Brigade at Bruges. Disposition of troops.
ENVIRONS OF GHENT.	continued covering the south of the town, held by a Brigade of French Marines (Territorials I believe). These latter were very jumpy and not at all backed by beating off a German infantry attack, in which action they did very well, killing some 200 of the enemy. On their right facing	French Marines in action

Army Form C. 2118.

WAR DIARY
or
INTELLIGENCE SUMMARY.

20th Brigade } Page 7.
7th Division

(Erase heading not required.)

Instructions regarding War Diaries and Intelligence Summaries are contained in F.S. Regs., Part II. and the Staff Manual respectively. Title pages will be prepared in manuscript.

Hour, Date, Place	Summary of Events and Information	Remarks and references to Appendices
10th October, 1914, cont.d (Ghent)	facing S.W. x W. was the 22nd Brigade.	
11th October 1914, GHENT.	Germans reported placing guns in position about MELLE which place was the scene of an action between combined French and Belgians and the Germans the day before our arrival in Ghent. All our outpost battalion patrols report Germans snipers and patrols. The SCOTS GUARDS claiming first blood, one of their scouts (Private Reay) reporting a patrol near LOOCHRISTY which he averred had lost one of their men upon his opening fire. Lieut. JOICEY of the Northumberland Hussars whose troop is permanently attached to our Brigade, did very good work, obtaining most useful information. He got his patrol out as far as Kilo. 12 on the LOCKEREN road. Inhabitants there reported a German force of all arms to be massing at LOCKEREN. Many refugees and Belgian soldiers escaping from ANTWERP in civilian clothes all report Germans troops proceeding in our direction. This is just what is required of them, namely to take attention away from the Belgian Army during their retreat from Antwerp, and sofar our mission seems to be succeeding.	First engagement. Lt Joicey's good work. (Northumbd Hussars). Retreat from Antwerp.

Army Form C. 2118.

20th Brigade } Page 8.
7th Division }

WAR DIARY
or
INTELLIGENCE SUMMARY.

(Erase heading not required.)

Instructions regarding War Diaries and Intelligence Summaries are contained in F.S. Regs., Part II. and the Staff Manual respectively. Title pages will be prepared in manuscript.

Hour, Date, Place	Summary of Events and Information	Remarks and references to Appendices
11th October 1914, cont.d (Ghent)	exceeding. GHENT is a lovely old town, its Hotel de Ville being a most beautiful old building — it is hoped the Germans will not shell it. Having drawn the formers from Antwerp and the Belgian army having made good its escape, orders were received in the afternoon for our force to withdraw, accordingly at 7pm. the Division moved off, headed by the 20th Infantry Brigade, our destination being SOMERGEN, some 9 miles to the West of GHENT. Arrived there just at daybreak on October 12th.	Withdrawal from Ghent.
12th October 1914, SOMERGEN	After a bitterly cold night's marching the troops were put into temporary billets to rest and sleep. The Germans had not followed us, but reports came in to say they had occupied GHENT. At midday we moved again and marched to THIELT, leaving the Northumberland Hussars to hold the line of the canal about SOMERGEN, a party of Royal Engineers being attached to them to blow up the bridges. The whole acting as a rear-guard whilst the Division got into billets at THIELT. The staff arrangements for getting into THIELT were very bad. The roads were blocked	Germans occupy Ghent. Brigade march to Thielt. Bad arrangements for routing.
" THIELT.		

Army Form C. 2118.

WAR DIARY
or
INTELLIGENCE SUMMARY.

(Erase heading not required.)

20th Brigade } 7th Division } Page 9.

Instructions regarding War Diaries and Intelligence Summaries are contained in F.S. Regs, Part II. and the Staff Manual respectively. Title pages will be prepared in manuscript.

Hour, Date, Place	Summary of Events and Information	Remarks and references to Appendices
12th October 1914, on 12 (THIELT) 10 p.m. until 10 p.m.	blocked for miles by guns and wagons and it was not until 10 p.m. we got our very tired infantry into their billets. Strong outposts were placed all round the town and all roads entering THIELT blocked by felling large trees across them to prevent any possible rush by large numbers of the enemy. THIELT is a pretty old town with an ancient church in the Market Place; the melodious chimes (which are very old) sounding like a toy musical box, chiming every half hour. The Germans are still following us and a force of all arms was reported as occupying SOMERGEN, where we noted yesterday. The Division moved off at 7 a.m. en	Defence of Thielt prepared.
13th October 1914, THIELT 7 a.m. — PITHEM	route for ROULERS. Upon our arrival at PITHEM a force of Germans was reported to be advancing from the N. and N.E., also some from the S.E., accordingly the baggage was sent on, and the 20th and 22nd Brigades were ordered to take up position in order to cover this move, a position being	German advance continuing.

Army Form C. 2118.

20th Brigade } Page 10.
7th Division }

WAR DIARY
or
INTELLIGENCE SUMMARY.
(Erase heading not required.)

Instructions regarding War Diaries and Intelligence Summaries are contained in F.S. Regs., Part II. and the Staff Manual respectively. Title pages will be prepared in manuscript.

Hour, Date, Place	Summary of Events and Information	Remarks and references to Appendices
13th October 1914 PITHEM.	Being reconnoitred near BERGHOLT. The Germans however did not come on and the march was continued to ROULERS	Reconnaissance near BERGHOLT
ROULERS 10 p.m.	Arriving there at 10 p.m. The roads were again blocked through want of system in getting troops to their different billeting areas. It was however not quite such a chaos as last night at THIELT. In spite of the late hour at which they billeted and their excessive fatigue, the troops are all in excellent spirits.	Arrival at Roulers

Spirits of the troops |
| 14th October 1914 YPRES | Division continued its march to YPRES, forming a strong rear guard. The Germans having occupied THIELT as soon as we had left it. On arrival at YPRES we discovered our Second Cavalry Division and a French infantry Division. We shall shortly form part of an new army. Our mission has been entirely successful, and the three Belgian Army has been enabled to retire from ANTWERP and Normandie on the coast upon the line NIEUPORT-DIXMUDE. Although we have had no fighting it has been a very hard time for the troops. They have had a great deal of marching, much outpost work, and very little sleep. In YPRES the border. | Germans occupy Thielt

Arrival at Ypres

Success of our mission

Hard work of troops |

Army Form C. 2118.

WAR DIARY
or
INTELLIGENCE SUMMARY.
(Erase heading not required.)

20th Brigade } Page 11.
7th Division

Instructions regarding War Diaries and Intelligence Summaries are contained in F. S. Regs., Part II. and the Staff Manual respectively. Title pages will be prepared in manuscript.

Hour, Date, Place	Summary of Events and Information	Remarks and references to Appendices
14th October 1914. 6:00 a.m. (Ypres)	Border Regiment relieved the 10th Hussars & their morning from round the town sent: the Grenadiers and Gordons were posted out on outpost on the south side of the town at KRUISSTRAAT and VOORMEZEEL, the former cutting up at VOORMEZEEL, the former cutting up and destroying a German patrol. The Borders were with the latter, the Scots Guards being in and out of duty at HAHLTE.	Brigade on outpost. Destruction of a German patrol.
15th October 1914. Near ZILLEBEKE.	The whole of the 20th Brigade ordered to entrench a position covering the south of the town. Dispositions as follows from right to left: Gordon Highlanders about DICKEBUSCH - PLAAS to VOORMEZEELE: Scots Guards about VERBRANDEN MOLEN: Borders about ZILLEBEKE, which lay found up with the French Grenadiers entrenching themselves in readiness. The wooded country to the eastward the town was full of German patrols and snipers. The Borders Regiment, under Lieut LAMB, did very good work accounting for some twenty odd snipers. Orders were received late in the afternoon for the Division to push out and occupy a line ZONNEBEKE	Brigade entrenched. Dispositions. Germans numerous. Lieut Lamb's work. (Border Regt.)

Army Form C. 2118.

20th Brigade } page 12
7th Division }

WAR DIARY
or
INTELLIGENCE SUMMARY.
(Erase heading not required.)

Instructions regarding War Diaries and Intelligence Summaries are contained in F.S. Regs., Part II. and the Staff Manual respectively. Title pages will be prepared in manuscript.

Hour, Date, Place	Summary of Events and Information	Remarks and references to Appendices
15th October 1914, cont.d	GHELUVELT – ZANDVOORDE. Our 20th Brigade held the line ZANDVOORDE (inclusive) to GHELUVELT (exclusive). A certain amount of sniping went on during the night, Captain EGERTON of the Border Regiment being shot prior to his own men on outpost duty, subsequently dying of his wound.	20th Brigade objective.
16th October 1914. ZANDVOORDE	The 20th Brigade proceeded to ZANDVOORDE, the 7th Brigade forming advanced guard under Lt. Col. M. EARLE. No serious resistance was encountered, touch being maintained throughout with the 22nd Brigade marching along in our YPRES – MENIN road to GHELUVELT. Arrived at ZANDVOORDE the Brigade took up the line to GHELUVELT, Grenadiers on right covering ZANDVOORDE, Scots Guards on left prolonging the line to GHELUVELT. Before joining up the line a Staff Officer rode out down the ZANDVOORDE GHELUVELT road to find out where to join up with the 22nd Brigade. A few minutes before his arrival a cyclist scout of the Bedford Regiment had been surprised by an Uhlan patrol, who kicked a certain prominent portion of his	Brigade at Zandvoorde. ——— New line taken up.

Army Form C. 2118.

20th Brigade
7 Division. Page 15

WAR DIARY
or
INTELLIGENCE SUMMARY.
(Erase heading not required.)

Hour, Date, Place	Summary of Events and Information	Remarks and references to Appendices
18 Oct 1914 Zandvoorde	Anderson took away his rifle and cycle and sent him back to his command. Fortunately the staff officer just escaped this undignified episode. The four days continuing entrenching our position. The British Cavalry continuing the line to our right, and having pushed out to the front at TEMPLELEN which is occupied by Civic troops.	Narrow escape of Brigade Major. Entrenchments complete
17 Oct 1914. ZANDVOORDE	The day was spent in improving and strengthening trenches. In the afternoon orders were received for two companies of each Guards to advance and occupy a commanding ridge at KRUISEIK. This detachment was commanded by Major Thom. H. Spencer. The position was very isolated and they were much worried by snipers and it was not until the village of KRUISEIK and neighbouring ???	
18 Oct 1914. KRUISEIK	Orders were received for the whole of the 2nd Brigade to advance and occupy the ground beyond KRUISEIK — AMERICA, linking back to ZANDVOORDE on the right. The left resting on the cross roads at life A on the YPRES - MENIN road. Dispositions of 2nd Brigade as follows:	Kruiseik ridge

WAR DIARY or INTELLIGENCE SUMMARY

Army Form C. 2118.

20th Brigade } page 14.
7th Division

Hour, Date, Place	Summary of Events and Information	Remarks and references to Appendices
October 17th KRUISEIK 18th	Followed about 9 am on Hill 64 holding the village and connecting up with 21st Brigade at Kts. 101 & the time being to however harden continuing line South to ZANDVOORDE. Now the Bays had their own groom check — firstly it was much too big for a Brigade to hold, secondly in order to maintain an efficient firing line no troops could be spared to form a reserve; secondly, the bend back from AMERICA to ZANDVOORDE formed a very sharp salient which was always a source of great weakness in our line, added to which, not the ground about this salient was very wooded, affording the enemy excellent opportunity of massing his troops in front of the weakest point in our defences. Hardly a house in AMERICA could be strongly held. Newport could mass and manoeuvre his men unobserved owing to the fact that all the ground was a fir-wood and was dead ground from the main position. The enemy at our abandoned position the Germans opened a very heavy shellfire from VIERICQ. 1½ Yathere or thereabouts supporting some counters. The	Dispositions — Defective line — Reasons for opinion — Germans shell from Vierica

Army Form C. 2118.

20th Brigade } page 15
4th Division }

WAR DIARY
or
INTELLIGENCE SUMMARY.
(Erase heading not required.)

Instructions regarding War Diaries and Intelligence Summaries are contained in F.S. Regs., Part II. and the Staff Manual respectively. Title pages will be prepared in manuscript.

Hour, Date, Place	Summary of Events and Information	Remarks and references to Appendices
October 19th continued 1914 (Kruiseik)	The shooting of the Germans was extraordinarily accurate along the KRUISEIK–WERVICQ road, doing some damage to Brigade Hd qrs and the 15th Company R.E.	Germans accurate shooting
October 19th, KRUISEIK	The Division is now occupying the following line: ZONNEBEKE–GHELUVELT–KRUISEIK–ZANDVOORDE. Our forward position at AMERICA which suffered to heavy shelling and it was decided that the line would be stronger if we gave up this position. Our new position is therefore as follows: Kilo 10 on YPRES–MENIN road, cross road just South of KRUISEIK–ZANDVOORDE. A strong column of the enemy were reported advancing westward through GHELUGHEM–NEGHEM and ANDOYEN and the 22nd Infantry Brigade were ordered to fall back on the line TERHAND–STROOIBOOMHOEK, the 21st Brigade to occupy the entrenched line YPRES–MENIN road to TERHAND, and our 20th Brigade ordered to occupy the trenches with two battalions, and send two battalions – Grenadiers and REUTEL to act as Divisional Reserve. Grenadiers and Borders occupy the trenches, Scots Guards and Gordons rest	New positions

Army Form C. 2118.

WAR DIARY
or
INTELLIGENCE SUMMARY.
(Erase heading not required.)

20th Brigade) Page 16.
7th Division)

Instructions regarding War Diaries and Intelligence Summaries are contained in F. S. Regs., Part II. and the Staff Manual respectively. Title pages will be prepared in manuscript.

Hour, Date, Place 1914	Summary of Events and Information	Remarks and references to Appendices
October 20th KRUISEIK	Sent back to REUTEL. Scots Guards and Gordon Highlanders return to the Brigade this morning. A reconnaissance was ordered to be carried out towards GHELUWE. This was effected by the Scots Guards and Gordon Highlanders, the former getting to within 1000 yards of that place. They were very heavily shelled from WERVICQ but did not suffer many casualties. At 1 pm they returned, reporting GHELUWE occupied by the Germans. Strong forces of the enemy were reported to be moving to the left of our position. The 21st Brigade was ordered to withdraw to its entrenched line on our left. The 20th Brigade was ordered to hold its trenches and keep up communication with the 21st Brigade. The 6th Cavalry Brigade are on our right at ZANDVOORDE, with an advanced troop of the Scots Greys at TENBRIELEN. At 2.30 pm a message was received from them that they had been ordered to withdraw, leaving one regiment for	Reconnaissance by Scots Guards & Gordons
2.30pm		

Army Form C. 2118.

WAR DIARY
or
INTELLIGENCE SUMMARY.
(Erase heading not required.)

20th Brigade } 7th Division } Page 17.

Hour, Date, Place	Summary of Events and Information	Remarks and references to Appendices
1914. October 20th cont. (Kruiseik). 3 pm. October 21st KRUISEIK	for an hour or two at TEMBRIELEN. This meant that the right flank of our Brigade would be left exposed, until the 3rd Cavalry Brigade (who were taking up a line from the canal near HOUTHEM to KORTEWILDE, which place is three miles from the right flank of our Brigade) could arrive in position. Lieut. Joicey and his troop of N.H. sent off to get connection with them at KORTEWILDE. At 3 pm the Grenadiers and Borders reported Germans advancing at 800 yards range, and had opened fire on them. The Scots Guards were sent off to act as Divisional Reserve near VELDHOEK, enemy occupying AMERICA. The German advance appears to be more in the nature of a reconnaissance than an attack. — The Scots Guards were sent to ZANDVOORDE to hold trenches there, and fill up gap between our Brigade and the 3rd Cavalry Brigade at KORTENWILDE. Lieut. Joicey and troop sent to establish communication with Cavalry. Gordons	 German advance

Army Form C. 2118.

WAR DIARY
or
INTELLIGENCE SUMMARY.
(Erase heading not required.)

20th Brigade }
7th Division } Page 18.

Hour, Date, Place	Summary of Events and Information	Remarks and references to Appendices
1914. October 21st continued. (Kruiseik)	Gordons report being attacked and all trenches report bodies of the enemy moving towards TENBRIELEN. At	
10.15 a.m.	half battalion of Scots Guards ordered to go to GHELUVELT to act as Divisional Reserve. At 10.30 a.m.	German general advance.
10.30 a.m.	The remaining Companies of Scots Guards were attacked by enemy between ZANDVOORDE and KORTENWILDE. The Germans commencing attack by heavy shell fire. In this attack Major Lord ESME GORDON-LENNOX was badly wounded, and his company suffered severely. The position at this juncture was rather critical as Lieut. TOICEY had not returned, and we were unable to ascertain if we had joined up with the 3rd Cavalry Brigade. Messages received from the Division stated that the 21st Brigade were being heavily attacked, and orders were received to send them half a battalion at 11 a.m. Two Companies of	Scots Gds suffer severely.
11 a.m.	Grenadier Guards were accordingly despatched to them. General Watts had already, earlier in the day, sent his reserve	21st Brigade attacked. Reinforced by portion of 20th Brigade.

Army Form C. 2118.

WAR DIARY
or
INTELLIGENCE SUMMARY.
(Erase heading not required.)

20th Brigade } Page 19.
7th Division }

Instructions regarding War Diaries and Intelligence Summaries are contained in F. S. Regs., Part II. and the Staff Manual respectively. Title pages will be prepared in manuscript.

Hour, Date, Place	Summary of Events and Information	Remarks and references to Appendices
1914. October 21st., continued. KRUISEIK.	reserve to the 22nd Brigade, who also were seriously engaged. The Grenadiers and Borders in neighbourhood of KRUISEIK report being heavily shelled with little damage. Message received at noon that the cavalry on our right heavily	Cavalry heavily engaged.
Noon.	engaged near HOUTHEM; it therefore appears that the Germans are attacking all along the line. The Divisional Cyclist Company ordered to strengthen our right flank at 1 p.m.	
1 p.m.	Lieut. TOICEY and No 4 Coy Northumberland Hussars established communication with cavalry, reporting this fact at 1.15 p.m.	
1.15 p.m.	We now feel more comfortable about our right, the N. Hussars being ordered to proceed there as well. The Gordons report they are much worried by German machine guns, which occupy farm house on their front. Borders report trenches blown in by shell fire. At 3 p.m. the Grenadiers reported	Trenches blown in by shell fire (Borders)
3 p.m.	they were heavily attacked, and the Yorkshires on their left were being very hard pressed, and at 4 p.m. Borders report they also were heavily attacked. This attack however was not pressed home, the enemy entrenching himself too close to our firing	

Army Form C. 2118.

20th Brigade } 7th Division } Page 20

WAR DIARY
or
INTELLIGENCE SUMMARY.
(Erase heading not required.)

Instructions regarding War Diaries and Intelligence Summaries are contained in F.S. Regs., Part II. and the Staff Manual respectively. Title pages will be prepared in manuscript.

Hour, Date, Place	Summary of Events and Information	Remarks and references to Appendices
1914		
October 21st continued. KRUISEIK 10 p.m.	firing line to be shelled by our Artillery. At 10 p.m. the Scots Guards were relieved by the cavalry at ZANDVOORDE. The Brigade had about 150 casualties today	Brigade casualties 150.
October 22nd KRUISEIK.	An air reconnaissance reports three German Regts. moving on WERVICK and three on GHELUWE road, and attack is therefore probable. Borders report being attacked and much harassed by machine guns; they also report enemy massing in dead ground near AMERICA. Snipers from our rear were very busy throughout the night, and enemy are pressing all along the line, with very heavy shell fire at intervals. The Scots Guards sent to VELDHOEK as Divisional reserve.	Borders attacked
October 24th KRUISEIK.	Following Intelligence report received: "The Division is fighting the 53rd and 54th Divisions of the 27th Reserve Corps. All prisoners testify as to heavy losses sustained yesterday and the day before." Scots Guards returned to the Brigade, having been lent to support the 21st Brigade. 2 Col: Bolton reports one Company "F" almost completely cut up	Scots Guards suffer

Army Form C. 2118.

WAR DIARY
or
INTELLIGENCE SUMMARY.
(Erase heading not required.)

20th Brigade } Page 21.
7th Division }

Instructions regarding War Diaries and Intelligence Summaries are contained in F.S. Regs, Part II. and the Staff Manual respectively. Title pages will be prepared in manuscript.

Hour, Date, Place	Summary of Events and Information	Remarks and references to Appendices
1914 October 24th, KRUISEIK. 3 p.m.	a/t, and Captn RIVERS-BULKELEY killed. About 3 p.m. the Grenadiers reported Germans attacking in force supported by machine guns. The Yorkshires on their left at the main cross-road also reported being heavily engaged, and this attack nearly succeeded in penetrating our line, being forward with great vigour. A counter-attack was launched however, which was gallantly led by Major COLBY, who drove the Germans back. In this action the attacking part lost four officers killed and 100 other casualties. The following officers were killed: Major Colby, Lieut. Antrobus. W. Somerset and Walter. Capt. Leatham was wounded. Lieut Sir P. Duckworth-King being the only officer to survive. The Brigade had some 200 casualties this day. No sooner had this attack been broken than the Borders reported several of their trenches blown in, and that they were seriously engaged with infantry and machine guns. Reports came in to say that the Germans were advancing through the breach in the trenches. This report luckily proved to be untrue. Two coys. of	German's press attack. Major Colby G.G. leads a gallant counter-attack. 4 officers killed, 100 other casualties. Brigade casualties 200.

Army Form C. 2118.

XXth Brigade } Page 22.
VIIth Division

WAR DIARY
or
INTELLIGENCE SUMMARY.
(Erase heading not required.)

Instructions regarding War Diaries and Intelligence Summaries are contained in F. S. Regs., Part II. and the Staff Manual respectively. Title pages will be prepared in manuscript.

Hour, Date, Place	Summary of Events and Information	Remarks and references to Appendices
1914. October 24th. KRUISEIK.	of the Scots Guards had already gone up to support the Grenadiers and Yorkshires, the remainder with one Company of Gordon Highlanders under Major Hon: Hugh Gordon went off to expel the Germans who were reported to have got through. They suffered some fifty casualties which was to be greatly regretted as the report was brought through by one or two fainthearted individuals who in a moment of intense terror had rushed back to Headquarters. The Grenadiers again report being hard pressed at 6 p.m. A message received that the 1st Division has come up and is attacking ZONNEBEKE on the left of our Division. It is to be hoped this will relieve the pressure all along our front, as at times the situation is most critical and it is as much as we can do to hold on. The Gordons on our right report they are also being attacked, but feel confident. The day closes with our line intact but all the trenches had received severe punishment. Meanwhile it has been decided to make a night attack on a house holding a German machine gun in front of the Gordons' trenches. Captain Peel, with some Divisional Cyclists, was detailed to carry this out, but they failed to get to the house and suffered severely. Capt: Peel did not return and it is feared was killed.	Grenadiers hard pressed ——— Critical situation ——— Capt: Peel's gallant night attack
6 p.m.		

Army Form C. 2118.

WAR DIARY
or
INTELLIGENCE SUMMARY.
(Erase heading not required.)

XX"Brigade } Page 23.
VII Division }

Instructions regarding War Diaries and Intelligence Summaries are contained in F.S. Regs., Part II. and the Staff Manual respectively. Title pages will be prepared in manuscript.

Hour, Date, Place	Summary of Events and Information	Remarks and references to Appendices
1914. October 25th KRUISEIK.	Enemy reported entrenching all along our south front and opposite ZANDVOORDE. The 21st Brigade report their line broken and the Division had arranged a counter attack, ordering us to hold on to the last gasp. The Connaught Rangers sent up to support the Grenadiers left near 21st Bde., and later on two companies of the Queens arrived. So far as we (20th Brigade) are concerned, except for being heavily shelled the day passed off with no further incident worth mentioning. About sunset however the Grenadiers left was again heavily attacked. The Connaught Rangers and Oxfordshire Light Infantry supporting, the attack was beaten off, and at this period our Division reported the 2nd Division to be making a counter attack through the 21st Infantry Brigade. During the day 4 heavy guns from 2nd Division and 4 heavy guns 6th Division came up to support us. Two officers, Capt. Gordon and Lieut. Clancy, killed in Pondero. Germans continued to attack all night Grenadiers and Pondero. 200 casualties today and 150 yesterday; great difficulty experienced in getting them removed.	21st Brigade line broken. Grenadiers again attacked Guns support our line. Casualties today 200

Army Form C. 2118.

XX Brigade } Page 24
VII Division

WAR DIARY
or
INTELLIGENCE SUMMARY.
(Erase heading not required.)

Instructions regarding War Diaries and Intelligence Summaries are contained in F.S. Regs., Part II. and the Staff Manual respectively. Title pages will be prepared in manuscript.

Hour, Date, Place	Summary of Events and Information	Remarks and references to Appendices
1914. October 26th 12 m.n. KRUISEIK.	Shortly after midnight on the night 25/26th reports came in to say the Germans were through the trenches and were attacking the trenches from behind, having got through between the Scots Guards and Borders, Lieut. LODER coming down in person to explain situation. There were three companys of Scots Guards in reserve, one Company however being only 45 strong, as it had been badly cut up when acting with the Divisional Reserve in POLYGON wood. Major Hon. N. FRASER took two of the Companys to make a counter attack to turn out the Germans who had got through. The night was very dark and rain was falling in torrents. On arriving in the neighbourhood of the trenches Major Fraser went forward with 40 men to see if he could retake a trench they were said to be occupying, on finding & take the trench from the rear, missing his way in the dark he got in front of the trench and came under a very heavy fire, only a small party of five men getting back. Major Fraser, unfortunately, was killed. Visct. Dalrymple then took command, and finding a house full of	Germans penetrate trenches. Major Hon. H. Fraser's gallant night attack.

Army Form C. 2118.

WAR DIARY
or
INTELLIGENCE SUMMARY.
(Erase heading not required.)

XX Brigade } — Page 25
VII Division

Hour, Date, Place	Summary of Events and Information	Remarks and references to Appendices
1914 October 26, continued. <u>KRUISEIK</u>	of Germans sent Captain Fox along the road to flank it, and advanced on it himself with 50 men. When within 50 yards they opened fire on him through a hedge, but charging the house our men got in with the bayonet, killed the Commanding officer and captured 200 men. Meanwhile Captain Paynter, Scots Guards was surrounded by the Germans in his trench, many of them coming up from behind him, calling for him by name and representing themselves to be reinforcements. This ruse however did not come off, and Captain Paynter fought his trench till daylight, when the Germans (Prussian Guard from the 4th Battalion) retired. As day wore breaking Lieut. Hope of the Grenadier Guards arrived and reformed all the Grenadier trenches intact, and the entire line was once more re-established. Dalrymple occupying a kind of which was full of dead and wounded (Germans and our own men) from Major Brooks body lying close by. The Company of Scots Guards which had learned the prisoners back turned up at this juncture and helped reinforce the	Viscount Dalrymple captures 200 prisoners after a good fight. Capt. Paynter S.G. surrounded by enemy. Gallant stand by his command. Entire line re-established.

Army Form C. 2118.

WAR DIARY
or
INTELLIGENCE SUMMARY.
(Erase heading not required.)

XX Brigade
VII Division } Page 26.

Hour, Date, Place	Summary of Events and Information	Remarks and references to Appendices
1914 October 26th (continued) KRUISEIK. 7 a.m.	the line. Unfortunately it was too late to go into the village in rear, as daylight prevented much movement outside the trenches. At 7 a.m. the Germans began shelling the trenches. The fire increasing to such an extent that occupants of the line counted as many as 60 per minute on each small trench. The men gallantly held	
10 a.m.	on till 10 a.m. in spite of the shells repeatedly blowing in the trenches and burying five and six men at a time, each man having to be dug out with a shovel — in some cases as much as three feet of earth being on top of the men. Many of course were suffocated before they could be extricated. At this period the South Staffords (who had relieved some of the Borders in their trenches) retired closely followed by Germans who now began devoting their attention to firing at the remainder of the trenches occupied by rearguards, the enemy being in rear of the latter. About 3.30 p.m. the Germans were so completely round them, and in such numbers that they were captured. Meanwhile a second line in rear had been established	Heavy shelling by enemy
3.30 p.m.	running from the left of the Gordons back in an arc (bent outwards) to GHELUVELT. The Gordons had not suffered much. The remainder of the troops who had retired being collected together to form the new line. One line was the	Scots Guards surrounded

Army Form C. 2118.

WAR DIARY
or
INTELLIGENCE SUMMARY.
(Erase heading not required.)

XX Brigade
VII Division
Page 27.

Hour, Date, Place	Summary of Events and Information	Remarks and references to Appendices
1914. October 26th continued.	The remnants of the 100th Grenadiers, Borders and S. Staffords. At 3.15pm the guns were ordered back to a position on the SCHERPENBERG – BASSEEVILLE. The Grenadiers retired to this position to cover a possible retirement from our recently held second position; the Germans however evidently has no desire for further fighting, and never seriously threatened that second position. At 5pm our position was considered to be so isolated that it was decided to fall back onto the BASSEEVILLE river, which more was carried out without any further fighting. The men were almost completely worn out, many of them having been in the trenches for five days and nights without relief. They were constantly shelled throughout the day, harassing with a very severe nights and day fighting, and yet their spirits and discipline were not at all upset. Before 24 hours in our Brigade more were casualties for the last 24 hours in our Brigade more were 2000, or very nearly half our total strength.	Spirits of the men. Brigade casualties 2000.
October 27th BASSEEVILLE	Orders were received from the Division for the Brigade to go into billets at the 5 Feb. to reorganise and report casualties.	

Army Form C. 2118.

WAR DIARY
or
INTELLIGENCE SUMMARY.
(Erase heading not required.)

XX Brigade
VII Division
Page 28

Hour, Date, Place	Summary of Events and Information	Remarks and references to Appendices
1914 October 27th BASEVILLE	casualties and deficiencies. The Brigade was accordingly withdrawn from BASEVILLE river, and the day spent in reorganising the companies. The two battalions having suffered most severely were the Scots Guards (who mustered 12 officers and 450 men) and the Borders (12 officers and 538 men) Captain Paynter commanded the Scots Guards and Lt. Col. Wood the Borders.	Reorganisation Heavy losses of Brigade
October 28th GHELUVELT.	The Brigade now musters as follows:- Officers. Other ranks. 1st Batt. Grenadier Gds. 20 670 2nd " Scots Guards 12 460 2nd " Gordon Highlanders 26 812 2nd " Border Regiment 12 538	(Nominal strength of a battalion 30 officers 977 o.r.)
3.30 p.m	The Brigade rested all day and at 3.30 the following was received from G.H.Q. per 7th Division. "It is reported from reliable source that the 24th German Reserve Corps has been ordered to take the Cross Roads S.E. of GHELUVELT to day. 1st and 7th Division please report situation on your front."	
4.30 p.m	At 4.30 p.m our Brigade was ordered to send two Battalions to those Cross roads to be there at 6.45 p.m. And at 5.30 p.m.	

Army Form C. 2118.

XX Brigade
VII Division — Page 29

WAR DIARY
or
INTELLIGENCE SUMMARY.
(Erase heading not required.)

Instructions regarding War Diaries and Intelligence Summaries are contained in F.S. Regs., Part II. and the Staff Manual respectively. Title pages will be prepared in manuscript.

Hour, Date, Place	Summary of Events and Information	Remarks and references to Appendices
1914. October 28. continued.	5.30 p.m. a message from the Division came to say that an intercepted wireless message ordered an attack by the 27th German Reserve Corps to take place against the Cross Roads on the 28th according to the [illegible] Brigade and the 2nd Gordon Highlanders were ordered out to take up a position from the Cross Roads to the track running S.W. from GHELUVELT. The Scots Guards and Borders to support them by night near GHELUVELT. In view of the absence of any prepared position or trenches at that spot, they were ordered to withdraw at daybreak if there was no German attack, in order to evade shell fire. The Scots Guards on the way up to their position were unlucky enough to have a shell burst right into one of their companies (which was in close order) causing some twenty casualties, 2nd Lt Gibbs Smith Rifles, and Lt Bosley Bathonie and Capt Kemble been wounded.	Operation near Gheluvelt Shell causes heavy losses
October 29th VELDHOEK.	No attack by the enemy having been launched at daybreak, the Scots Guards and Borderers withdrew to VELDHOEK. About 7.30 a.m. the Germans opened a tremendously heavy shell fire, which proved to be the prelude to their main attack on the cross roads – on which road the left of the grenadiers. Beyond the cross roads [illegible]	Germans prepare attack

7.30 a.m.

Army Form C. 2118.

XX Brigade } Page 30
VII Division

WAR DIARY
or
INTELLIGENCE SUMMARY.
(Erase heading not required.)

Instructions regarding War Diaries and Intelligence Summaries are contained in F.S. Regs., Part II. and the Staff Manual respectively. Title pages will be prepared in manuscript.

Hour, Date, Place	Summary of Events and Information	Remarks and references to Appendices
1914. October 29th continued VELDHOEK.	connecting up with the Grenadiers was the first Brigade on whose right was the Black Watch, whilst on their right was the Gordon Highlanders. The morning was very foggy and before the troops could realize what was happening they were suddenly rushed by overwhelming numbers. The enemy who penetrated the line between the Black Watch and Grenadiers. The Grenadiers reserve was then put led by Major Stucley drove out the Germans who again attacked, bringing up still more troops into the assault, and once again they succeeded in breaking through. Again, however, Major Stucley led a counter attack against them, but they were two numerous and Major Stucley was killed whilst gallantly trying to erect a force which outnumbered his small reserve by at least ten to one. The enemy now began to press in on the Grenadiers all along their front. Capt. Lord Richard Wellesley was killed in a counter attack led by him, delivered on the right of the Grenadiers and the reserve of the Gordon Highlanders came across from the right rear to try and stem the overwhelming numbers of the enemy who were now engaging the Grenadiers at close quarters from the front and rear, their supports being as closely engaged as their firing line. At this period the Brigade on their left were forced back, and the Grenadiers	Enemy rush trenches. Counterattack by Major Stucley GG Second counter attack by Major Stucley, who gallantly led against overwhelming numbers. Counter attack by Capt. Lord Wellesley

Army Form C. 2118.

XX Brigade
VII Division } Page 31.

WAR DIARY
or
INTELLIGENCE SUMMARY.
(Erase heading not required.)

Instructions regarding War Diaries and Intelligence Summaries are contained in F. S. Regs., Part II. and the Staff Manual respectively. Title pages will be prepared in manuscript.

Hour, Date, Place	Summary of Events and Information	Remarks and references to Appendices
1914. October 29th continued VELDHOEK	Grenadiers were beaten back on to the high ground to the east of GHELUVELT, where they were reinforced by the Borders. Here the German advance was checked and were beaten back time after time throughout the day. During this fight one company of the Gordons under Capt. Pryse Gordon held and fought their trenches throughout the day, 240 dead Germans being counted in front of one platoon alone. Meanwhile the 1st Division on our left had been equally strongly attacked, and the 1st Brigade had all been forced back with the exception of the 1st Batt. Scots Guards. The 1st Bn Coldstreamers having been annihilated to a man. Reinforcements were collected as quickly as possible. The 2nd Batth Green being sent to us. The Scots Guards supported by the Sussex, were sent through the N. of GHELUVELT and engaged the enemy all day, holding a position on the N.W. side of the town. About 4pm they advanced and got back to the original line held by the Grenadiers in the morning, capturing two machine guns just before dark. Here they discovered the company of Gordon Highlanders still holding their own, having inflicted a terrible punishment on the Germans. Evening closed in with the 20th Brigade holding the same ground which it had occupied in the morning.	Grenadiers beaten back. Germans in turn beaten back. Heavy slaughter by Gordons. Coldstreamers suffer heavily. Capture of German machine guns.
4pm		

Army Form C. 2118.

WAR DIARY
or
INTELLIGENCE SUMMARY.
(Erase heading not required.)

XX Brigade } Page 32
VII Division

Hour, Date, Place	Summary of Events and Information	Remarks and references to Appendices
1914 October 29th (continued) VELDHOEK.	At nightfall orders were sent out to establish an outpost line from GHELUVELT towards KRUISEIK and back right-handed to ZANDVOORDE. The 20th Brigade being withdrawn to VELDHOEK. Rain was coming down in torrents and the troops did not get back to the latter place till nearly midnight. Of the 20 officers and 670 men in the Grenadiers who had started the day, only 5 officers and 200 men were left, the dark figures being Capt. Rasch, Lt. Pilcher, Lord C. Hamilton, Lt. Hope, 2nd Lt. Danby and some 200 men were left, the dark figures had 70 casualties. The Borders 250 and Gordons 100. On withdrawing from their forward position the dark figures were heavily fired on by the Queens who mistook them for Germans in the dark. The following was the officers casualty list: Lt. Col. M. Earle D.L.O. wounded and missing. Major Ker ?; Lt. Shelley killed; Major Hon. A. O'Neill-forcott wounded. Capt. Lord R. Molkeley killed; Capt. Ronn M. (severely wounded); Capt. G. Rennie wounded and missing; Lt. Hon. A. G. Douglas Pennant wounded and missing (reported killed); Lt. P. Van Neck wounded and missing; Lt. Aubrey Fletcher wounded Lt. L. Fries, wounded. Lt. Harcourt Powell wounded; 2nd Lt. R.O.A. Kerperman wounded remaining; 2nd Lt. S. Lambert wounded.	Grievous losses of the Brigade.

WAR DIARY
or
INTELLIGENCE SUMMARY.
(Erase heading not required.)

Army Form C. 2118.

XX Brigade } Page 33.
VII Division

Hour, Date, Place	Summary of Events and Information	Remarks and references to Appendices
1914 October 29th cont?	wounded. Lt. Butt, R.A.M.C., missing	
October 30th ZANDVOORDE	At 6.20 a.m. a message came from the Division to say the 20th Infy. Brigade would probably be sent to ZANDVOORDE-KLEINE-ZILLEBEKE road, and that the Scots Guards who had been withdrawn the previous evening would be required to get in touch with the Cavalry Brigade and be prepared to re-capture ZANDVOORDE if the Cavalry were driven in. This message was cancelled but the Gordon Highlanders were ordered to report themselves to General Bulfin, commanding the second Brigade in the woods just S.W. of ZANDVOORDE near the BASSEVILLE RIVER to fill up a gap in the line on his right. The 2nd Brigade was also pushed up, three being relieved later by the 4th Guards Brigade. The 22nd Brigade then being forced on a position above the BASSEVILLE RIVER on the left of the 2nd Brigade. The remainder of our Brigade was placed in rear of this line, as a reserve. Throughout the day the Germans made repeated efforts to penetrate this line, each attack being prepared by a very heavy shell fire, the ground in rear of our forward	Disposition of Brigade German attacks

Army Form C. 2118.

XX Brigade }
VII Division } Page 54

WAR DIARY
or
INTELLIGENCE SUMMARY.
(Erase heading not required.)

Hour, Date, Place	Summary of Events and Information	Remarks and references to Appendices
1914 Oct. 30, continued. ZANDVOORDE	forward line being well searched by shells during their attack, apparently with a view to harassing any reinforcements we might be sending up to our firing line. At nightfall our Brigade (with the exception of the Gordon Highlanders who were left in position on the right of the 22nd Brigade) was withdrawn to VELDHOEK. At 10 p.m. the following message was received:- "Fresh troops of the enemy are reported to have engaged us today. The right wing of our troops (composing 1st + 2nd Divisions with the Cavalry Brigade) is attacking in the general direction north by a line between the Canal and ZANDVOORDE. This attack will pass our front at 6.30 p.m. The Artillery of the VII Division will co-operate and support the attack. Immediately Gen. Bulfin's Brigade vacate the trenches they now occupy, the Gordon Highlanders will close to their left, prolonging the line of the 22nd Brigade. The 20th Brigade will remain in its present position until 6.30 a.m., when it will leave one Battalion in support of the left portion of the line, and move the remainder to a central position where it can rapidly support any portion of the line held by the 7th Division. Troops will occupy their present position and will best resist the attack by receiving any counter attacks that might be made against them." The	Brigade withdrawn to Veldhoek

Army Form C. 2118.

WAR DIARY
or
INTELLIGENCE SUMMARY.
(Erase heading not required.)

XX`th` Brigade } page 36
VII`th` Division }

Instructions regarding War Diaries and Intelligence Summaries are contained in F.S. Regs., Part II. and the Staff Manual respectively. Title pages will be prepared in manuscript.

Hour, Date, Place	Summary of Events and Information	Remarks and references to Appendices
1914 October 30th. continued	The Division now held the following line:—	
	21st Brigade: left resting YPRES-MENIN road in front of the cross roads at VELDHOEK to a point about 1000yds due South.	
	22nd Brigade: thence to a point about 500 yards N. North of ZANDVOORDE.	
	The Gordon Highlanders were to close in on the 21st Brigade advancing, and thus prolong the right of the 22nd Brigade	
October 31st ZANDVOORDE	At one a.m. it was decided to push the Scots Guards and Borderers, and entrench them close behind the left of the 21st Brigade. Accordingly they took up a line along the eastern edge of the wood running North and South from the VELDHOEK cross roads. Orders came in early to say that the Gordon Highlanders would be under General Bulfin. As soon as day broke the Germans began a terrific shell fire all along the line. The Brigade Headquarters Staff moved to Music Chateau as no protection could be given to the House of the horses above the House. It is staff time on the 21st Brigade in the road at CHATEAU HERENTHAGE where the Divisional reserves (reserve)	Terrific shell fire Brigade H.Q. shelled out

See Next

Army Form C. 2118.

XX Brigade } page 36.
VII Division }

WAR DIARY
or
INTELLIGENCE SUMMARY.
(Erase heading not required.)

Hour, Date, Place	Summary of Events and Information	Remarks and references to Appendices
1914. October 31, continued. ZANDVOORDE.	By 1 a.m. the bombardment became so terrific that shells were bursting over and on the line in one unceasing flow. Towards noon word came in to say that the 21st and 22nd Brigades had been shelled out of their position, and had been forced to retire. The Scots Guards and Borders still held their line in rear of the 21st Brigade, and the Grenadiers were led up in prolongation of this line by their Brigadier in person, in hopes of stemming the German advance. On gaining the ridge through the wood it was found that in order to be of any use it would be necessary to push them forward to occupy the empty trenches of the 21st Brigade. This was effected with some difficulty owing to the very heavy shell fire, and three or four of the men forward thereto on the right of the 21st and left of the 22nd Brigade were occupied just in time to meet a portion of the main German attack which was now being delivered on the GHELUVELT – ZANDVOORDE frontage. The small portion of Grenadiers were now confronting some thousands of Germans, their right being exposed, as the 22nd Brigade trenches	Retirement of 21st & 22nd Brigades. Unequal forces: fine stand by Grenadiers

WAR DIARY
or
INTELLIGENCE SUMMARY.
(Erase heading not required.)

Army Form C. 2118.

XX Brigade
VII Division } Page 37

Hour, Date, Place	Summary of Events and Information	Remarks and references to Appendices
1914 October 31st, continued ZANDVOORDE	Trenches were now unoccupied. Although the Germans were wonderfully brave it was fortunate for us that their attack appeared to be utterly disjointed and unorganised. No officers could be seen leading their men, who (as lots of the trenches) were simply mown down by the fire of the Grenadiers. All seemed to be going on well to our front, when the right hand trench reported the Germans to be streaming through a wood and crossing the VELDHOEK - ZANDVOORDE road, working their way into the large wood immediately in our rear, and matters began to look very ugly. A staff officer escorted down & made a reconnaissance to the right and saw the Germans in great numbers massing in the wood. All reserves had then used up by this time, and apparently the only thing to be done was to hang on till nightfall and let the Division know the situation at once. No means of communication having been established since their re-occupation, the staff officer	German tactics Wholesale slaughter by our men Reconnaissance by Brigade Major.

Army Form C. 2118.

XX Brigade
VII Division

Page 38.

WAR DIARY
or
INTELLIGENCE SUMMARY.
(Erase heading not required.)

Instructions regarding War Diaries and Intelligence Summaries are contained in F.S. Regs., Part II. and the Staff Manual respectively. Title pages will be prepared in manuscript.

Hour, Date, Place	Summary of Events and Information	Remarks and references to Appendices
1914 October 31st, continued ZANDVOORDE	Officer got out of the trench, and went off to inform the Division. Finding a loose horse he galloped off and found Major General Capper, who immediately went to find General Ruffin and his second Brigade who were in the neighbourhood of KLEINE ZILLEBEEK. On returning here General Capper found the 4th Guards Brigade already advancing to make a counter-attack through the wood. This attack was shortly afterwards reinforced by General Ruffin who prolonged the line to the left with the 2nd Brigade. On returning to the Grenadiers in their trenches, the Staff Officer discovered them still holding their own and quite happy! They were successfully beating off the futile German attacks to their front. The Germans who had entered the wood on the right rear of the trenches were soon busily engaged meeting the attack of the 4th Guards Brigade and the 2nd Brigade. At 6 p.m. it was decided to withdraw the Grenadiers, and the 3rd Brigade received orders to take over the trenches occupied by the 2nd Guards and Borders, prolonging the line down the east of CHATEAU	Attack by 4th Guards Bde. Plucky defence by Grenadiers.

WAR DIARY
or
INTELLIGENCE SUMMARY.
(Erase heading not required.)

Army Form C. 2118.

XX Brigade
VII Division

Page 39

Instructions regarding War Diaries and Intelligence Summaries are contained in F.S. Regs., Part II. and the Staff Manual respectively. Title pages will be prepared in manuscript.

Hour, Date, Place	Summary of Events and Information	Remarks and references to Appendices
1914 October 31st continued CHATEAU-HERONTHAL	CHATEAU HERONTHAL wood, the 20th Brigade being ordered to join up on their right with the left of the 22nd Brigade, which was somewhere — no-one knew quite the exact spot! — in the middle of the wood. Two guns belonging to the Battery had been left out in rear of the left of the 22nd Brigade trenches. A party of 40 men from the Scots Guards, together with some Bedfords, were taken out and man-handled the guns back behind our trenches, all the men and horses originally belonging to the guns having been completely annihilated, their bodies spread round the guns bearing eloquent testimony to faithful service. At the close of the day the situation remained very much the same as at the commencement as far as our brigade was concerned, and the Germans, in spite of attacking all day in vastly superior numbers, were no nearer taking YPRES. This day they had brought up numbers of new guns, and the shelling was the worst we had so far experienced, nearly all our casualties having been caused by shell fire. Its German infantry can neither shoot or make	Two guns retrieved by Scots Guards & Bedfords, man-handled by the party under command of Brigade Major, Capt Paynter & Capt Brooke. Ypres still intact.

Army Form C. 2118.

WAR DIARY
or
INTELLIGENCE SUMMARY.
(Erase heading not required.)

XX Brigade } Page 40
VII Division

Hour, Date, Place	Summary of Events and Information	Remarks and references to Appendices
1914. October 31st continued CHATEAU-HERONTHAL	make any use of the ground over which they manoeuvred. Had they been of any use at all they must have swept us out of existence by sheer weight of numbers and advanced into YPRES. So critical did the situation become at one time that the Division issued a provisional order at 8 p.m. ordering us to fall back on a new line from one mile E. of ZILLEBEKE to the 57 Kilo: on the YPRES – MENIN road, should we be unable to hold on to our line. This however was unnecessary, as the Germans never succeeded in establishing themselves on our line. At midnight the 21st Brigade relieved Scots Guards and Borders of their trenches, and they were withdrawn to CHATEAU – HERONTHAL. Our greatest difficulty was to find the left of the 2nd Brigade, with whom we had to join up. Col. H.M. Montgomery G.S.I. on the Divisional Staff gallantly rode in the dark through the wood (which was known to be full of the enemy) and eventually returned having discovered where the left of the 2nd Brigade rested. News came in during the night that GHELUVELT had been	Situation critical Col. Montgomery's night ride

Army Form C. 2118.

XX Brigade
VII Division } Page 41

WAR DIARY
or
INTELLIGENCE SUMMARY.
(Erase heading not required.)

Instructions regarding War Diaries and Intelligence Summaries are contained in F. S. Regs., Part II. and the Staff Manual respectively. Title pages will be prepared in manuscript.

Hour, Date, Place	Summary of Events and Information	Remarks and references to Appendices
1914 October 31st continued CHATEAU-HERONTHAL	been recaptured by the Grenadiers (presumably the first Brigade) The line being now established, the Scots Guards and Borders dug themselves in during the night. The Grenadiers (who were in reserve in the CHATEAU HERONTHAL wood) were reinforced by 175 French Cavalry on foot, their Captain informing us they were unable to obtain any more horses in France!	Line again re-established

The 20th Infantry Brigade (Guards) of the 7th Division.

by M.Genrl Sir H. Ruggles-Brise

In September, 1914, the units detailed to form the Brigade - The 1st Bn. Grenadier Guards, the 2nd Bn. Scots Guards, the 2nd Bn. Border Regiment, and the 2nd Bn. Gordon Highlanders - were assembled in the New Forest, and in accordance with privilege and custom Officers of the Brigade of Guards were selected for the various appointments on the Brigade Staff. At first the Brigade was nothing more than a collection of four individual units, but the acquaintance formed during the training quickly ripened into a mutual feeling of trust and friendship. Reports of the early fighting in France showed conclusively that the physical endurance of the troops had been subjected to a severe strain. Consequently no efforts were spared to harden all ranks, and render them fit to face the trials that were in store. The difficulties in the formation of signal companies and in the collection of ordnance stores and transport were gradually overcome, ahd in a short time all anxiously awaited the summons to proceed to the relief of their much tried comrades overseas.

The call came suddenly; On Sunday, October 4th, orders for a divisional field day were issued for the Monday, but at 3 p.m. orders were received that the Brigade was to embark at Southampton that very night for an unknown destination. The embarkation was complete by daylight, and after dark on the evening of the 5th the transports moved into the Solent, called at Dover on the 6th, and were berthed at Zeebrugge early on the 7th, on which day the Brigade was trained to Bruges and was billeted there for the night.

The wanderings of the Brigade in Belgium can be shortly described, the tiring march from Bruges to Ostend, the entrainment to Ghent, the outpost position on the Eastern outskirts, the retirement under cover of darkness, and the eventual arrival at Ypres on the 14th of October by way of Thielt and Roulers. At Thielt, the Grenadiers had the satisfaction of claiming the destruction of a German aeroplane. Needless to add, the claim was much disputed.

So far, the Brigade had responded splendidly to the calls made on its physical endurance, it had made long and tiring marches by day and night with occasional turns of outposts and entrenching. All ranks were short of sleep during the retirement before a superior force, and, though the confusion in the towns was indescribable owing to the crowds of refugees and the disorganisation of the Belgium administration, discipline was fully maintained and the men were in excellent spirits. It was now to face the severest ordeal imaginable; the battle against vastly superior numbers, supported by an overwhelming artillery.

On the 16th October, the Brigade marched out of Ypres, and entrenched on the line Gheluvelt - Zandvoorde. On the following day, half a battalion of the Scots Guards were sent forward to occupy the high ground at Kruiscik, and on the 18th, the whole Brigade advanced and entrenched on the line Kruiscik - America - Zandvoorde. This line it successfully maintained till midnight of October 26th in spite of an intense and accurate artillery fire by day and in spite of infantry attacks by day and night. Owing to the extended line not being continuously entrenched, the snipers at first were troublesome, crawling through the intervals between the trenches and firing from well chosen positions in rear of the front line trenches. A Russian student of battle has said that "on the same spot you must eat and starve, drink and thirst, sleep and die." This was truly the experience of the holders of the front line trenches.

On October 26th at midnight, it was reported to the Brigadier that the Germans had broken through the line, and were in occupation of some houses in rear of the front line trenches. Two companies of the Scots Guards were at once ordered to re-establish the line, no easy matter as the night was exceptionally dark and the rain was falling in torrents. The counter-attack was right gallantly carried through and completely successful, and over 200 prisoners were captured. By daylight, the line had been re-established.

At 7 a.m. the Germans recommenced their attack with a violent artillery fire, the trenches were practically levelled the enemy again broke through and surrounded the trenches occupied by the Scots Guards who fought on till about 3.30 p.m., when the few remaining unwounded were overpowered and taken prisoners. But their stern fighting saved the rest of the Brigade, the Germans made no attempt to follow up their success, and the remnants of the units were collected after dark and were marched to the West of the ridge in rear which was held by another infantry Brigade.

After a day spent in resting and re-organising, the Brigade was ordered on the 28th, to take over a new front line, and entrench it just S.E. of Gheluvelt. The two strongest battalions were detailed, the Grenadiers and Gordons, the line was taken up in the dark and entrenched.

The morning of the 29th was very foggy, under cover of the fog and of a heavy artillery fire the Germans broke through the Brigade on the left, and attacked the Grenadiers from the flank and rear. The Battalion fought with the

greatest gallantry; repeated counter-attacks were made on the
iniative of individual officers; any retirement was at once
followed by a renewed advance; the losses were so constant and
severe that at about 11 a.m. the remnants of the Battalion
were ordered to fall back on to a line in rear held by other
troops.   So impressed were the Germans with the unconquerable
spirit of this Battalion that they made no attempt to advance
or even to hold the ground on which they received such a
severe punishment. On its right, the Gordons had held their
own, and inflicted terrible losses. The original line was
practically recovered that evening by the weak and exhausted
relics of the Brigade, who that night were ordered into reserve.

The whole Brigade was now reduced to the strength
of a weak Battalion. The Grenadiers barely mustered 100
fighting men; the Scots Guards were organised into one weak
company, while the effectives of the two other Battalions had
been almost as largely reduced.

But a well earned rest was not yet their reward.
On the following day the Gordon Highlanders were detached to
assist the 2nd Brigade, while the Scots Guards and Borders
dug themselves in behind the centre of the 7th Division.
On the 31st, the day opened with a heavy artillery bombardment
on the trenches, followed by a massed infantry attack. The
small band of Grenadiers - the only Brigade reserve - was
called upon to make a counter-attack at 2 p.m.   For this it
was commended by the Divisional Commander, and - now reduced
to about 50 men - held a portion of the front line
trenches against all attacks, till it was recalled at
nightfall. On its return it assisted the Scots Guards
to drag in two of our guns which had been abandoned owing
to the detachments and horses having been annihilated.

From November 1st to the 5th, the Brigade held a portion of the front line trenches, was repeatedly shelled, and often attacked. But it never gave way, the Border Regiment being highly praised for maintaining its trenches, though for a time unsupported on its right.

On the 5th, the Brigade was relieved, and started to march back to Meteren. The Brigade Major had succeeded to the Command, three of the Battalions were commanded by Captains and one by a Subaltern. Since the 18th of October it had lost 74% of its effectives, and in spite of the heavy concentration of artillery fire on its trenches was always eager and ready to meet the German infantry, who with an enormous superiority of numbers never broke its stubborn spirit.

7th Division.

B.   H.   Q.

20th INFANTRY BRIGADE

NOVEMBER 1 9 1 4

WAR DIARY
or
INTELLIGENCE SUMMARY.
(Erase heading not required.)

Army Form C. 2118.

XX Brigade
VII Division

Page 42

Hour, Date, Place	Summary of Events and Information	Remarks and references to Appendices
1914 Nov. 1 CHATEAU HERONTHAL	News came in that our Gordon Highlanders had been fiercely engaged all day yesterday and only three officers and 200 men were left of them. Our Brigade now consisted of the following: 1st Grenadier Guards, 5 officers 200 other ranks (commanded by Capt. G. Paech). 2nd Scots Guards, 5 officers 250 other ranks (commanded by Capt. G. Paynter). 2nd Border Regiment 5 officers, 310 other ranks (commanded by Capt. Warren). 2nd Gordon Highlanders 3 officers 200 other ranks (commanded by D. Hamilton). The morning began with a trench shell fire from the Germans on the CHATEAU HERONTHAL occupied by Brigade Headquarters one shell (Jack Johnson) stripping the entire back off the hotel. Headquarters removed to the dug-outs in CHATEAU HERONTHAL woods when the Household Guards and French Cavalry Detachment were in position. The shelling soon became so bad that it was thought desirable to move the whole and it was accordingly placed in a wood just off the road to KLEINE ZILLEBEKE and immediately in rear of the light	

Army Form C. 2118.

XX Brigade
VII Division } Page 43

WAR DIARY
or
INTELLIGENCE SUMMARY.
(Erase heading not required.)

Hour, Date, Place	Summary of Events and Information	Remarks and references to Appendices
1914 November 1, continued	right of our line. At 9.40 a.m. reports came in that the enemy were again massing in front of us on the woods preparatory to an attack. As usual the attack was preceded by a very heavy shelling from the enemy in the trenches, which however did very little damage. Their infantry making a feeble sort of advance which was easily beaten off by us. The 2nd Brigade on our right were more furiously engaged and had some difficulty in retaining their line, but the 2nd Grenadier Guards from the 4th Guards Brigade made a counter attack and saved the situation.	
November 2, 1914.	After a very quiet night improving the trenches adjusting the line, and were entangling the front, the enemy opened a very heavy shell fire on our right, and the left of the 2nd Brigade. At 10.40 a.m. a message came in from Brigadier General Fera Cowan to say that the Northants Regiment on his left were unable to hold their left hand trench any longer and they were being withdrawn into the wood. This left the right of the trenches (held by the Bedfords) exposed. At 12.40 p.m. a message came in to say that the enemy had broken through the gap caused by the Northants having retired. One company

WAR DIARY or INTELLIGENCE SUMMARY.

Army Form C. 2118.

XXth Brigade
4th Division

Page 44

Hour, Date, Place	Summary of Events and Information	Remarks and references to Appendices
1914. November 2nd, Continued	Company of the Bedfords, the 2nd Brigade and a half Battalion of Worcesters were sent up, and eventually relieved them. But the Borders had a bad time from enfilade fire though they gallantly stuck to their trenches. At times the situation was critical and it was doubtful if it would be possible for them to retain their position, all ended well and the Borders were their ground until the enemy was driven out. Throughout the day the 1st Division had been heavily engaged with the enemy on our left though still holding their own. At 10.30 p.m. the following message was received from the C.O. "Stout action of Border Regiment in maintaining its trenches throughout the day, although for a time unsupported on its right is much commended. Congratulate Borders from me, and tell them I am making a special report on their conduct through Corps Headquarters". At 12 midnight the following report of the situation came in "We have maintained our line against very severe attacks throughout the day. On the right the French have made some progress and have taken over 100 prisoners. On our left the French have maintained their line. The enemy attacks the 3rd Corps unsuccessfully. The line will be maintained tomorrow at all costs." During a heavy shelling on our trenches, the Brigadier General H. Ruggles Brise was badly wounded in both arms and the shoulder. Half Major A Cair, the Brigade Major, first on command of the	

Army Form C. 2118.

XXIth Brigade
VII Division

Page 4 5

WAR DIARY
or
INTELLIGENCE SUMMARY.
(Erase heading not required.)

Hour, Date, Place	Summary of Events and Information	Remarks and references to Appendices
1914 November 3rd Continued. The Brigade. November 3rd. 1914	Heavy shelling all the morning. Lieut D Drummond Scots Guards was killed by a sniper. At 1.30 pm the Division sent the following message. "1st Division who's enemy's infantry advancing from Wood just South of GHELUVELT and swinging slightly south. 22nd Brigade has been ordered to support 2/1st Brigade. We have ample support for you too. If any further signal exists where you want it, and if your Trenches want strengthening. Watch gap on hill near Bedfords and woods south of it. Guns are in position ready to shell wood." We felt quite confident the German Infantry would be unable to make much impression on our line, as it was now well wired in front and the Trenches continuous and good ones held by the Grenadiers on the right and the Scots Guards on the left. The only weak spot was just on the right of the Grenadiers next the woods, and this was well covered by the Coldm. Highlanders in rear. The Borders being retained in local reserve in case of counter attack if necessary. At 3.55 pm the Scots Guards reported the enemy to be massing in the wood in front of them. Carriers were ordered moving towards out right but not enough to expect immediate attack. Our guns turned on a heavy shell fire in the wood which apparently had the effect of dispersing the enemy and no	

Army Form C. 2118.

WAR DIARY
or
INTELLIGENCE SUMMARY.
(Erase heading not required.)

XXII Brigade
VII Division
Page 46

Hour, Date, Place	Summary of Events and Information	Remarks and references to Appendices
1914. November 3rd, Continued.	No attack of any importance was made by them; a few advances, but it was more a matter of reconnaissance than an attack. At 8.30 P.M. we got the following report of the situation. "The French attack on our right was not attacking and further large reinforcements are reported at once. The Belgians have also had a marked success N. of DIXMUDE. The Division will remain as it is & in which will be further strengthened during the night."	
November 4th, 1914.	A draft of an Officer (Lieut. Mitchell) and 100 other ranks arrived to Reinforcements. Nothing of importance occurred throughout the day. The Germans continued shelling all day and again massed some Infantry on the woods opposite our front.	
November 5th, 1914.	During a very heavy shell fire the men in the some trenches were relieved into some dug outs, & occupying them again in ample time to meet a futile German advance, we could hardly call it an attack so easily was it beaten back by our rifle fire. At 12 noon a message came to effect now was the return at nightfall by the XXI Brigade. The strength of our Brigade was called to to which was as follows:— 1st Bn Grenadier Guards. 5 Officers 305 other ranks 2nd Bn Scots Guards 4 officers (which includes a draft of 1 officer & 60 men) & 260 other ranks 6 Officers 406 other ranks. Officer [?] 60 m Cain and 100 other ranks after arrival the 2nd Border Regt. date.	

Army Form C. 2118.

WAR DIARY
or
INTELLIGENCE SUMMARY.

(Erase heading not required.)

XX th Brigade } Page 49.
VII Division

Hour, Date, Place	Summary of Events and Information	Remarks and references to Appendices
1914. 5th November, continued	2nd Bn Border Regiment, 9 Officers & 324 Other ranks 2nd Bn Gordon Highlanders, 4 Officers & 316 Other ranks Desultory shell fire continued throughout the day and Borders injured a German Field Gun 200 yards in front of them put out of action by shell rifle fire. The Germans again attempted to attack and again were repulsed. The Yorks Brigade arrived and at 11 pm our 2nd Trench was retaken.	
November 6th, 1914.	After marching all night the Brigade arrived at LOCRE at 6 a.m. On arrival found every available house and shed occupied by the French, who had the church opened and put the Grenadiers and 2nd Scots Guards there, remainder had to bivouac in the adjoining fields much to their disgust as the neighbourhood of LOCRE was very much fouled by the French troops. The latters sanitary arrangements being practically nil. At 2 p.m. the Brigade resumed its march to METEREN via BAILLEUL and went into Billets for rest and refitting.	
November 7th, 1914.	The morning was spent in reorganising the Battalions. Companies were remade and commanders of platoons appointed. The rifles were thoroughly gone through and cleaned many of them having got into a very bad state in the trenches.	Nov: 8th

Army Form C. 2118.

WAR DIARY
or
INTELLIGENCE SUMMARY

(Erase heading not required.)

XXth Brigade
VII Division } Page 48

Hour, Date, Place	Summary of Events and Information	Remarks and references to Appendices

November 8th, 1914.
Divine service was held at 10 am, the R.C's attending the METEREN Church Service. Church of England had a parade under the O.C the Brigade, no Chaplain being available.

November 9th, 1914.
Most of the day spent in cleaning up and refitting. Each Battalion did one hours steady drill. In the afternoon the Brigade was drawn up in a Square formation facing inwards. The G.O.C came down and spoke first to each Battalion in turn and then addressed the Brigade as a whole. He reviewed the approved and administration of the way in which they had fought round YPRES telling them that they had in every way upheld the traditions of their Regiments. The 28th Batty of London Regiment (the others) attached to the Brigade.

November 10th, 1914.
Strength of Brigade now as follows:—
Headquarters: 5 Officers   50 other ranks
Grenadier Guards: 6 Officers   404 other ranks
Scots Guards   6 Officers   400 other ranks
2nd Border Regt.   11 Officers   422 other ranks
Gordon Highlanders.   5 Officers   443 other ranks

Brigade Machine Gun teams under Lieut A Taylor Scots Guards. Began to be reorganised but only two complete sections could be formed. These were formed by massing the

Army Form C. 2118.

WAR DIARY
or
INTELLIGENCE SUMMARY

(Erase heading not required.)

XXth Brigade } Page 49
VIIth Division }

Hour, Date, Place	Summary of Events and Information	Remarks and references to Appendices
1914.		
November 10. Continued	The numbers of the guns and names of the Machine Gun Sections of the entire Brigade and forming them with the complete sections.	
November 11th, 1914.	Call roll of the Brigade made up to date.	
November 12th, 1914.	Forward orders from the Chief's Office sent to each Battalion of the Brigade in a similar proportion with a view to giving them commissions. The following drafts arrived to the Brigade, Grenadiers 4 officers 400 men, Scots Guards 7 officers 250 men, Gordon Highlanders 1 officer and 50 men. A line from NEUVE EGLISE — KEMMEL reconnoitred with a view to the Division being required to occupy it at short notice.	
November 13th, 1914.	Field Marshal Sir John French visited the Brigade and saw each Battalion in its Billets. He complimented the officers and men on the fine work they had done round YPRES. Orders received that the Division will move tomorrow to occupy trenches in neighbourhood of FLEURBAIX. Our Brigade to relieve the 19th Brigade.	
November 14th, 1914.	Marched to SAILLY, where the 19th Brigade. Grenadiers on the right, Scots Guards centre — Border Regiment on the left. The trenches taken over by the Grenadiers an absolute disgrace to any British Regt.	

Army Form C. 2118.

Page 50.

WAR DIARY
or
INTELLIGENCE SUMMARY XXIst Brigade
VIIth Division

Hour, Date, Place	Summary of Events and Information	Remarks and references to Appendices
1914 November 14th continued	British Regiment. Two who had been in occupation of the ground for three weeks and apparently have done no digging, a entanglements 10 yards of it all and the trenches had been left in a very dirty state. The distance from the German trenches vary from 5 to 6 hundred yards to one hundred and fifty. The Germans have been fairly active in front both with their shelling and from their trenches. Every house within a mile of the trenches has been levelled by their guns. Brigadier General F. Heyworth, D.S.O. arrived from England to take over the Command of the Brigade.	
November 15/16, 1914.	The 21st Brigade which had been left behind at NEUVE EGLISE rejoined the Division. They we have two days rest and then take over the centre section of our line. This will give us up 2,500 yards to hold instead of 3,500. On our right are the Indian Division. They kept up an incessant roar of musketry all night. They will shortly to be relieved by the 8th Division. This will get the IV Corps all together for the first time and it has been formed. The Germans are busy digging saphheads out towards us. Lieut. G. Ward — Grenadier Guards, wounded. Our Staff Captain — Captain Brooks, leaves us to take over Brigade Major, 101 Brigade.	Nov: 16th

Army Form C. 2118.

WAR DIARY
or
INTELLIGENCE SUMMARY

XXth Brigade, VII Division Page 51

(Erase heading not required.)

Instructions regarding War Diaries and Intelligence Summaries are contained in F. S. Regs., Part II. and the Staff Manual respectively. Title pages will be prepared in manuscript.

Hour, Date, Place	Summary of Events and Information	Remarks and references to Appendices
November 16, 1914.	The following is now the strength of the Brigade. Grenadier Guards. 9 Officers 980 men Scots Guards 21 Officers 1042 men Borders Regt. 6 Officers 400 men Gordon Highlanders 4 Officers 500 men Inhabitants in neighbourhood of Zinchio being removed. Snipers and spies reported to be plentiful in rear of the trenches.	
November 16, 1914.	The increased downfall of rain is making the trenches very bad. Scots Guards sent in a good report of German trenches. Lieut. L. Cain going out in the dark and making a personal reconnaissance. The Germans are sapping forward and making parallels from their saphead. One parallel opposite the right of the Scots Guards has now advanced to within a hundred yards of them.	
November 17, 1914.	Steady rain and some snow fell. Water lying in the trenches much hampered us. the snow shows the men up to a great extent.	
November 18th, 1914.	More snow fell and cold continues. Some men frost bitten.	
November 19, 1914.	Following drafts arrived.	1st Grenadiers

Army Form C. 2118.

WAR DIARY
or
INTELLIGENCE SUMMARY XXth Brigade. } Page. 52
(Erase heading not required.) VIIth Division.

Hour, Date, Place	Summary of Events and Information	Remarks and references to Appendices
1914. November 19, Cambrin.	1st Grenadier Guards. 6 Officers 100 other ranks Border Regiment 12 men. London Highlanders 12 men. The following officers arrived with 100 Grenadier draft; Captain the Earl Stanhope, Captain Morrison, 2nd Lieut Lord Bingbourne, Lord W Percy, 2nd Lieut Rhys Williams. &c. Whale smocks issued for troops to reconnoitre in the snow.	
November 20, 1914.	The troops are now doing seven days in the trenches and three days off. Boders and finding where the troops bivouac. Cold spell very severe. Several cases of frost-bite in the trenches. A good report of the German Trenches sent in from the Scots Guards from information collected by one of their Scouts Pte Reay, who crawled out in a snipers nightshirt. Braziers are being collected and issued to the trenches, the difficulty is fuel and to keep them going.	
November 21, 1914.	A draft of 1 Officer and 100 men arrived for the London Highlanders.	
November 22, 1914.	(See app Page) Grenadiers reported 30 cases of frost bite in their Battalion in the trenches. The lines of their trenches have two bad salients in them and they	

Army Form C. 2118.

WAR DIARY
or
INTELLIGENCE SUMMARY

XXII Brigade } Page 53
VII Division

(Erase heading not required.)

Instructions regarding War Diaries and Intelligence Summaries are contained in F. S. Regs., Part II. and the Staff Manual respectively. Title pages will be prepared in manuscript.

Hour, Date, Place	Summary of Events and Information	Remarks and references to Appendices

1914.

November 22 (continued) (See of 1 in 1, p 23.a).
and they are now digging a new line slightly in rear so to do away with the salient as no plan

— Old Line.
--- New Line.
Rough Scale
200 0 200 400 600

Germans reported to be entrenching the parallel at their own heads opposite left of Gunaducu.
Rifle grenades wanted to the Trenches.

November 23, 1914.
Reports from Trenches state the Machine guns are continually being fryer also the Rifle Oil. The new rounds of boots are very bad, they are made of very insufficient leather and the sole come away from the uppers. The wiring in front of the Trenches has been allowed to get in very bad a way the continual firing cut it up.
Orders issued for the R.E. to put it in good order the troops in the Trenches to be made responsible for repairing subsequent damage.
The Brigadier conducted Church Service to Church of England.

Army Form C. 2118.

WAR DIARY
or
INTELLIGENCE SUMMARY

XXth Brigade } Page 54.
VII Division

(Erase heading not required.)

Instructions regarding War Diaries and Intelligence Summaries are contained in F.S. Regs., Part II. and the Staff Manual respectively. Title pages will be prepared in manuscript.

Hour, Date, Place	Summary of Events and Information	Remarks and references to Appendices
1914. November 23, Continued	Church of England men. The Germans putting in their Shrapnell Shells close by while the service was going on. Our snipers shot a German observation officer.	
November 24, 1914	A cold thaw set in. Captain Paynter commanding Scots Guards went sick with Bronchitis and a temperature of 103°. Command of the Battalion taken over by Captain Don; R Cope with Lieut Law as adjutant. Major Trotter Grenadier Guards injured. Godin Highlanders Machine Gun killed two Germans. A patrol of the Grenadiers killed three.	
November 25, 1914.	Still thawing and the trenches are becoming a stream of liquid mud. Stridor in everywhere much as usual. Very heavy gun fire heard in direction of YPRES.	
November 26, 1914.	Germans evidently had the jumps last night as they opened a very heavy fire about midnight which lasted two hours. Lieut Rugers and a German Clerk getting to the Scots Guards. Scots Guards had two men killed in the night.	
November 27, 1914.	Scots Guards made a very successful small raid on the German trenches. Lieut Sir E Hulse and eight men crawled up and fired into their trenches apart	

1247 W 3299 200,000 (E) 8/14 J.B.C. &A. Forms/C. 2118/11.

Army Form C. 2118.

XXII Brigade } Page 55
VII Division

WAR DIARY
or
INTELLIGENCE SUMMARY
(Erase heading not required.)

Hour, Date, Place	Summary of Events and Information	Remarks and references to Appendices

November 27 continued. A party of about 20 Germans were setting round a fire into these they discharged a Rifle Grenade. They got back under a very heavy fire with the loss of two men missing. The following information was obtained by them. The German Trenches are so slingly as our own.

Their sentries are not over vigilant. There is no obstacle in front of their Trenches.

Their loopholes are placed very low in the parapet, and they are sited obliquely.

November 28th, 1914. Shell loopholes served out to the Trenches. We visited our Brigade Headquarters and found them absolutely bullet proof. At ranges of 60 and 100 yards the plate was not even dented.

November 29, 1914. G.O.C inspected the Grenadiers who were in Divisional Reserve. Church of England Divine Service conducted by the Brigadier. Major Ross commanding 55th Company R.E. which have been attached to the Brigade throughout the whole war — was killed last night putting up the wire outside the Trenches a great loss. Neither he nor his Company had shown themselves in keeping with our Trenches and wire entanglements this whole war. He was a man full of resource and courage.

Nov 30

Army Form C. 2118.

WAR DIARY
or
INTELLIGENCE SUMMARY XXII (Brigade) VII Division

(Erase heading not required.)

Page 56

Hour, Date, Place	Summary of Events and Information	Remarks and references to Appendices
November 30, 1914.	Lieutenant Colonel Noah Rowe, arriving to take over command of the 1st Bn. Grenadier Guards, Lt. Colonel Corry, who was temporarily in command of the Battalion during Captain Paynter's absence, was wounded. Lieut. Loder took over command of the Battalion.	

Report by Capt E.L. Speirs.

30th November 1914.

German attack on ECURIE N. of ARRAS on 27th, 28th, and 29th inst.

1. The German attack on the trenches N. of ECURIE was carried-out by elements of the 12th, 13th, and 3rd Bavarian Reserve Regts. and by 1 Battalion of Sappers.

2. The French defending troops belonged to the Algerian Division.

3. The German attack progressed by sap heads which, being worked by sappers advanced with great rapidity, the sap heads were connected by trenches.

4. The sap heads in the course of an afternoon progressed under the wire entanglements and some got to within 5x of the French trenches.

5. During the whole afternoon of the 27th the French were subject to Artillery fire while the sap heads progressed con-centrically towards ECURIE-When the Germans were so close that their Artillery could no longer fire the French were subjected to such a violent fire from Grenades and Minenwerfers that they had to evacuate their trenches for a length of some 300x.

6. A counter attack was at once organized, the lost trenches were recaptured as well as the sap heads and some German trenches, but these had been mined and were now blown up by the Germans. The French retired to their 2nd line.

7. A counter attack on the same night had to be given up owing to the moon-light.

8. On the afternoon of the 29th the lost trenches were occupied but are only to be held till a better position in rear can be prepared.

20 Inf Bde

For your information.

Ian Stewart Major.
General Staff, 7th Division.

7th Division.

B. H. Q.

20th INFANTRY BRIGADE

DECEMBER 1 9 1 4

W A R   D I A R Y.

Headquarters, 20th Infantry Brigade.

December 1914.

December 1st, 1914.	His Majesty the King arrived at Divisional Head quarters and gave D.S.O's and D.C.M.s away. He was accompanied by President Poincaré, General Joffre, The Prince of Wales and Sir Pertab Singh.
December 2nd, 1914. (December)	Captain James arrived to take over duties of Communication Officer vice Lieut Palmer who is now attached to Divl Staff Captain. A draft of 4 Officers and 540 men arrived for the Border. One Officer and 60 men for the Grenadiers. The Germans attacked & have me out of ammunition which fiercely armour'd plate. One of our men killed today through the armour'd plate looph'ole.
December 3rd, 1914.	Everything much the same as usual in the trenches. A German shouted across to the Scots Guards do "Don't you wish you were in London doing Guards." The G.O.C held a conference re attacking German trenches. All the Brigade Staff's attending. Heavy Rain. Dec 4th

1247 W 3299 200,000 (E) 8/14 J.B.C. & A. Forms/C. 2118/11.

Army Form C. 2118.

XXth Brigade } Page 59.
VIIth Division }

WAR DIARY
or
INTELLIGENCE SUMMARY
(Erase heading not required.)

Hour, Date, Place	Summary of Events and Information	Remarks and references to Appendices
1914. December 4, 1914.	The G.O.C. had all the Brigade and Artillery staffs out to watch Mortar Guns and Hand Grenades. The experiments taking place at BAC ST MAUR. Quite one of the most "engrossing" mornings of the campaign. The Mortar Guns were field experiments with, we two French Guns dated 1848. The 1st shot proved quite successful being fired with a light charge and the round shot was not charged with gun cotton. It went some 900 feet in the air and landed about 160 yards away. Encouraged by this a heavier charge was used and the gun gave more elevation. What happened to the shell we don't know, the gun went off with a roar, there was a crack amongst the bystanders of an apple tree above the heads of the spectators standing behind and the gun were seen to be horning the reverse way, to which it had turned. Several more shots were fired with different charges none were very accurate and it appears that the gun was very unreliable. No two shots with the same charge and elevation getting the same range, but the gunners seem to think they will be able to get it going all right after they have had some more practise experiments. We then tried the hand grenades. Two types were home made " by the R.E. and one a french one. The first we tried were made of a gun cotton with the plumers inside lit by a fuse timed for four seconds. The	

WAR DIARY or INTELLIGENCE SUMMARY

Army Form C. 2118.

XXth Brigade
VII Division

Page 58

Hour, Date, Place	Summary of Events and Information	Remarks and references to Appendices
1914 December 4th continued.	The second "the Hairbrush" so called because of its shape, also fired with a second fuze. The third kind, the Trench Mortar, was the best. A large thing is attached to the Hungarian fuze which goes off out of the bomb when thrown, the explosion taking place in two seconds. The "jam pot" kind were not much use but the Hair Brushes were good, bursting with a tremendous explosion. The recent heavy rain is causing a lot of the trenches to fall in. One man in the Border Regt. trenches at A.1 was suffocated before he could be got out.	
December 5, 1914	Very heavy rain all day making the trenches knee deep in slush and mud in places. The 6th Bn. (Tewkesbury) Gordon Highlanders arrived and are attached to this Brigade. Captain Withered to command the Scots Guards.	
December 6th, 1914.	Church of England service conducted by the Brigadier at 11 a.m. New books made out for the trenches. The Grenadiers and Scots Guards relieving each other in No "W" section. No 2 Subsection being found by 5 Bn. of Brd Gordon Highlanders, 5 Bn. Borders, and 200 men of the 6th Bn. Gordon Highlanders. The Germans have put out "chevaux-de-frise" in front of all their trenches.	Dec 4th

WAR DIARY or INTELLIGENCE SUMMARY

Army Form C. 2118.

XXth Brigade } VIIth Division Page 59.

Hour, Date, Place	Summary of Events and Information	Remarks and references to Appendices
1914 December 7th, 1914.	Blowing a gale and very wet. The Prince of Wales and Major Barry came to Brigade Headquarters just after the German shot a "Jack Johnson" which burst outside the house.	
December 8th, 1914.	Still very wet, and we are having a hard time fighting the trenches from falling in. Practically the whole of them have to be rerooted with wood. Our artillery fair.	
December 9th, 1914.	Trench's rain alight when blazed all day. Major Ottley went out on a sight close up to the German trenches. He heard two officers discussing matters about a "dug-out". The sentries challenging in English "'Who goes there' Halt wer is Dar" so "Halt who goes there". Another wet day.	
December 10th, 1914.	Experiments carried out on bomb throwing and cutting wire entanglements.	
December 11th, 1914.	Very heavy rain all night. The communication are so full of mud that three men of 6th Bn Gordon Highlanders had to be dragged out as they were unable to move. The Highlanders choro out guide walks in the mud drags them off and they get lost in the dark. The Gordons lost fifteen fuae last night.	
December 12th, 1914.	A draft to the Grenadiers under Lieut Hon. H. Douglas Pennant arrived. More rain and more trenches falling in.	

Dec 13th

Army Form C. 2118.

Cap 60

WAR DIARY
or
INTELLIGENCE SUMMARY

XXII Brigade
VII Division

(Erase heading not required.)

Hour, Date, Place	Summary of Events and Information	Remarks and references to Appendices
December 13th, 1914.	The 91st Brigade withdrawn from the trenches in support in attack the 3rd Corps are going to carry out. Our Brigade takes over the right half of their line and the 22nd Brigade takes over the left. The Germans shelled our area for a while in the afternoon. No damage done, in spite of "Black Johnsons" landing quite close to our transport lines.	
December 14th, 1914.	Heavy rain all night. Trenches in a very bad state in consequence. The Germans were engaged heavily with gun and rifle fire to prevent them throwing their line to reinforce where we are going to attack. The 6th Bn Gordon Highlanders are beginning to feel the strain of the trenches, all their men are very young and their Drachen turns much to be desired.	
December 15th, 1914.	Brigadier Ottley took doolie Encaros sent a good report on the German trenches, when close up to them in the night they fired a star shell, by which light he discovered he was lying on a dead German. He reached the shoulder straps. The myn belonged to the 12/of Regiment 25th Brigade VII Corps, commanded by the Duke of Wurtemburg. The G.O.C. held a conference at 6.15 pm about attacking the German trenches, methods on a plane being discussed.	Dec 16th.

Army Form C. 2118.

Page 61

WAR DIARY
or
INTELLIGENCE SUMMARY XXth Brigade VIIth Division

(Erase heading not required.)

Hour, Date, Place	Summary of Events and Information	Remarks and references to Appendices
December 16th, 1914.	Nothing of importance occurred, the Germans shelled us a short while in the afternoon.	
December 17th, 1914.	Rather an unfortunate day, the Germans being very active. 1 Officer Lieut Coch. Gordon Hdrs. being killed. 1 Officer Lieut. 6 A.M. Cap Scots Guards wounded in addition to Lieut. and 2 men Scots Guards killed and 2 men of the Bordw. and Gordons wounded. The Scots Guards Machine Gun Detachment had a lucky escape a German shell destroying the barn in whose top they were billeted too, which place they had only left four minutes before to go and do some Machine Gun drill. Lieut. The Earl of Kintore, Scots Guards did a fine piece of shooting this morning just after daybreak. Three Germans got out the trenches opposite him. He dropped two of them. At 12.15 a.m. Major Stewart R.S. 210 the Devons called to tell us our Major were ordered to make a move, but during the night an aide came in to say there would be no more doing the night, but the R.O.C. wrote it to see the Brigadier at 9 a.m. He returned at 9 a.m. with orders for an attack to be carried out this evening. The General idea being that at 4 p.m. all the guns of the Division were to open fire on the German trenches opposite.	

1247 W 3290 200,000 (E) 8/14 J.B.C.& M. Form C. 2118/11.

WAR DIARY
INTELLIGENCE SUMMARY

XXth Brigade
VIIth Division

Page 62

Hour, Date, Place	Summary of Events and Information	Remarks and references to Appendices
1914 December 18th continued	Officers of the 22nd Brigade, who were to attack the Germans at 4.30 p.m. At 6 p.m. Our Brigade was to attack with two half Bns on the right of our attack being along the edge of the SAILLY–FROMELLES road. The 21st Brigade who will returning to the DIVISION during the night, were to occupy their old line on the trenches and attacking during the night probably at 10 p.m. The Scots Guards were now in occupation of the right subsection (No 1) and the left (No 2) subsection. Also half the 2nd Brigade line was held by 2 Companies each of the 2nd Borders, 2nd and 6th Bn of the Gordon Highlanders. The 6th Batt: Gordon Highlanders were thought to be too inexperienced to use in the firing line so they were withdrawn to the "Rue Tilloi" and unnamed in Rear, their two Companies being relieved by the 2nd Bn Gordon Highlanders. It was decided to double man the trenches of the front of attack, so the Scots Guards were all withdrawn from the right of No 1 Subsection being relieved by the Grenadiers and Irish Gardes were closer to the right to join at 6 p.m. with the Scots Guards. The plan being that at 6 p.m. a given signal for the attack to commence the two Companies of each Battn who were carrying out the attack were	

Army Form C. 2118.

WAR DIARY or INTELLIGENCE SUMMARY

XXth Infantry Brigade
VIIth Division

Page 63.

(Erase heading not required.)

Hour, Date, Place	Summary of Events and Information	Remarks and references to Appendices

1914
December 18th Continued

were to be hurried up the trench out of their trenches by their Coy Coys who were remaining in the Brigade Headquarters were themselves down to trenches. Brigade Headquarters were themselves down to LA CORDONNIÈRE FARM so as to be in close touch with the trenches. The whole time 10 guns a heavy fire and kept the Germans pinned down to their trenches and prevent them from reinforcing the trenches and being short of ammunition they were front. The guns had the effect only were not going to open on a message to the 10th more their bombardment fire till 4.15 pm so as to make their bombardment of the German trenches all the more violence fire to the attack by the 22nd Brigade. Time was all too short to make much more than a hasty plan of whom The Grenadiers had to go down and relieve the Scots Guards in No 1 Subsection in broad daylight and The unfortunate artillery for No 2 Subsection. The included the above all day by the Batteries all round to shew unusual activity on the part of our troops. About 6.30pm we heard that the attack delivered by a Battn and a half of the 22nd Brigade had failed. At 6 pm in a judgement signed of a white being sounded the Scots Guards attached their attack. Either from not having the wheats is not being ready the Bodies failed their started till 6.30pm. The Scots Guards attack was under Captain G Paynter. That of the Bodies being led by Captain Cotton. The Scots Guards advanced as quietly

WAR DIARY or INTELLIGENCE SUMMARY

XXth Brigade
VII. Division

Page 64.

Hour, Date, Place	Summary of Events and Information	Remarks and references to Appendices

1914.
December, 18th Continued.

so quietly as possible could close up to the German trenches being lucky enough to find very little wire in front of them. They then rushed the trenches and bayoneted all the Germans who were in occupation, completely surprising them until they were almost in their grasp. In place though, parties of them got up again & strong parties were entanglements and tore heavily wooden hoardings. The night was very dark and the German trenches were not taken in isolated patches. The enemy had a machine gun in the right trenches which caused great havoc among the men who were held up by the barbed wire entanglements. The reign of the attack failing to get through, Brigadier Officers were sent forward with as many men as could be spared from the trenches to support the front. He was severely wounded and most of the men were killed and wounded. On gaining the trenches the men then made the positions as well as they could in the meal face of the enemy's trenches but the trenches were very deep and as our men could not see out of them to reply, the Germans [in many of them climbed out and made a few frank fire, taking on the parapet the men on each front firing down the trenches to their right and left respectively. The Germans then brought up very strong reinforcements from their second line of trenches and aided by their machine gun which was now enfilading their parapet (on which many of our men were lying) retook some of their trenches at 11.30 p.m.

Army Form C. 2118.

Page 65

WAR DIARY
or
INTELLIGENCE SUMMARY

XXth (Brigade)
VIIth (Division)

(Erase heading not required.)

Hour, Date, Place	Summary of Events and Information	Remarks and references to Appendices
1914. 18th December continued	At 11.30 p.m. The attack of the Borders on the 3rd Guards left having failed and the Engineers who were to have been in their support to close the trench they had taken by blocking it with sandbags and defending the flank with hand grenades, having not got up, their officer Captain Boscawen wounded, it was thought, to be wiser for men to have retained the attack. The German howevers were unable to dislodge the men from the centre of the trenches. CO communicating cap was placed out to it and Lieutenant Warner was sent out with a party to unblock the trenches in which Lieut Duncan Marsares who were the men under Lieut Graham trenches. Finding it was impossible to get the out through the enemy trenches by daylight and the party their held, it was weak to withstand any attack, they held, it was decided to withdraw them. Captain Walsh got the men back with very little loss carrying Lieut Bacmars, wounded in a stretcher with them. The following were the casualties amongst the two companies of the Scots Guards:—	

Officers
Missing:
Wounded.

1. [illegible] 2. Capt. H. Taylor. Lt. R. Nugent.
3. Lieut Sir J Fitz Wigram Lieut Ling Baumann Lieut Ottley.

Wounded and Missing

Army Form C. 2118.

Page 66

WAR DIARY
or
INTELLIGENCE SUMMARY XXch Brigade
VIth Division

(Erase heading not required.)

Hour, Date, Place	Summary of Events and Information	Remarks and references to Appendices
1914 18th December continued	Wounded and missing.. Lieut Hon J Hanbury Tracy. Other ranks Killed 29. Wounded 69. Missing 40. Wounded and missing 44. Total 186. The Border Casualties were. Captain N Askew. Wounded and Missing (Dead) Captain C Lamb DSO. Wounded (Died) Lieut N Crofts, " R.S.M. McKendry, " Other ranks Killed 7. Wounded 40. Missing 64. Total 115. Of the missing in the above lists it is impossible to find out who amongst them were killed and who wounded. The following was the description of the German trenches. Depth 6 to 4 feet. Width about 5 feet. Two steps on the forward face for the firing position. Loopholes were low down made by sinking a conical hot narrow at out end and broadening over the narrow end nearest the enemy. Bullet proof plate Macdonalds broad end. At the loopholes.	

WAR DIARY
INTELLIGENCE SUMMARY

XXII Brigade
VII Division

Page 64

Army Form C. 2118.

Hour, Date, Place	Summary of Events and Information	Remarks and references to Appendices
1914 December 18th Enclosure	loopholes set slightly obliquely to the line of fire. Wire was running along the inside of the trenches. (Telephone or mine) Trenches every ten yards. Men and rifles of the trench bombed. Dug out in rear of the trench. Opposite the local Guards the Germans behaved well and allowed them to bring in their wounded, but threw the bodies of the wounded men in many cases shot whenever they moved. One man who was shot through both thighs dragged himself as far as our parapet and was then led just as he reached it. Most of these were shots at 65 to 80 yards. There was no firing going on at the time, and they were all deliberate shots. Nothing of importance occurred during the remainder of the day. Our Casualties on the Brigade say 11 Officers and just over 300 other ranks. Although not much has apparently been accomplished in our raids we have kept the Germans on their guns & tired and prevented them from reinforcing further south where the French are undertaking a big advance in the neighbourhood of ARRAS. We also learnt a few hints for future guidance of any advance amongst others chiefly as follows. Activity amongst our troops was much to be apparent when we moved troops down to reinforce the trenches. This together with	

WAR DIARY or INTELLIGENCE SUMMARY

XX th Brigade
VII Division

Army Form C. 2118.
Page 68

Hour, Date, Place	Summary of Events and Information	Remarks and references to Appendices
1914 December 18, continued	with the heavy shelling from our guns, gave the German ample warning of something on. The attacks were not simultaneous. The rifles got so clogged up with mud that only one in four could be used. The signal for the attack was not heard by all the troops. The men all lost their spades and sandbags. Arrangements must be made for the men to get through their own wire entanglements simultaneously before they start. Small isolated attacks are useless.	
December 20th 1914	All quiet in front. A lot of my dead are still being picked up by our Thirty four men missing of the Bodies returned. They had lain out all day in a small duck between the two lines of trenches and got back under cover of darkness. The constant rain is melting the trenches almost invisible, and the communicating trenches (mostly improved ditches) are now impassable. To reach the troops in the trenches one takes the early fetching them four hours. They have only to go back a mile. It's now a choice of two evils for any one entering the trenches. They can either use the communicating trench which goes up the knees deep in mud and water, or go over the top of the	

WAR DIARY or INTELLIGENCE SUMMARY

XXII Brigade, VII Division

Page 69

Hour, Date, Place	Summary of Events and Information	Remarks and references to Appendices
1914 December 20 continued	over the 10th of the ground which is well swept by the rifle fire of the enemy. The RIVER DE LAYES, a deep ditch which draws all the surrounding country, has risen six inches in the last 48 hours. Our new Church of England Chaplain Captain Abbot, held a service for the troops. The first we have had with a proper conducting the service since we left ENGLAND.	
December 21, 1914.	Two wounded men of the Bodies discovered to be still out in front, close under the German parapet. Impossible to get them in until tonight. The R.E. all trying to make a scheme for draining off the water from the trenches but as the country is dead flat for miles and only 16 feet above the sea level we have not much hope of matters getting much better. All the inhabitants tell us that this country gets absolutely water-logged in winter.	
December 22, 1914.	The two men wounded on the night of the 18-19 brought in one off the head and the other quite unable. The latter told us the Germans shot at all the wounded who showed any sign of movement. In front of their trenches. He himself feigned death and dragged out of a fusilade at night. Both men's toes do had gangrened. News came in that the Indians	

WAR DIARY
INTELLIGENCE SUMMARY

xxiv Brigade
VIII Division

Page 40
Army Form C. 2118.

Hour, Date, Place	Summary of Events and Information	Remarks and references to Appendices
1914		
December 22, Enterred	Indians have left their trenches and that the 100 Sepoys had been sent to reinforce them and counter-attack the Germans.	
December 23, 1914	The RIVER-DE-LAYES rising a lot, water coming down the communication trenches and part of the trenches have a foot of water in them. Fatigue parties all night clearing and deepening ditches to try and get the water to run off.	
December 24th, 1914	Nothing of importance happened. The Grenadier Regt. [?] more two and a half of their platoons from the fire trenches as the men were up to their waists in water. A new form of trench dug to cover the gap caused by the floods. A change in the weather, very sharp frost.	
December 25th, 1914.	Last night one of our Sgts. Sir Mister of the 100 Guards was out. He heard a voice from the German trenches shouting that the Germans would like a "party". A man came out to him and said they wanted to have a quiet Xmas Day, all their men were sick of the war. They had lost twenty two killed in last Sundays attack; On an officer approaching, the man changed his conversation and pretended being about Xmas. The officer gave our four some cigars and sent a message to say that if we agreed not to shoot today they the Germans would do the same and Xmas Day	

WAR DIARY or INTELLIGENCE SUMMARY

Army Form C. 2118.

XXth Brigade } Page 4/.
VIIth Division }

Hour, Date, Place	Summary of Events and Information	Remarks and references to Appendices
1914 December 25. Continued	Xmas Day might be hoped in peace. The Day passed off with not a shot being fired after 9 am by either side. About 10 am both sides appeared outside their trenches. An officer went across and met the German commanding officer and they agreed to bury all the dead which was lying out between the trenches. The dead were collected and a bit German and British were buried side by side. Captain Chaplain of the force Adam conducting the burial service which was interspersed by a German student of Divinity whaling it after him. The following report was given by Captain Indian Commanding the Q Detachment "The commandant of the German forces immediately in front of my subsection came in of two French about 10 am. I met him two half way between the two lines of trenches. We agreed to bury the dead, any bodies of our men on the half way line should be carried across by their men and vice-versa, so that there was no possibility of viewing the trenches. This was done and all the dead have now been buried. I would like to point out that the Bodies who made their night attack were informing of great German dead and I would add that the Germans made a counter attack to record the following immediately holding the points of the line</tbody>	

WAR DIARY
INTELLIGENCE SUMMARY

XXIII Brigade } Page 72
VIII Division

Army Form C. 2118.

Hour, Date, Place	Summary of Events and Information	Remarks and references to Appendices

1914.
December 25th. Continued.

immediately in front of my subsection:- The Saxon Corps, 52½ and 109th Bavarians. The men are mostly young but of good physique. I noticed the majority of them carried hand grenades at their sides, several of them showed me the "Iron Cross" which they had received which would make it appear that they had very fighting in other parts before coming here. I obtained information about Captain Eaker and Bowers Regt. He was in their trenches, lying, his revolver at them, when he was killed. Captain Hanbury-Tracey, 2nd Coldstream Guards, was captured by them (wounded) and lived for 6 hours. The officers gave him off. They said only seven prisoners were taken by them. He said during the night attack of the 18th. I am quite confident none of the Germans attacked our trenches and men were in observation in the trenches all day."

Captain Taylor's body was also found and the Germans reported they captured an officer, wounded officer which must be Lieut. R. Nugent, Scots Guards, as he is the only one not accounted for.

December 26, 1914. The day passed off quietly nothing of note hung and forth

Army Form C. 2118.

WAR DIARY or INTELLIGENCE SUMMARY

XXth Brigade
VII Division

Page 43

Hour, Date, Place	Summary of Events and Information	Remarks and references to Appendices
1914. December 26. Continued	both sides outside their trenches walking about. The Germans complained that they had no meat. Some of the men sent them over some of their "Bully Beef". They all could have fought for the "Hie Tigro". Most of the men reported "missing" after the fight on the night of 18-19 were now accounted for. The Germans say they only took ten prisoners. The remainder were all killed or died of wounds. A great many of the dead both British and German were found lying together on the ground between the trenches, & men of various of the fiercer contest which must have taken place in the trenches. The Germans testified that most of their wounds were caused by bayonets. This is accounted for by the fact that our men when rifles were not clogged up with mud they were unable to fire with them. Means to avoiding this evil has now been adopted. Each man is now being served out with a loose rough canvas bag to slip over the muzzle of his rifle and which is able to be pulled off instantly the rifle is required for use. Every if the rifle is required on the shew of the moment it does no harm to fire it off with the bag still in position on the rifle. A large number of men were employed in cleaning	

Army Form C. 2118.

Page 94

WAR DIARY
or
INTELLIGENCE SUMMARY   XXth (Brigade)
                        VIth Division
(Erase heading not required.)

Hour, Date, Place	Summary of Events and Information	Remarks and references to Appendices

1914.
December 26, Continued. | Clearing out the RIVER-DE-LAYES in the hopes of being able to drain some of the water out of the trenches. Every day more of the latter are being inundated with water by the rain incessing floods. In consequence of so many men being killed and wounded up arriving and putting plate work out in front of the trenches, most are now being made. They are wired up before being placed and rolled out; men crawling out to peg them down when in position. False alarm at 11 p.m. of an intended German attack. All was quiet however throughout night. |

December 27th, 1914. | Many of the trenches fell up, and the day was further employed repairing them. The Germans tried to come over and enjoy another days "parallel" armistice, but were informed that they must keep in their trenches. They seemed to be quite indignant and said they wouldn't fire if we didn't, but if we had orders to fire |

1247 W 3299 200,000 (E) 8/14 J.B.C. & A. Form/C. 2118/11.

WAR DIARY or INTELLIGENCE SUMMARY

XXII Brigade ? VII Division

Page 45.

Army Form C. 2118.

Hour, Date, Place	Summary of Events and Information	Remarks and references to Appendices
1914 December 27, Continued	Those signed to them with their colleges first fired into the air.	
December 28, 1914	Last night the Germans enticed four door's Guards Fusiliers to come into their trenches - & say they have not returned. C Company of 150 men tried to bomb throwers under Br Lieut Chip William T.C. Gunadier Guards took two fames a shell time and are making excellent progress. Two Company supplies two men per platoon when in the trenches. One hundred men have also been permanently attached to the 65th Field Company R.E. to work under them in the trenches. These men are composed of men who in civil life are miners.	
December 29, 1914 20 and 31st	Nothing of importance occurred, the constant heavy rain playing havoc with the trenches. The country has now become completely waterlogged. the fact that the water is dammed up and purified out of one portion of the trenches it breaks through in another place. This	

Army Form C. 2118.

WAR DIARY
or
INTELLIGENCE SUMMARY

(Erase heading not required.)

Instructions regarding War Diaries and Intelligence Summaries are contained in F. S. Regs., Part II. and the Staff Manual respectively. Title pages will be prepared in manuscript.

Hour, Date, Place	Summary of Events and Information	Remarks and references to Appendices
December 29, 30 and 31st continued	The Germans are in the same plight and can be seen at pumping operations daily. It has now become impossible to dig any trench below a depth of two feet, water forming in the bottom at once if a greater depth is dug. In very bad spots it has been necessary to revet and build breastworks behind those parts of the trenches which have been made untenable by the floods.	

20th Infy. Bde.

    The G. O. C., has had great pleasure in forwarding to Head Quarters, 4th Corps, a despatch (of which this is a copy for your retention) testifying to the devoted conduct of the Officers and men of the Brigade under your command during the recent operations near YPRES.

    He hopes you will take occasion to bring his remarks to the notice of the Officers Commanding Battalions concerned.

18th December 1914

    Major
A.A. & Q.M.G., 7th Division.

20th INFANTRY BRIGADE.

This Brigade had, eventually, the most difficult task to perform: as it had to hold the exposed position of KRUISEIK hill. It was impossible to abandon this point without prejudicing not only the rest of the line, but also the pivot of all contemplated offensive action.

In spite, therefore, of its natural unfavourable situation, KRUISEIK hill had to be held.

The 20th Brigade did this itself, under constant violent Artillery fire by day and often by night.

The defence was by no means passive, but counter attacks were frequently and successfully made.

Later on in the fighting, this Brigade showed the same tenacity in defence, and on one critical occasion (31st October) by its forward action, was mainly instrumental in restoring the fight.

The losses of this Brigade were very heavy.

W20th Infantry Brigade

1st Battalion Grenadier Guards.

This battalion fought with the utmost tenacity and determination in a most exposed position at KRUISEIK in front of YPRES, being subjected to almost ceaseless heavy artillery fire and repeated attacks of the enemy for a week. Owing to the length of front to be held no reliefs could be found for troops in the trenches. During this fighting Major COLBY'S Company of this Battalion counter-attacked the enemy who had almost successfully attacked the line. In this counter-attack this Company lost 4 officers killed and wounded, only one officer and 45 men returning unhurt; but this company succeeded in driving back a very much larger hostile force. This battalion lost very heavily in the three weeks fighting before YPRES.

I consider that the resolution and gallantry of this Battalion, obliged to take its share in holding a height which was the pivot of all the operations in this part of the field was most Noble and devoted, and worthy of its highest traditions.

Later on in the same operations, though weakened in numbers, and with few officers, the Battalion exhibited gallantry in a counter attack near GHELUVELT, where it was mainly instrumental in restoring the battle South of the main YPRES-MENIN road; and, subsequently, the same tenacity as it had shown at KRUISEIK, in holding a very difficult and exposed part of the Brigade line in the final position in front of YPRES.

2nd Battalion Border Regiment.

This battalion held a portion of the KRUISEIK position in front of YPRES during which it was exposed to particularly heavy shell fire for 5 days and nights. Many of the trenches were blown in but no trench was given up by any portion of the battalion.

On 2nd November this battalion formed the right of the Brigade at VELDHOEK. Owing to troops on the right giving way the enemy was able to occupy some woods and so surround the right of the Border Regiment. Nevertheless the Battalion held its line for some hours until the enemy could be driven from those woods by relieving troops.

During the fighting this battalion lost very heavily.

The devoted and firm conduct of this Battalion, repeatedly called forth the admiration of the Brigadier and of Officers in other Battalions in the same Brigade: and I, myself, can testify to its fortitude and determination to maintain its position at all costs; a spirit which saved a difficult and critical situation.

It is impossible to praise this Battalion too highly for its firmness and battle discipline.

2nd Battalion Gordon Highlanders

This Battalion assisted to hold the exposed position of KRUISEIK from the 18th to 26th October.

On 29th October one company under Captain B.G.R.Gordon maintained a very forward position, although completely isolated, until relief arrived. This Company inflicted very heavy loss on the enemy.

Later on this Battalion became detached and fought with troops of the 2nd Infantry Brigade, where it had much severe wood-fighting.

A captured German Officer gave testimony as to the excellent shooting of this regiment.

Throughout all the fighting before YPRES, this Battalion nobly upheld its high traditions, inspite of grevious losses in officers and other ranks.

When withdrawn from action, it was commanded by a Subaltern Officer, but had retained all its cohesion and discipline.

Addendum "B."

FRENCH ATTACK NEAR ST. MENEHOULD.

The attack described below was carried out by the IV. French Army in the neighbourhood of St. Menehould and was completely successful.

Success was mainly due to adequate and well organised artillery preparation and support, to a definite objective being allotted to each body of troops and to the distribution and formations adopted by the attacking infantry and engineers.

ATTACK ORDERS.

In accordance with the orders given by the General Officer Commanding the Colonial Army Corps an attack on the hostile positions will be made on the objectives opposite the section occupied by the 6th Brigade.

Objective.—The enemy's trenches marked D.E.B.M. on the sketch, which are situated opposite our trenches 5, 6, 7, 8 and 9.

Troops for the attack.—The troops for the attack will be composed as follows:—

    2 Battalions of the 33rd Colonial Regiment.
    2   ,,   ,,   7th   ,,
    1   ,,   ,,   22nd   ,,
    1   ,,   ,,   24th   ,,
    2 Companies of Engineers.

Distribution of the attack.—They will be formed into 2 groups which will attack supported by a reserve.

1st group (on the left) { 1 Battalion of the 22nd Colonial Regiment.
                                { 1   ,,   ,,   33rd   ,,
                                { ½ Company of Engineers.

2nd group (on the right) { 2 Battalions of the 7th Colonial Regiment.
                                  { ½ Company of Engineers.

Reserve { 1 Battalion of the 33rd Regiment.
        { 1   ,,   ,,   24th   ,,

Direction of the attack.—The first group crossing our trenches Nos. 5 to 8 on flying bridges will attack trenches D and E of the enemy, will drive out the defenders, and will occupy the communicating trenches sufficiently in advance to cover themselves. One part detailed in advance will face towards the West, another detailed in advance will face to the East, in order to attack trench B in enfilade with the assistance of a section of machine guns.

The second group, as soon as the first group has succeeded in getting a footing in the enemy's trenches, will advance from trenches 8 and 9 and in the intervals between them and will attack M and W, putting in its columns successively one after the other in order to re-inforce them; it will employ all its efforts to advance its attack in an easterly direction towards the ravine of L'Etang.

At the same time the first group will attack trench B.

If success crowns the efforts of the assailants they will endeavour to advance up to the ravine of L'Etang by trenches S, T, V, Y and Z, which will allow them to attack trenches R and Q in front and flank and perhaps to capture them.

As soon as the columns of which they form part are in the trenches the Engineers, according to instructions which will be issued to them in advance, will endeavour to discover the position of any mines which have been laid and to cut the wires.

As soon as the enemy's trenches have been occupied, the infantry will endeavour as soon as possible to put them in a state of defence. For this purpose it will hold about 50 metres in front by means of small parties of selected men all the communicating trenches leading out from the trenches, organizing thus a first line under the protection of which the remainder of the work can be carried out.

In order to put the trenches in a state of defence the infantry will utilize materials on the spot; it will also use rolls of wire, sandbags, chevaux de frise and various other materials which have been prepared in advance close to communicating trenches of Nos. 6, 7, 8 and 9.

Machine Guns.—Machine gun sections of the first group detailed for the destruction of the wire entanglements will become available to support the columns, and will establish themselves without delay in trench E in order to hold the front. One of them must try to attack hostile trench B in enfilade. Machine gun sections of battalions of the 7th Colonial Regiment will follow the supports of the column, and will establish themselves in trench MS and will endeavour to fire on B, R and Q.

Flanks of the attack.—Beyond the flank columns, which are detailed to face outward as soon as they arrive at the trenches, infantry attacks will be flanked in the first case by fire from trenches 1, 2, 3 and 4, and by the machine gun established there; secondly, by fire from trench 9, so long as it is not masked by the attacking columns and by the trenches of Hill 180; thirdly, by the 87 and 65 mm. guns established on Hill 180, and on the saddle 165*, and by the batteries of 75 mm. guns.

* Not marked on the map.

Organization of the Columns.—Columns will debouch 3 companies at a time in four columns of ½ section per company, followed almost immediately by the other ½ section. Each column will have at its disposal 2 flying bridges for crossing each of our trenches.

The columns will consist of 1 squad at the head, followed by a group of sappers and then a second squad. The second ½ section will follow in the same formation. The men will be furnished with portable entrenching tools carried on the waistbelt, and one out of three with picks and shovels from the Engineer tool carts.

Each man will also have a sandbag.

Six men of the first squad will have a hurdle for crossing wire entanglements.

The men will carry their packs except those of the first ½ section of each column, i.e., the section at the head of the column.

The 6 leading men of each column will be furnished with wire cutters.

Assembling of Columns before the attack.—The companies will be assembled before the attack in the communicating trenches, and in the places of assembly close to our trenches in the first line. The sections for the attack will be organized in advance as has just been indicated.

The point reserved for each battalion forms the subject of a special instruction.

Preparation.—The attack will be prepared as follows:—

(1) By the artillery. In a general manner this will act with batteries against each hostile battery which is opposed to it.

A special group of artillery is charged with the duty of firing on the wire entanglements in order to form a passage through them and to break them up, and also on the hostile trenches in order to blow them in.

(2) By the artillery of 57 and 65 mm. guns. It will endeavour to destroy the machine guns and shields.

The hand grenade throwers will direct their efforts to destroying the defenders in the trenches.

(3) By machine guns in position which will form passages through the wire entanglements on all points where they can be seen sufficiently clearly.

When all these machines have produced their effect the attacking artillery will lengthen its fuze. On a signal which will be arranged between the commander of the attack and the commanders of the various groups the infantry will assault.

Execution.—The attack on the trenches constitutes an assault which demands for success rapid execution carried out with the whole energy of which the men and the formations are capable. It is a question of crossing defences which have been destroyed or overthrown, of jumping into the trenches, of killing the defenders and of organising as rapidly as possible against counter-attacks, whether delivered at once or after a short interval.

Reserves.—Battalions in reserve will remain during the attack at the ravine of Marson, the battalion of the 33rd on the West and a battalion of the 24th on Hill 180.

When the attack has been delivered the battalion of the 33rd will be ready to move by the communicating trenches or in extended order near trenches 6 and 8. The other battalion will remain under cover.

Retirement.—If the attack is compelled to retire, which will cause us more losses than in holding our ground, it will be covered by the troops occupying the trenches.

Materials.—The materials provided by the Engineers will be collected by the side of the exits of the trenches and near to trenches 6 - 8.

Ammunition.—The men will carry 200 cartridges, and a reserve of 300,000 cartridges will be established in rear of the trenches under cover of the Marson Brook (left poste de commandement).

Employment of Battalions of the 22nd and 24th Regiments in the trenches.—During the attack the sub-sections on right and left of the Brigade will each be held by 2 battalions. These troops will have the following role to carry out:—

(1) To flank the attack, especially the defenders of trenches, 1, 2, 3 and 4 on the West. The defenders of trenches 10 - 20 will have the same task so long as the attack does not mask their fire.

(2) The defenders of 20 - 26 will fire on any part of the enemy which endeavours to debouch from the Valley of L'Etang and from the ravine to the North of Medius and finally to fire on the enemy from the trenches of the Index in order to compel him to remain under cover.

Precise orders will be given to the trench commanders so that their fire may be directed on the hostile trenches which are not attacked by us as soon as our attack starts.

From trenches 25 and 26 special observers will follow the progress of the attack with great care.

Poste de commandement of the Colonel commanding the attack, 1,200 metres West of Minaucourt, near the Calvary.

(Sd.) MAZILLER, Colonel,
Commanding the Attack.

17-12-14.

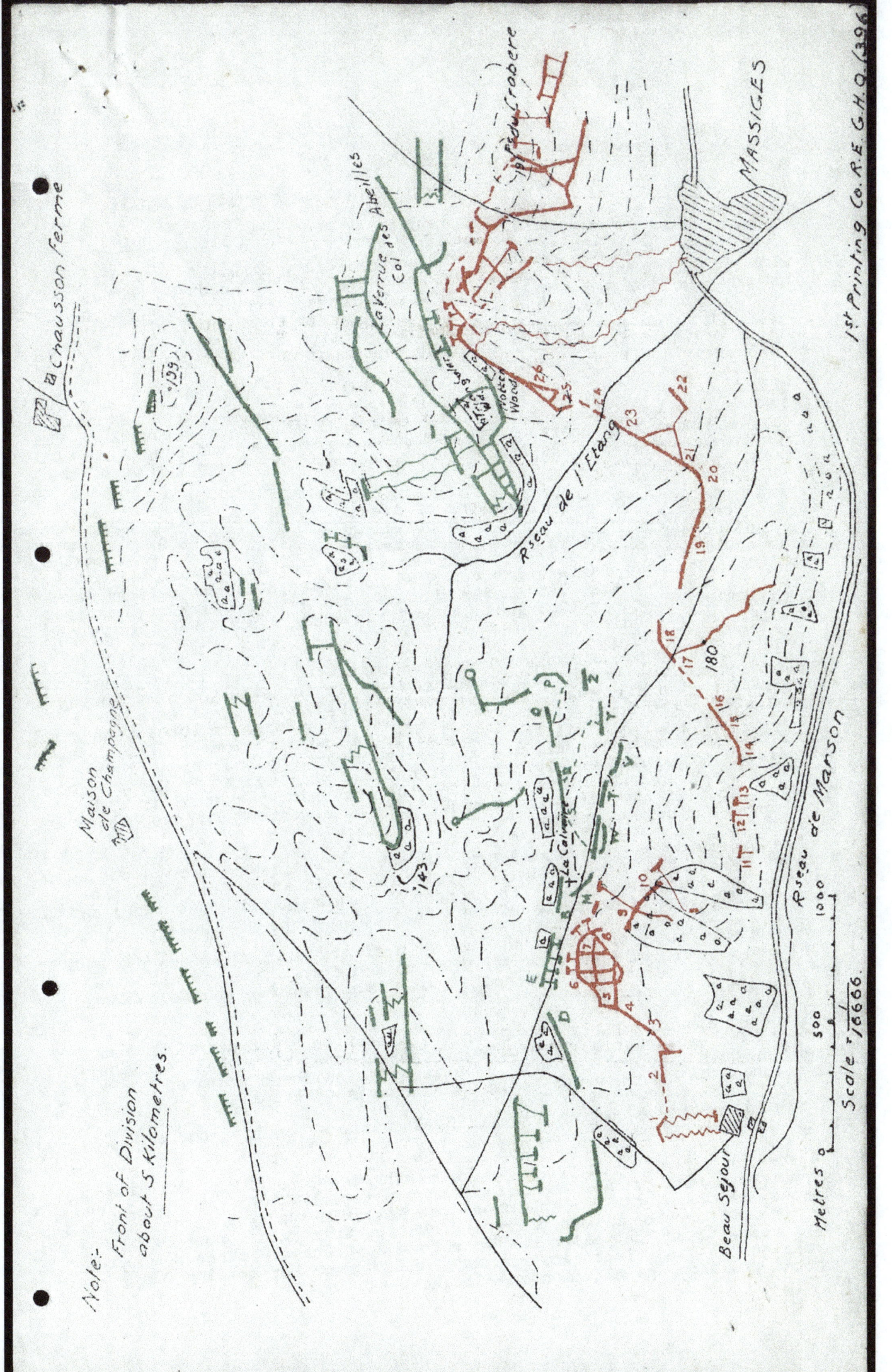

(Translation of a German Document)

VII Corps H.Q., PHALEMPIN. 25-12-14.

THE CAPTURE OF THE ENGLISH POSITION EAST OF FESTUBERT on 20-12-14.

The front of attack was about 900 metres wide, situated on a flat ridge which commands the ground east and west of it. About 50 metres behind the position was a well-built English cover trench. Between the first line and the cover trench, and parallel to them, runs a natural ditch, which had not been touched. The position of the 2nd and 3rd Battalions of the 57th Infantry Regiment was about 80 - 150 metres in front of the enemy's firing line.

Here, as well as in the neighbouring sectors, saps had been dug out from our line to within, in places, 3 metres of the enemy's position. The enemy, who were very active in throwing hand grenades, had forced us to cover in our sapheads. He himself had made no saps in the region of the attack.

From the 10 sapheads in the zone of attack, mines were laid under the enemy's trenches, each charged with 50 kilogrammes of explosive. To ensure the ignition of the mines, the attack was arranged for 9 a.m. so that the leads could be tested by the Company Commander and his second in command and that any improvements which appeared necessary could be made by daylight. A mine was also laid under a house held by the enemy on the right of the front of attack (Quinque Rue) and was charged with 300 kilogrammes (660 lb.) of explosive.

All the telephone communications were manned to ensure the neighbouring sectors commencing the attack simultaneously in the event of their being any delay in the explosion. Actually, the explosion did not take place till 10.25 in the morning owing to special difficulties in connection with one of the leads. When it was reported to the senior pioneer officer on the front of attack that all the mines were ready, he had three flare signals fired simultaneously. This signal was only meant for the pioneers, who then fired all the mines including the one under the house in the Quinque Rue. At the same time a number of "Minenwerfer" directed their fire on to the cover trench.

The explosion was the signal for the attack, which was carried out as follows by the 2nd & 3rd Battalions of the 57th Infantry Regiment, the 2nd and 3rd Companies of the 7th Pioneer Battalion (less 2 sections) and the 1st Battalion of the 19th Pioneer Regiment (less 1 company).

A storming party of half a section of infantry with 12 pioneers was in readiness in each of the 10 saps. They rushed into the enemy's trench, searched it for mines, and cleared it with hand grenades and incendiary torches (Brandrohren).

A second storming party (in strength, a section of infantry between every 2 saps) rushed simultaneously across the open from their own position on both sides of the saps (sortie steps had been prepared for this) and reached the cover trench behind the enemy's position.

A third party - a company from each battalion - occupied our own trench in case of a counter-attack.

A working party in reserve - the remaining sections of the six attacking companies with pioneer detachments and materials for providing cover (shields, sandbags, etc.) - followed the attacking party into the enemy's cover trench for the purpose of reconstructing this into a new position facing west. Every battalion had, therefore sent forward three companies in echelon for the attack and retained one in rear for holding our original position against counter-attacks.

Up to

Up to the moment of the explosion, the allotment of targets and the task of the artillery remained the same as they had been on the previous days, so as not to excite the attention of the enemy.

Not until the mines were fired were the neighbouring sectors to engage the enemy by increased fire action. Use was to be made of any advantages which appeared abtainable. The medium "minenwerfer" were to attack the enemy's machine guns, which were dug in and arranged for flanking fire in the neighbouring sector to the left. The field artillery was to shell the enemy's approaches. The 21 cm mortar battery was to subdue the enemy's artillery and machine guns, which were intended to afford flanking fire from positions known to us in the village of GIVENCHY; 3 batteries of heavy field howitzers were held in readiness to return the fire of any new hostile batteries which might come into action.

The whole operations was carried out according to plan. The 10 mines exploded simultaneously. With the help of the over-powering effect produced by them, our attacking parties, who had immediately rushed forward, succeeded in getting into the enemy's cover trench with few losses, and took up a position there. The enemy, English and Indians, who fled from the position suffered heavy losses.

The forces in both the neighbouring sectors joined in the attack, for the most part by means of a charge across the open, which led to the capture of so-called "Heckenhaus" in the Rue de Caillaux and of the English position east of GIVENCHY. On the previous day the "Heckenhaus" had been destroyed by a heavy "Minenwerfer"; on the day of the attack gaps were made in the wire entanglement round it by means of two mines, each with a 50 kilogramme (110 lb) charge, and its garrison was rendered "ripe for attacking" (sturmreif) by two rounds from the "Minenwerfer" being directed on to the ruins of the "Heckenhaus".

The effect of the attacks on the enemy were such that he immediately brought up the 9th Indian Cavalry Brigade which was in reserve near BETHUNE, and part of the 142nd French Territorial Regiment and "alarmed" the 1st Infantry Division (English) which belonged to his Army reserve and was in the vicinity of HAZEBROUCK. This division was brought up by rail and motor to BETHUNE and used for heavy counter-attacks on the 20th, 21st and 22nd, all of which were repulsed with heavy losses.

Six machine guns and eleven small trench mortars were captured and 19 officers and 815 men taken prisoners. According to a reliable estimate, over 3,000 of the enemy lay dead upon the battlefield.

In the dug-outs of the trench which was destroyed by the mines, a large number of Indian corpses was found still sitting: they had apparently been suffocated. In view of the success we obtained, our own losses in this attack (10 officers and 452 men wounded, now in the hospitals of the Army Corps, 459 slightly wounded, and about 250 killed) were not great and in the actual assault itself they were inappreciable. Apart from the bravery of the troops, success was due to the minute and detailed tactical preparation by both the infantry and the pioneers and to the accurately timed co-ordination of the mines, "Minenwerfer", infantry assault and artillery fire.

A plan was for a moment considered for drawing the enemy into his front trenches by increasing our fire before exploding the mines, and thus attracting larger bodies of the enemy over the mines. This, however, was discarded because it was feared that we should, in consequence, meet with so much opposition to our attack against the front trenches as would delay us from penetrating into the cover trench, which was our objective. Also, we wished to avoid attracting the enemy's attention prematurely.

(Signed) v. CLAER,
General Officer Commanding.

The following account of a French attack is of interest and we can learn something from it :-

The French and German lines were approximately as shown on the attached diagram.

The opposing lines were about 300 to 400 yards apart. Along the whole front of the French lines there was a wire entanglement, which would have prevented the French troops moving forward to the attack; so the French dug another line in front of their wire. This trench was not very deep in order to allow the infantry to get out very quickly.

The French brought up a mass of artillery (about 150 guns or so), amongst them some heavy batteries.

Artillery observers were in the trenches.

Orders were issued for the attack to be delivered on the following line:-

20 minutes heavy bombardment.
10 minutes interval.
20 minutes heavy bombardment.
4 minutes intensive bombardment (by field guns only)

The interval was allowed as it was hoped the Germans would think the bombardment was over and that their troops would leave their bomb-proofs and support trenches, and go forward into the fire trenches in order to meet the expected infantry assault.

The bombardment, and in fact, all the arrangements, were worked by the clock - (watches being, of course, carefully set beforehand).

Towards the end of the second bombardment the French infantry got out of their front trench and lay ready to advance.

At the exact moment fixed for the intensive bombardment the French infantry rose and advanced. They ran forward at as good a pace as they could, and under cover of the intensive bombardment pushed up as close to the German trenches as possible and lay down. Some of the French shells were falling short of the German trench, and where that occurred the advancing infantry halted a little further back.

The four minutes intensive bombardment stopped by the watch, and the French infantry, after allowing a
suitable

suitable pause, rushed to the assault. Some of the heavier French artillery continued to fire at objectives further to the rear and at certain other targets on the flank (i.e., enemy's trenches, machine guns, and artillery positions).

The infantry rushed the front trenches and dropped into them with a sigh of relief. The trenches were practically empty, as the Germans, during the artillery bombardment, had retired into support trenches and bomb-proofs.

Up to this moment the French casualties had been slight. The front line of hostile trenches were all captured except a small length on the right of the German line.

Apparently the German support trenches and bomb-proofs were quite close to their front line. (I gather within 25 yards in places, but am not sure of this), and communicating trenches led into the firing trenches.

When the bombardment ceased and the French were in occupation of the front trenches, the Germans began to put their heads up and in a very few minutes had opened a very hot rifle fire on the French. The latter found it very difficult to reply as the trenches were made to fire the other way.

Attempts were made to advance up the communicating trenches, but the Germans checked this by placing a maxim at the far end. (apparently some at any rate of the communicating trenches were straight, not zigzagged).

The Germans now began to bomb the French. In some cases the bombs were thrown from the support trenches, and in other cases the Germans worked up the communicating trenches. The Germans appeared to have an endless supply of bombs, but the French supply gave out very quickly. The French losses now began to be serious, and reinforcements were sent up. These men lost very heavily in crossing the space between the trenches; so much so that the French dug two long communicating trenches (marked A A on sketch). These took about four hours to dig and were carried out successfully.

In the meantime, the French troops had been bombed so heavily that the men left the trench and dug themselves in about 40 or 50 yards away. It is difficult to explain how the French were able thus to dig themselves in in the open. Probably the German guns were unable to fire as the opposing infantry were too close to one another, and the French were out of bombing distance and they were probably able to look after themselves as regards rifle fire from the Germans in the trenches.

The

The fighting ended in the French establishing themselves firmly on the line they had dug just in front of the German lines. (This line is marked B B B on sketch). The Germans continued to hold their original line.

What will be done in the future remains to be seen, but the French are confident that they will shortly retake the German trenches, and this time they mean to hold them.

There are one or two obvious lessons to be learnt from these operations, and from some of our own experiences:-

(i). The necessity for a carefully thought out plan. The timing of the bombardments and the advance of the French infantry worked without a hitch. Small details are often very important.

(ii). The effect of a properly directed artillery fire is very great. But the artillery observers must be right up in the front trenches, and there should be quick (telephonic) communication from them to the guns.

(iii). Some of the guns, at any rate, should be firing at close range. This enables the gunners to keep close observation of their own infantry, and the guns can be turned quickly on any hostile counter-attack or fresh target.

(iv). The capture of the enemy's trenches is often easy enough. The problem usually is "How are we to keep them?" This requires thinking out beforehand, and nothing should be left to chance.

(v). The French were "bombed" out of the trenches they had captured. (This has happened to us in the British Army during the last fortnight - and will happen again unless we have thought out a plan to compete with the "bombers").
First of all we must arrange to have a plentiful supply of "bombs" of our own.
Then we must think out how we are going to deal with the communication or other trenches from which the enemy can throw bombs into the trench we have captured.

Can

Can we put maxims to enfilade the trench up which the bombers must come? If it is a straight trench this is possible; but it is a question of who establishes his maxims first — the enemy or ourselves. If it is a zig-zag trench, then we should push men down the trench and block it (with sandbags probably) so as to keep the enemy beyond bombing distance.

(vi). We must be prepared for the enemy to emerge from his support trenches and bomb-proofs, and we should attack him at once either by fire or with the bayonet.

(vii). We must have everything cut and dried for supporting our troops in the captured trenches — by artillery (single guns pushed up close can do much to help) by concentrated maxim and rifle fire, and by all other possible means.

(viii). It will often be advisable to start digging a communication trench directly the trench is captured.

(ix). Everyone (officer and man) should know what he is to do. This is very important.

Then we should think over the matter as regards the defence. What can we do not only to prevent the enemy capturing our trenches, but if they do make a lodgment, how are we going to turn them out?

Have we bombs and "bombers" ready?

Where are our troops going to go if the enemy bombard the front trench severely?

Are our bomb proofs and support trenches connected up with the firing trench?

In the event of the enemy making a lodgment can we enfilade the captured trench with our machine guns or artillery, or both?

It is unlikely that the enemy will be able to bring off a successful surprise attack. Generally speaking there will be indications to warn us of an attack — either a bombardment, or a massing of the enemy's sap infantry, or the close approach of the enemy's saps. Anyhow, a careful officer will seldom be surprised, and he will usually be well advised to move his reserves as close as possible to the threatened point.

If the enemy make a lodgment or push on beyond the front line, he should be counter-attacked <u>at once</u>; there is no time to be lost.

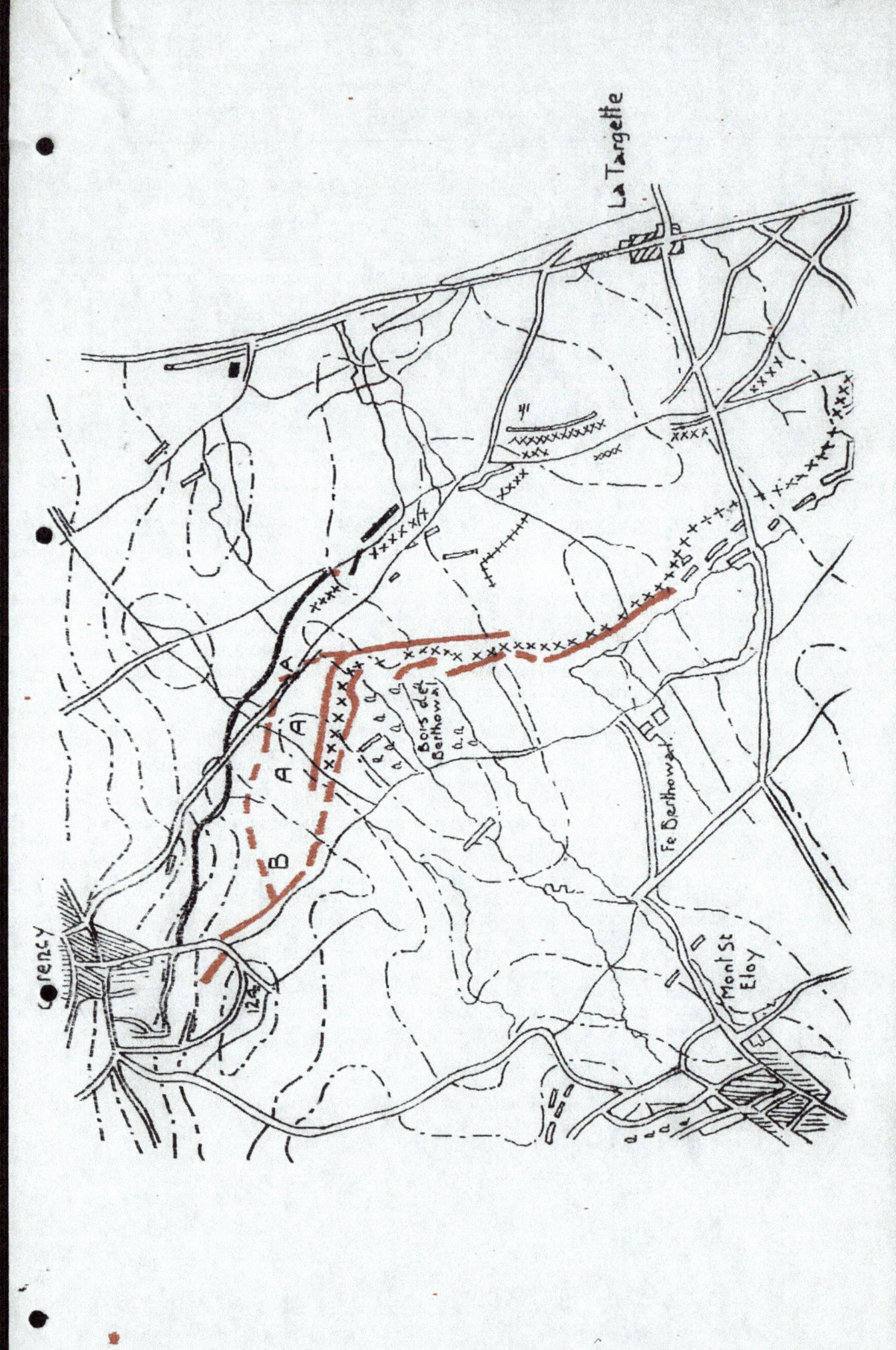

Notes on recent German methods of Attack.

During the last few days the enemy have made attacks against the 1st Division at the villages of Givenchy and Cuinchy and also against the French at the village of Zonnebeke near Ypres.

There are several points in connection with these attacks to which the 4th Corps Commander desires to draw special attention, as useful lessons may be derived from them for future guidance.

GERMAN ATTACK ON ZONNEBEKE.

1.—At Zonnebeke there was no artillery preparation whatever. The Germans, strength about a battalion, got out of their trenches in daylight about 8 a.m. and advanced in close formation against the French line which was well protected by wire and distant between 200 and 300 yards. Another battalion is said to have been in support and a third battalion in reserve.

2.—The French were on the look out and well prepared. They met the attack with rapid and sustained fire causing heavy loss to the Germans, some of whom reached the wire entanglement, but none of whom succeeded in crossing it.

3.—The French artillery kept up continuous bursts of fire on the supports and reserves which, in consequence, made no attempt to reinforce the battalion already launched to the attack.

4.—The lessons to be learned from the defeat of this attack are :—

Firstly, the necessity of keeping constantly on the watch and of being able to bring an overwhelming volume of fire to bear on the enemy at very short notice. The careful selection of machine gun positions will enable Commanding Officers to reduce the number of men kept in the fire trench. This number should also vary with the state of the ground in front of our trenches, i.e., whether it is deep and heavy or hard and can be advanced over rapidly.

Secondly, the need of having a sufficient force of artillery in close support of the infantry line and ready at short notice to open rapid bursts of fire on any part of the ground which intervenes both between the two lines of trenches and in rear of them where supports and reserves are likely to assemble.

THE ATTACK ON GIVENCHY.

5.—At Givenchy the two lines of trenches were so close together that efficient wire entanglements had not been constructed. The attack was preceded by heavy artillery bombardment for more than an hour and the infantry assault was delivered by four or five companies with great dash and vigour. Several assaults were repulsed, but finally the Germans succeeded in gaining an entrance into the village through which they advanced until they struck the Keep or reduit which had been thoroughly prepared and wired in at the near end of the village. They attacked but failed to capture it.

6.—A counter-attack was at once delivered by the South Wales Borderers and Welsh Regiment before the Germans had time to make good their position, with the result that the enemy was soon forced out of the village again, leaving about 100 dead and 100 prisoners in our hands.

7.—The lessons to be learned from this attack are :—

Firstly, the need of good wire obstacles in front of the fire trenches. If a proper entanglement cannot be constructed on account of the proximity of the enemy's trenches, then "chevaux de frise" made of wooden supports and wire twisted across them can be pushed out in front of the parapet and anchored.

Secondly, the importance of constructing a strongly constructed Keep or reduit as a supporting point in rear of the front line of trenches as a pivot of manœuvre.

Thirdly, the imperative necessity of launching a counter-attack at the earliest possible moment after the front line has been broken and before the enemy has been able to construct any kind of improvised defences.

THE ATTACK ON CUINCHY.

8.—The attack was delivered after very heavy and sustained bombardment by artillery at 8.30 a.m. in daylight and was immediately preceded by fire from a Minenwerfer and the throwing of bombs. The front trenches were speedily captured by the Germans notwithstanding that the defenders had half-an-hour's warning of the impending attack.

9.—The Germans followed up their success, but on reaching the Keep, some hundred yards in rear, failed to make further progress and proceeded to dig themselves in.

[P.T.O.]

10.—There were no guns of the defenders in close support so that artillery fire was not brought to bear on the attackers after their success, and they therefore proceeded at once to entrench themselves. No counter-attack was made for four hours after the assault, but the Keep held out and when the counter-attack was made it failed to re-establish the line.

11.—There were no splinter proofs or shelter of any kind near the front trenches in which the defenders could take shelter during the bombardment.

12.—The lessons to be learned from this attack are :—

Firstly, the immense importance of a counter-attack being delivered at the earliest possible moment after the line has been broken.

Secondly, the imperative need of close artillery support and guns being at once brought to bear on the lost trenches and the intervening ground by artillery officers in observation posts which can see the ground well.

Thirdly, the value of a strong Keep well wired in all round.

Fourthly, the need of splinter proofs in which the defenders can take shelter during the artillery bombardment.

Fifthly, the value of bombs and hand grenades with which to reply to the enemy when they begin bomb throwing.

A good supply should be kept in the support trenches, to be available for a counter-attack should the fire trench be captured by the enemy. The positions of these supplies must be known to all concerned.

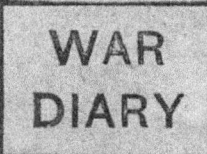

Headquarters,

20th INFANTRY BRIGADE.

(7th Division)

J A N U A R Y

1 9 1 5

Appendix.

The Officer,
Official History of the War,
Military Branch, C.I.D.
Audit House,
Victoria Embankment

THE WAR OFFICE.

Army Form C. 2118.

WAR DIARY
or
INTELLIGENCE SUMMARY.

(Erase heading not required.)

Hadqrs 20 R Inf Bde

Instructions regarding War Diaries and Intelligence Summaries are contained in F.S. Regs., Part II. and the Staff Manual respectively. Title pages will be prepared in manuscript.

Hour, Date, Place	Summary of Events and Information	Remarks and references to Appendices
	1 9 1 5. ---ooo0000000ooo---	
January 1st to 7th.	On inquiring what was the heavy firing at midnight on the 31st – 1st it was reported both sides were firing into the air to celebrate the New Year. From Headquarters it sounded as if a heavy battle was in progress. The Germans fired a number of rockets all down the line. The Germans opposite us seem very loathe to commence fighting again and sniping from them has ceased entirely. Defensive posts as pivots are now to be made in rear of the trenches. On January 3rd, the Scots Guards received a party of one Officer (Lieut Seymour) and 45 men discharged from Hospital and rejoining. 2nd Gordon Highlanders – 1 Officer and 50 men. Captain Douglas Gordon arrived, appointed Adjutant to 2nd Battalion Scots Guards. Captain Loder who has been carrying out these duties since October 25th applied to Brigadier-General Commanding and General Officer Commanding, 7th Division, to retain the post of Adjutancy. Captain Gordon ordered by General Officer Commanding 4th Corps to withhold his appointment and not take over his duties till further reports have been received from home as to why Captain Loder should not retain his post. Stringent orders issued to bring the informal truce to an end. Men not allowed out of the trenches. All Germans above ground to be shot at.	
January 8th to 15th.	Trenches flooded. To retain the line it has been found necessary to hold isolated posts of 1 N.C.O. and 10 men at intervals of about every 50 yards. The posts so held being dammed up at both ends and the water pumped out between the dams. Between these posts retrenchments are dug outside and just in rear of the trenches. sic. This design	

Army Form C. 2118.

WAR DIARY
or
INTELLIGENCE SUMMARY.
(Erase heading not required.)

Instructions regarding War Diaries and Intelligence Summaries are contained in F.S. Regs., Part II. and the Staff Manual respectively. Title pages will be prepared in manuscript.

Hour, Date, Place	Summary of Events and Information	Remarks and references to Appendices
January 8th to 15th continued.	This design is the least noticeable to the enemy, the parados requiring very little alteration. In addition, redoubts are being made as "supporting points" at intervals in rear. These "supporting" "points" are to be self-contained, and capable of holding garrisons of 20 to 40 men. The Germans are evidently in the same plight with regards the water and can be seen and heard pumping and baling water out of their trenches incessantly. In rear of our line of trenches we are making five redoubts. Between these redoubts houses are being put in a state of defence and small breastworks made. This method of holding the trenches has also the additional advantage of being able to reduce the garrisons. So at present the men can be relieved every 12 or 24 hours, get into billets and get dry and warm before going in again, hitherto they had been doing four days on and off duty in the trenches.	
January 16th to 20th.	The Brigade re-organised for the purposes of relieving trenches. The Grenadier Guards and Scots Guards relieving each other in No 1 Subsection. The Border Regiment and the 2nd and 6th battalions Gordon Highlanders (the two latter formed into one unit for the purposes of holding the trenches) relieving each other in No. 2 Subsection. Lieutenant-Colonel Wood, Border Regiment, reassumed Command of his Battalion having recovered from wounds received at YPRES. Pumps issued to the trenches, 10 to each subsection, a great help and enabling us to retain the line, in many places there is 3 feet 6 inches of water in the trenches. The Germans are using a new shell in their guns, painted red and made of thick roughly smelted iron. Very few of which burst.	
January 21st to 31st.	A great improvement in the weather, the water in the R.LAYES dropping 1½ feet. This enabled us to reclaim a good many of the trenches in No 1 Subsection. No.2,However, is still hopeless. The posts in rear considerably improved daily. The flooded trenches in front of them forming itself a formidable obstacle. This together with the wire in....	

WAR DIARY
or
INTELLIGENCE SUMMARY.
(Erase heading not required.)

Instructions regarding War Diaries and Intelligence Summaries are contained in F. S. Regs., Part II. and the Staff Manual respectively. Title pages will be prepared in manuscript.

Hour, Date, Place	Summary of Events and Information	Rem
~~February 1st to 28th inclusive~~ January 21st to 31st continued	wire in front makes their positions fairly secure, the acute salient there makes it difficult to make it really strong. The Cellar Farm in rear together with the Fort "E" make a strong supporting point there. The Germans have considerably increased their shell fire daily. The RUE PETILION, CELLAR FARM, and Batteries in rear being their chief objects. Many of their shells are blind and they have done little or no damage.	

APPENDIX.

Secret.

20th Infy Brigade.

Attached is forwarded for your information and retention.

It is considered that all Battalion Commanders should have an opportunity of studying this interesting document at your Head Quarters, but it must not leave your possession.

Please acknowledge receipt

4.1.1915.

Ian Stewart Mey, Colonel,
General Staff, 7th. Division.

Notes on the effect of French Artillery Fire, issued
by the Staff of the French 4th Army, January, 2nd, 1915.

****

The examination of prisoners made since the resumption of our offensive has given an indication of the material and moral effects of our artillery which are summarized below. It applies especially to the VIIIth Active Corps and VIIIth Reserve Corps. The enemy was living in a state of peace and quiet. The men had been more or less quiet for the last three months; captured note-books made mention from time to time, in a casual way, of a cannonade without serious effect; prisoners talked only of the dampness of their dug-outs and of the lack of variety in their rations.

The re-openeing of our artillery fire created great consternation, as much by the effect of its surprise as by its violence and effectiveness.

Prisoners made since the re-opening of the fight present an entirely different appearance. They appear bewildered; and two or three days after being captured they have not pulled themselves together again.

"I have been through the whole campaign, I was present at the battle of the MARNE where our losses were terrible, but that was nothing compared to the artillery fire to which we have been subjected the last few days, both from the point of view of the accuracy of the fire, and the destructive effect of the shells", said a soldier of the VIIIth Active Corps in the neighbourhood of PERTHES.

"I am glad to think I got out of that hell and I do not think myself a bad German for saying that I consider I have paid my debt to my country by having been exposed to such artillery fire; I wonder how it is that my reason has not given way; it was a perfectly damnable day".

The Lieutenant of Engineers captured on hill 200, like the Infantry Subaltern taken prisoner N.E. of PERTHES, displayed astonishment not to say stupefaction at the extraordinary accuracy and violence of the fire; the trench bombarded is entirely knocked to pieces.

"We saw rifles and men flying through the air" said a soldier, "the defenders are either blown to pieces or buried alive, the only ones to escape were those that took refuge in the mine galleries like the Engineer Officer and his men or in a dug-out like the Infantry officer and his four men".

It is nearly certain that in the reserve units, men tried to abandon the trenches which were being bombarded, in order to take refuge in rear of their reserve trenches but the fugitives fell while on the run. Shells pursued them, said the prisoners, it was better to stick to the bottom of the trench and trust to God than to attempt to fly said a N.C.O.

A plan which seems to have created discouragement and demoralization while it also inflicted extreme fatigue on the men consists in bombarding the same trenches two days running.

In the interval, the night is devoted to putting these right again in as far as can be done at a cost of unheard of fatigue and then next morning the work of destruction begins again.

"The man who comes to clear up the trenches that have been bombarded and has seen the lamentable spectacle of his comrades buried or torn to pieces works franctically all night, and then feels his courage leaving him when the guns open again the next morning".

One more expression of a man of the 65th Reserve Regiment –
"One would think that your gunners had measured the range of our trenches to a yard".

As regards the effect of the bombardment of the ground in rear of the trenches not much is known at present as the prisoners taken up to the present all come from the trenches themselves, none belonged to a unit in reserve.

Only two indications have come to hand:-

Firstly, on asking a Lieutenant, who had been taken prisoner, why units in reserve do not come to the assistance of the Companies who are defending the trenches, he replied "As long as the artillery fire goes on it is impossible to attempt to send up reserves for hardly has the last round from the guns been fired at the trench, than your infantry are upon us".

Secondly, "On the day when the attack took place against the 29th Reserve Regt. East of PERTHES". said a N.C.O. of the 65th Reserve Regt, "we were also bombarded but we felt it was only to keep us occupied; all the efforts of your artillery were directed to our right against the 29th Reserve Regt; my company left its shelters to join the battalion and go to the help of the 29th. During the time it took us to get out we had 12 men put out of action and 4 killed".

Another cause of the exhaustion of the troops will be noted. Since the day when the enemy had knowledge of our intended attack, (prisoners declared that they were warned about the 20th December to re-double their watchfullness for fear of attack), the whole of the troops were kept in a state of instant readiness (Hochste gefechtsbereitschaft); at the first shell every man stands to arms, the local reserves (in the vicinity of the trenches) then have as hard a time as the men in the trenches themselves.

As regards losses, it has not been possible so far to estimate them, but one point is known for certain. In the course of the attack carried out against the 28th Active Regiment N. of PERTHES the 3rd Company of this regiment (having about 100 rifles in the trenches) was annihilated, all except 10 men and the Lieutenant Commanding the Company. The 4th Company prolonging the line to the East must have shared the same fate, declared the Lieutenant.

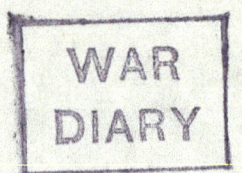

Headquarters,

20th INFANTRY BRIGADE.

(7th Division)

F E B R U A R Y

1 9 1 5

Appendices.

Historical Section
2 Whitehall Gardens
S.W.

ON HIS MAJESTY'S SERVICE.

NATIONAL ECONOMY. FASTEN Envelope by gumming this Label across Flap. OPEN by cutting Label instead of tearing Envelope.

(2986.) Wt. 84286/204. 4,000,000. 12/18. P.P.Ltd. Est. No. 4213.

BY HAND.

HISTORICAL SECTION
(MILITARY BRANCH)
AUDIT HOUSE,
VICTORIA EMBANKMENT,
E.C.4.

Headquarters, 20th Infantry Brigade.

February 1915

February 1st to 7th.

The week spent in strengthening the strength salient near CARDONNERIE FARM. A strong line being made across the base of the salient. The SAILLY - FROMELLES road considerably strengthened by fresh wire being put out in front of the barrier opposite the German Lines.

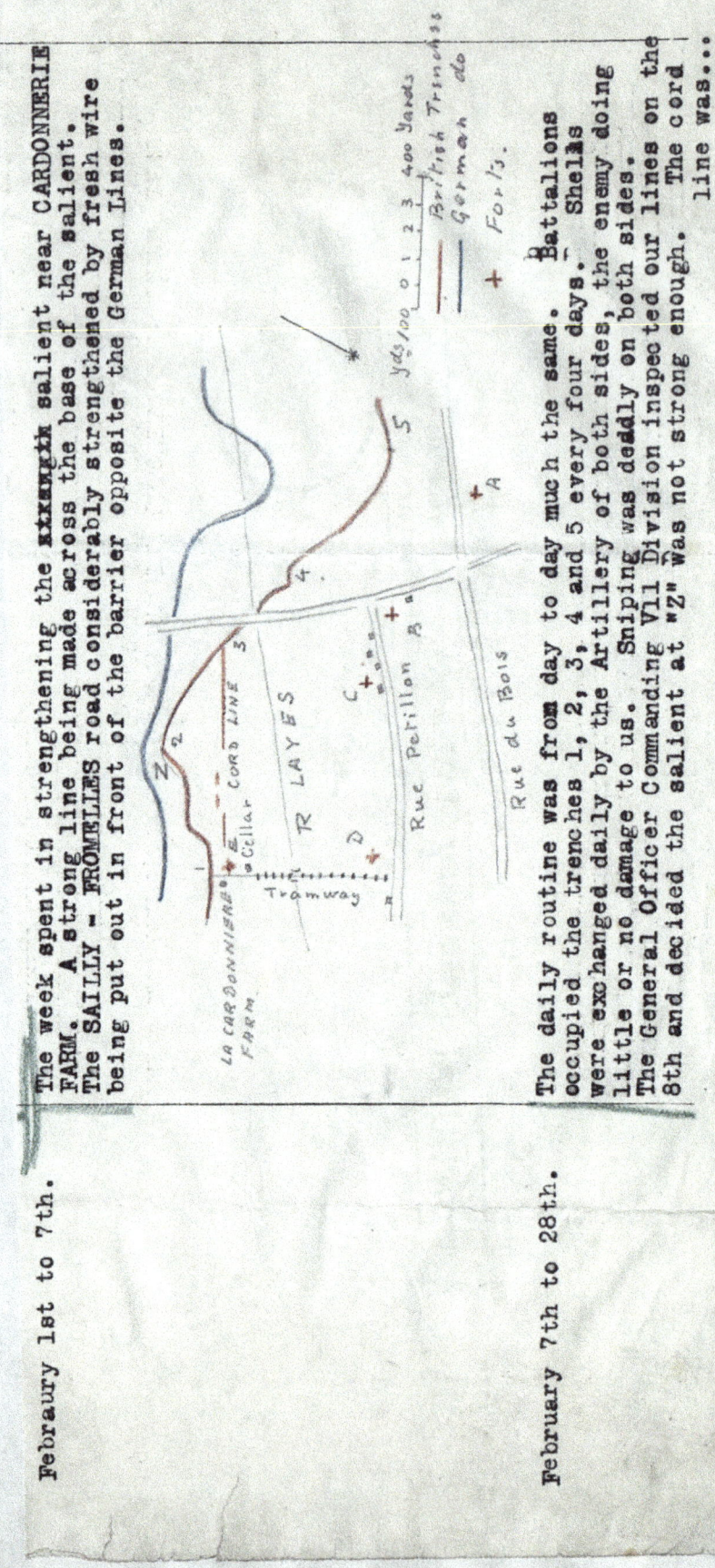

February 7th to 28th.

The daily routine was from day to day much the same. Battalions occupied the trenches 1, 2, 3, 4 and 5 every four days. Shells were exchanged daily by the Artillery of both sides, the enemy doing little or no damage to us. Sniping was deadly on both sides. The General Officer Commanding VII Division inspected our lines on the 8th and decided the salient at "Z" was not strong enough. The cord line was...

WAR DIARY
or
INTELLIGENCE SUMMARY.
(Erase heading not required.)

Instructions regarding War Diaries and Intelligence Summaries are contained in F.S. Regs., Part II. and the Staff Manual respectively. Title pages will be prepared in manuscript.

Hour, Date, Place	Summary of Events and Information	Remarks
February 7th to 28th continued.	line was made and a continuous breastwork immediately in rear of the trenches as per dotted line in diagram. Fresh wire was put out nightly and the defended localities at A, B, C, D and E, were strengthened, each locality being surrounded by a strong barbed wire entanglement. The Farm (LA CARDONNERIE) at "E" was put in a state of defence, breastworks being put all round it. Two hundred and forty men were sent out nightly in four hour reliefs to effect all this work.	

APPENDICES.

SECRET.   18th Division No. G. 810

    20th Infantry Brigade.
    ~~22nd.~~   -do-.
    ~~53rd~~   -do-
    ~~54th~~   -do-
    ~~55th~~   -do-

The following extracts from 10th Corps Operation Order No.11 are forwarded for your information:-

1. In order to assist the French attack south of the SOMME a demonstration will be carried out by the 10th Corps on the 4th and 5th instants.
   This demonstration will consist of

   (a) The concentration of a specified number of guns on the German trenches opposite our trenches 49 to 56.

   (b) A bombardment of points selected by G.O.C's. of Divisions.

2. X   X   X   X   X   X   X   X   X
3. X   X   X   X   X   X   X
4. X   X   X   X   X   X   X

5. The Zero hour at which the bombardments are to commence will be notified later.

        1st Day.

  0.00) Bombardments (a) and (b)
  2.00)

  4.00) Bombardments (a) and (b).
  6.00)

        2nd. Day.

  0.00) Bombardments (a) and (b).
  2.00)

  2.00) (a) An intensive bombardment at the rate of one round per gun per minute.
  2.30) (b) Continues at ordinary rate.

  2.30) (a) Lifts to support and communication trenches.
  2.40) (b) continues.

  Rifle and Machine Gun fire are opened and arrangements made to simulate an attack on (a).

  2.40) Front trenches in (a) again intensely bombarded - one round per
  2.50) gun per minute.
  (b) continues.

  2.50. Fire ceases.

6.
7.   X   X   X   X.   signed A.R.CAMERON, Brig.General.
8.   General Staff, 10th Corps.

Reference para.1 (b) of the above orders, the G.O.C. 18th Division has selected the following points for bombardment on the 4th February:-

    (1) "Y" Sap.
    (2) X.20.a.4.6. to X.20.a.0.8.
    (3) X.20.a.8.2. to X.20.a.95.35.

The points selected for bombardment on the 5th February will be notified later.

    ACKNOWLEDGE.

February 4th.1915.   Major,

20th Infantry Brigade.

      Although in the notes that were written to you this morning the opinion of the Divisional General was expressed that the system of the retrenchment should be continued, he does not want there to be any misunderstanding as to the importance of reclaiming more trench so that the existing islands may each be prolonged as far as possible on either side. It is obvious that the system of islands is a sounder method of defence than a system of high commanding entrenchments provided the weather and ground conditions admit.

Div H.Q.
4-2-15.

Ian Stewart Maj.
for Colonel,
General Staff, 7th Division.

The Brigade Major
20th Inf Bde.

With reference to the provision of look out holes in the parapets of the "retrenched" portions of the fire trenches. I find that fixing pipes, or wooden channels down in the parapet is not likely to prove very successful as the field of view must be very limited.

I am making a sample to show you, but I do not think you will like it.

2. I think a loop hole, like the sample in the RUE PETILLON fixed inconspicuously at the ends of the retrenchments would prove more valuable.

3. If periscopes cannot be used over the tops of the parapets, could they not be used at the ends of the traverses? or through a nick in the parapet.

A. Brough
Maj RE
OC 6th Inf Bde

4/9/15

95

① The Brigade Major
        20th Inf Bde

With regard to sapping I
calculate the following working
parties will be required.—

① For one relief of 4 hours
one N.C.O and 8 men are
required. To give reasonable
intervals of rest it would
be necessary to allot four
such parties for 24 hours work.
(2 reliefs each for 3 parties + one
spare). For one sap
the strength of parties would
be 4 N.C.Os + 32 men
digging only.

② For four saps for digging
only 16 N.C.Os + 128 men
would be required.

The present establishment
of sappers is only 7 N.C.Os +
84 men. So for digging only
9 N.C.Os + 44 extra men
would be required
In addition some 60

2/

2/ men would be required to stand by to replace casualties. & These could primarily be utilised as carrying parties for removing earth. but the number would have to be increased as saps progress, & men get hit or injured.

Stores / &c (3). I propose to send the following stores down (as soon as arranged for), for immediate issue.
25 branch gallery running cases.
200 planks & 200 posts for shoring. if required

Tools (4). Tools I am making & keeping here for issue —

Explosives (5) I am indenting for extra explosives in case of need.

3/

6. Would you consider it advisable to tell off some bomb throwers to be ready near each sap, in case the sap head be rushed?

7. I have shown the detail of working parties & the O.C. miners

A. Brough
Major R.E.
O.C. 53 Field Co.

5/2/15

2nd Bn. Border Regt.

The GOC VII Division has sent the following remarks after his inspection of No 2 Subsection.

Line of Defence — The Retrenchments should be continuous. They are very conspicuous where detached. If continuous troops can work freely behind them. Command & control facilitated if officers can move over their line. It facilitates the reinforcing the front line by day or night. Where retrenchments are close to "islands" communication between the two should be established by the skilful arrangement of communicating trenches.

Design of Retrenchment — The design of the Retrenchments are bad & conspicuous. The tops & sides are very straight instead of being broken by irregular bullet proof heaps of earth. Sandbags are not coloured or muddied. Parados should be made to protect men & troops from shell explosion. Look out holes should be formed. Carefully constructed loopholes protected by iron plates & blinded used for snipers should be constructed.

Organization of Garrison — Each post should have 2 Bombers a Verys Light Pistol, a Periscope. Garrison said they had orders to remain motionless by day. If this is so the day time becomes a complete rest & there is no reason why they should not work at night.

Listening Posts should be established.

In view of the attached the B.G.C. desires each Post to be given a definite task to be accomplished in the 24 Hours. There are 10 men in each post these men will start by increasing the length of the retrenchments so as to eventually join up with each other & make the retrenchments continuous. Each post should do at least 5 yards per night. There being 18 retrenchments this would mean 90 yards per night or 360 yards done by each Battⁿ on its tour of 4 days duty. By this means the retrenchments will soon be made continuous.

Up to the present there has been no progressive system of work in No 2 Subsection. Will you please order your Company Commanders to report every morning what work on each post has been done on the retrenchments & islands. This work to be marked up on the attached Form. At the end of each tour in the trenches the Form to be sent to BHQ for the B.G.C's inspection, who will then return it to you.

W.M. Fator Major
Brigade Major
xx Inf B^{de}.

France
5-2-15

3.

Instructions in case of attack.

Men posted in the Trenches and in the Reserve dugouts will be under the command of the O.C. the Subsection in which they are posted.

48 men and 8 N.C.O in billets will form part of the Brigade Reserve and in case of the Brigade Reserve being called out will at once proceed to Brigade Head Quarters. with 250 Grenades.

14 men and 2 N.C.O will form part of the Divisional Reserve and proceed to with 100 Grenades.

2 store keepers will remain at the Magazine to guard the explosives.

Boxes containing the above Grenades will be stored near the door of the Magazine ready for action, painted "Brigade Reserve" "Divisional Reserve".

Rhys Williams
O.C. Grenade Co
20th Brigade

Total Grenades in Magazine 1062
Rifle Grenades 320
1382

Total in Trenches & Magazine 2754.

(2)

Present Position of Grenade Co
and Grenades. Feb 4th 1915.

No. 1 Subsection

In Trenches 14 men & 2 N.C.O.
In Reserve Dugout 9 men & 1 N.C.O

Total 23 men 3 N.C.O

Grenades
In Trenches   128 grenades
In Reserve Store 260 —
In Fort C.   200
             ———
             588

No. 2 Subsection

In Trenches   40 men   6 N.C.O
In Reserve Dugout 9 men   1 N.C.O

Total 49 men   7 N.C.O

Grenades
In Trenches   206 grenades
At Cellars Farm 120 —
In Reserve Dugout 260 —
In Fort D.   200
              ———
              786

In billets at Sailly 64 men 10 N.C.O.

(1)

SECRET.

H.R.S./51.

IVth Division.

The attached Notes, compiled by Lieutenant-General H.Wilson during a recent visit to distant points in the French line, are forwarded for your information.

H.Q. IVth Corps.   Sgd° A.G.Dallas, Brig-General,
5th Febry,1915.   General Staff, 7th Division.

(2)

20th Infantry Brigade.

For your information.

           Ian Stewart [?] Colonel,
Div H.Q.   General Staff, 7th Division.
6-2-15.

SECRET.

Some Notes on the French System of Defence in Second and Third Line.

1. The whole scheme is based on the defence of tactical localities, or "centres de resistance", and not on one continuous line of trench work and I thought I saw, in addition to this fundamental principle, an inclination, if not a decision, to select tactical points at such a distance in rear of the front line as would make it necessary for the Germans to move the whole of their Artillery, and, not only to move it but, move it to positions with which the French were already cognisant.

2. In general the works at these "centres de resistance" were made to hold about one battalion with a front line capable of employing half the force and supporting trenches for some three quarters of the force.

3. These "centres de resistance" were, on an average, about 1,000^x to 1,500^x apart.

4. All works were very heavily wired, and I often noticed masses of wire entanglements in hollows and in woods, in positions which were denied to the enemy's guns, or at least to well-observed fire.

5. Most of the work I saw was of excellent description, a field of fire of 200^x to 300^x being considered ample, the siting was good, the depth of the trench, communicating trenches, revetting, head cover, and supporting trenches all admirably thought out and constructed.

6. Gun emplacements were specially treated and, of course, quite apart from the siting of the "centres de resistance". The whole field of fire and cross fire, invisibility, ranges, likely positions for the enemy's artillery (when moved), lines of retirement from present to rearward positions, all most carefully worked out and prepared.

7. Machine gun emplacements and sitings prepared with a view, I think in every case I saw, to bring cross fire to bear on ground over which the enemy must advance and in every case the greatest care taken to secure invisibility. I saw no case of machine guns being placed in trenches for direct fire. All for cross fire which, again, in many instances, was made more effective by wire and obstacles contracting the front of the enemy's advance.

8. I never heard a word, nor saw a sign, whcih led me to believe that the French were ever going to occupy these rearward lines; on the contrary, I was much impressed by their self-assurance and feeling of power to stand where they now stood; but they all told me the same story, voz., that the present line could be, and was being, held with much greater confidence by the men because they knew that in the event of some unforeseen occurrence there was a strong second line ready for occupation at a moments notice.

9. I saw flat ground, open ground, hilly ground and forest all treated in the same manner as regards the principle of defence being by "centres of resistance" on selected tactical points and not by continuous lines of trench.

10. As was only natural, some of the works which stood out from the general line were more carefully prepared, more heavily wired, even to being wired all the way round, deeper in profile and with greater head cover than others on more favoured xxxxxxx sites.

11. Villages were used and brought into the general line in many instances, the trenches being some 50^x to 100^x outside the village perimeter.

Streams used and banks wired and abbattised.

12. I saw a few cases of "troups de loup" and of sharpened stakes, but in general wire and abbattis were the chief material obstacle, cross fire from guns and machine guns the chief distant threat, and tactical positions held and strongly entrenched the main factor in the defence of the line.

13. Each "Army" drew up its own line, made its own arrangements and carried out its own works, but, in order to make sure that there was no weak point in the long line, the proposals of the "Armies", especially at those points where flanks of "Armies" met, were submitted to General Joffre and approved and altered by him.

14. In short my visit showed me that the French have constructed a second (and in certain places a third) line in a most systematic and soldierly manner, and that unless something quite unforeseen happens to the French Army they have there a defensive line of almost semi-permanent works, of great strength, and capable of prolonged resistance.

1st February, 1915.   (intd) H.W.

20th Infantry Brigade.

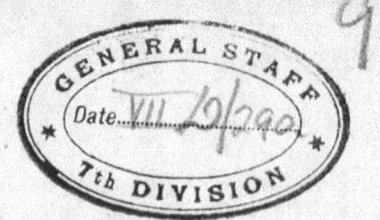

1. After the conversation of yesterday afternoon, the Divisional General agrees to the following arrangement.

When the 2/Scots Guards are in the trenches, a portion of the troops, who at the same time form the Divisional Reserve unit found by your brigade, may be retained by you. This amount must not, without approval of D.H.Q., exceed one Company.

With this additional strength you will be able to render sufficiently secure the "supporting points" and such parts of the "localities" as you may, under present conditions, consider that it is necessary to hold as a precaution, without interfering with your present arrangements for front line defence and local counter action.

You will, no doubt, ensure that this Coy, which would otherwise be in Divisional Reserve, obtains as much rest as is compatible with the conditions, and that this duty falls as equally as possible on all units.

It is to be quite understood that this arrangement must in no case weaken the determination to hold the present front line, or the determination to regain any portion of it which the enemy might temporarily succeed against. The whole object is to avoid any chance of the enemy, if successful against the front line, getting any lodgment in the localities, and thus affecting the success of local or Brigade counter-attacks. In no case should any portion of the Brigade Reserve be locked up in passive defence.

2. With regard to the CORDONNIERE farm, it now appears that your Engineer Officer does not think that mining arrangements

which /

which are not put into active operation until the enemy actually enters the farm, are likely to be successful. At the same time you wish to retain the shelter of the farm as a screen.

Under these conditions, the only thing to do is to include LA CORDONNIERE in your "E" locality.

This could be done without much work, and without much locking up of force, as "E" Work could then be rather more lightly held.

Very careful plans must be made for any work at LA CORDONNIERE, so as to maintain and keep fire and bomb superiority over any attacks. For this reason it must be considered how much of any existing communicating trenches about this farm must be included. The wire system can easily be increased to include LA CORDONNIERE.

3. The Divisional General would be glad to know what you decide to do about (1) and (2).

a. R. Hoskins

Div. H.Q.
7-2-15.

Colonel,
General Staff, 7th Division.

20th   Infantry Brigade.

       The Divisional General wishes constant practice to be carried out in attack formation under varying circumstances with Bomb throwers, Wire Cutters and all the various parties which the attack may require. A system of trenches should be attacked and the communication Trenches dealt with practically. All such exercises should be carefully watched and supervised by the Brigade Staffs who should see that the best formation of columns for the varying circumstances are adopted.

Div H.Q.
10-2-15.

                          Colonel,
           General Staff, 7th Division.

C O N F I D E N T I A L.

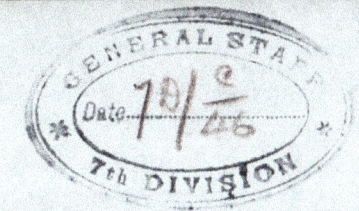

20th Infantry Brigade.

As you are well aware the Divisional General is much concerned as to the comparative weakness of the front line of No 2 Subsection of your Section of the defence. The Divisional General knows well that you too share this concern with him.

The reasons for this Subsection remaining weak are :-

(1) That it is a salient and so naturally weak.
(2) That it is close to the enemy and so difficult in this weather to make strong artificially.
(3) That the length of front, considering its difficulty, is great for the numbers available.
(4) That the troops who have to hold it, having suffered very great casualties, losing most of their officers and N.C.O's, have had great difficulties to contend with in re-establishing their regimental and company systems.

The Divisional General thinks, therefore, that you would be well-advised, in the interest of the safety of your front line, to make some re-adjustment as regards the length held by your No 1. and No 2. Subsection.

The Divisional General would be glad if you would let him know early what re-adjustment you make in this respect.

He is prepared to place at your disposal 100 men of the Northd Hussars to take over that part of the right of your line recently taken over from the 8th Division. These will be relieved periodically under regimental arrangements.

Div.H.Q.
16th February, 1915.

Colonel,
General Staff, 7th Division.

20th Infantry Brigade.

     The Northumberland Hussars will take over that portion of the right of the right section which was recently taken over from the 8th Division. For this purpose the O.C., Northumberland Hussars will place One hundred men at the disposal of the Brigadier-General Commanding 20th Infantry Brigade and report personally to him for instructions as to the taking over, which should be arranged for to-morrow night. These hundred men of the Northumberland Hussars will be relieved under regimental arrangements.

Div. H.Q.
16th February, 1915.

Ian Stewart Major
for Colonel,
General Staff, 7th Division.

20th Infantry Brigade.

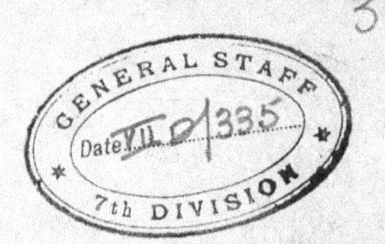

In considering any new trenches which may be made shortly in your Section the Divisional General wishes the following points to have attention :-

1. Trace should be slightly indented.

2. Plenty of <u>inconspicuous</u> alternative Machine Gun emplacements must be made, so as to bring enfilade fire along the front.

3. Loopholes to be made on a slant.

4. Snipers posts to be constructed at a <u>slant</u>, so as to keep hostile line under <u>oblique</u> fire throughout its length.
These posts must be inconspicuous.

5. Alternative loopholes and steps to be made. To every man one loophole and one step. Loopholes for day use. Step to shoot above parapet for night use; and close attack. This principle could be applied even to high command works.

6. Communicating trenches with old line to be frequent.

7. Wire to be erected as line is commenced, and at least 30 yards in front of line where this is possible. Where enemy is very close, aeroplane wire entanglement only can be used.
This must be pushed out as far as is reasonably possible.

8. Listening posts to be made at head of saps thrown out from line.

9. After completion of line, "T" heads should be thrown out for next line. These to be joined up later on.

A.P. Hoskins

Div.H.Q.
19-2-15.

Colonel,
General Staff, 7th Division.

71st Infantry Brigade Tramway Regulations

1. A reliable N.C.O. will be placed in charge, who will have **four** tramwaymen (Privates) under him. These will be permanently detailed by 71st Brigade.

2. The N.C.O in charge is responsible for arrangement of the traffic as ordered at stated times by G.O.C. 71st Brigade. No Officer N.C.O. or man is to interfere with him in the execution of his orders. Officers & N.C.O's in charge of parties are to take the advice of the N.C.O. in charge as to loads of trucks. They will also provide any labour needed for loading the trucks, and for haulage.

3. The trucks are not to be left at Cellar Farm, but are to be brought back to RUE PETILLON as soon as possible. Any loads to be brought back must be ready, so as not to delay the trucks. The two tramwaymen are responsible that trucks are brought back at once. These men will always accompany a train of trucks. Trucks can be used for conveyance of wounded on their return journey, under supervision of a Medical Officer. In emergency, a truck can be specially demanded by an Officer for this purpose.

4. Any damage to the line is to be reported to N.C.O in charge of tramway as soon as discovered. This N.C.O. will ask the representative of the R.E. Company in RUE PETILLON for any skilled labour needed to repair the damage.

5. All officers and N.C.O's will over the tramway officials all help in maintaining the line in efficient order and such protection and labour as may be necessary at any time.

6. No man is permitted to ride on the trucks.

7. Any soldier found removing wood from the tram line or any part of it will be most severely dealt with.

8. If wood is found to be removed from the tramway, the Battalion who is on duty at the Cellars and Rue Petillon will find permanent patrols and sentries on the line.

9. No truck to go down the line in daylight.

AW Cator, Brigade Major
71st Infantry Brigade

22nd February, 1915.

20th Infantry Brigade.

The Divisional General wishes me to inform you of his anxiety that the constant and thorough practice of the attack, under the somewhat new conditions which now prevail, and the rapid instruction and perfection of grenade throwers of Brigades and units, should engage the particukar attention of all responsible Commanders. He knows well that the Brigadiers of Infantry Brigades are taking a close personal interest in these matters, but he feels that they are of such importance that too much insistence cannot be laid onthem, and he hopes you will convey his wishes to those under your command.

Div.H.Q.
23-2-15.

Colonel,
General Staff, 7th Division.

SECRET.

20th Inf. Brigade.

Instructions have been received, that in order to avoid confusion and admit of ready reference to individual works, the following system will in future be adopted in the nomenclature of redoubts and supporting points in the first, second and third lines occupied by the 4th.Corps :-

1st.Line.

7th.Division. Lettered from the right, with the number of the Sub-Section prefixed to the letter, e.g., 1.A., 3.G.

8th.Division. Numbered from the right of each Section with the letter of the Section prefixed to the number e.g., A.1.,A.2.,F.3.

2nd.Line. Numbered consecutively from right to left of the Corps.

3rd.Line. Lettered consecutively from right to left of the Corps.

2. In accordance with the above instructions the nomenclature shown on the attached lists and diagram will henceforward be adopted for works in the 1st.line and in the 2nd or G.H.Q.line.

Letters will be assigned to works in the 3rd line later when the necessity arises.

Div.H.Q.
24.2.1915.

Colonel,
General Staff, 7th.Division.

SUBJECT.

	Contents.	Date.

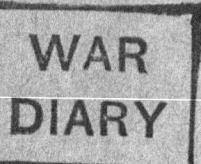

WAR DIARY

B. H. Q. 20th INFANTRY BRIGADE

MARCH 1915

Reports on Operations at NEUVE CHAPELLE.

Operation Orders.

- General.

REPORTS ON OPERATIONS AT

<u>N E U V E   C H A P E L L E</u>

20th Infantry Brigade.
1st Grenadier Guards.
2nd Scots Guards.
2ndcGordon Highlanders.
1/6th Gordon Highlanders.
2nd Border Regiment.

<u>Reports on Battalions</u>

20th Infantry Brigade

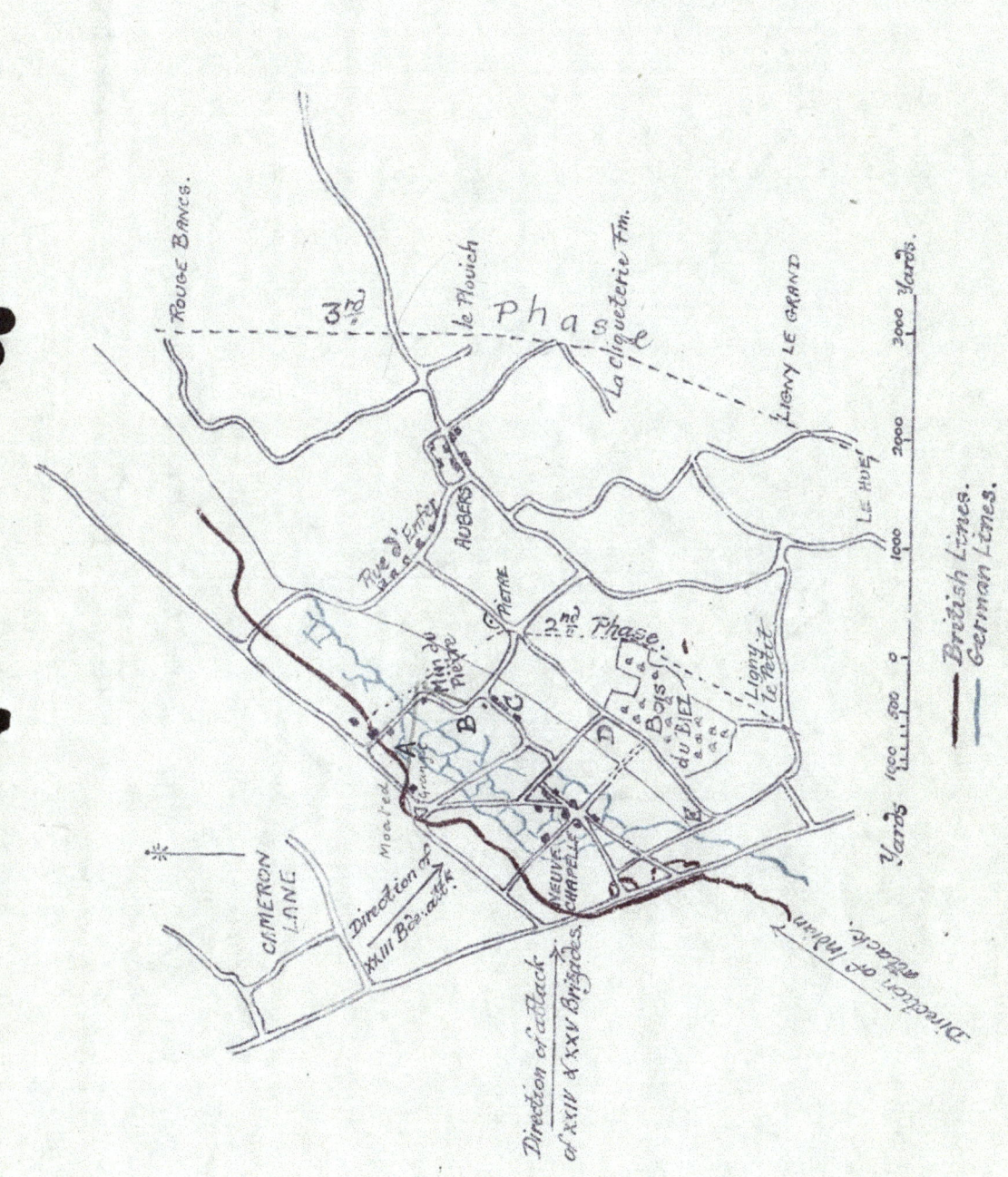

20th Bde

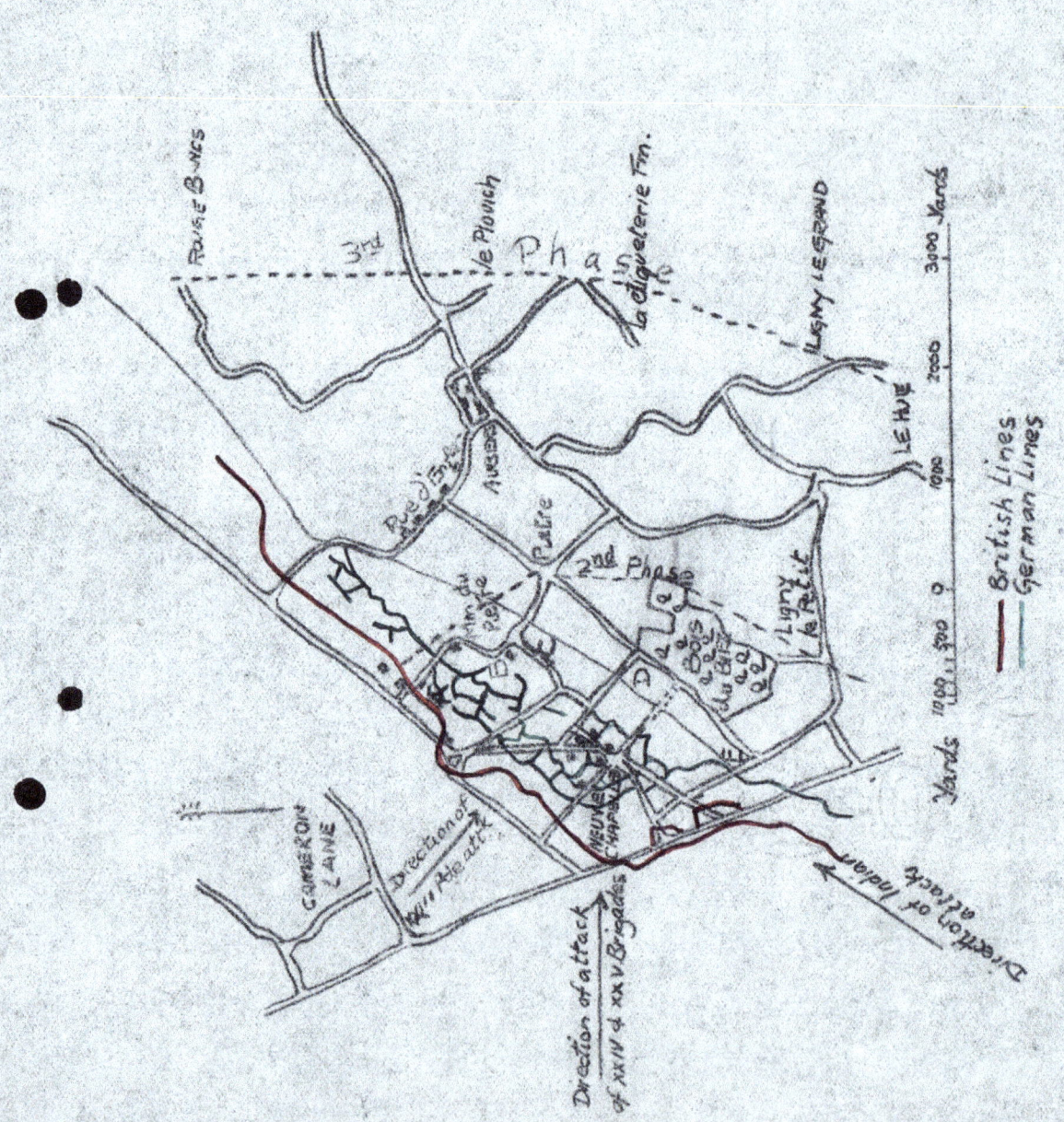

Report on the attack of 10th to 14th March, 1915.

On Tuesday the 9th Orders were received for attacking the German position about NEUVE CHAPELLE.

The plan of attack was as follows:-

(1) To capture NEUVE CHAPELLE.

(2) To advance to the line road junction S.W. of LIGNY LE PETIT - E. corner of BOIS DU BIEZ - Cross Roads W. of PIETRE to enemy's front line trenches E. of the PIETRE - RUE DU PACQUEROT road.

(3) To advance to the capture and occupation of the line LE HUE - LIGNY LE GRAND - LA CLIQUETERIE - LE PLOUICH - ROUGES BANCS. This included the complete capture of AUBERS. The capture of AUBERS was therefore our objective.

In the first phase of the attack the 8th Division attacked NEUVE CHAPELLE at 8 a.m. with two Brigades from the North West, their right Brigade, the 25th, capturing the German trenches West of the village by 10 a.m. Simultaneously the Indian Division attacked NEUVE CHAPELLE from the S.W. being equally successful. These attacks were preceded by a

bombardment of half an hour of the entire Artillery of the 7th, 8th and Indian Division. These guns being augmented by 4 Siege Batteries, two 9.2 Howitzers and one 15" Howitzer, altogether making a total of some 300 guns. The Batteries occupied positions on the N.E.-N.-N.W.-W. and S.W. of NEUVE CHAPELLE forming a big horse-shoe shape round it on three sides.

The bombardment commenced at 7.30 a.m. Meanwhile the 21st Brigade was in fire trenches in a position of assembly in CAMERON LANE, moving out to the 8th Division support trenches in RUE DE TILLELOY and vacated by their

23rd Brigade/

Sheet 2.

23rd Brigade as it moved forward to the attack. We - the 20th Brigade filling up the fire shelters as they were vacated by the 21st.

Owing to the fact that the Artillery had failed in their endeavours to cut the German wire in front of the 23rd Brigade, their attack got hung up for a while and it
1.25 p.m. was not until 1.25 p.m. we got the orders to close up our last Battalion into CAMERON LANE and there await orders
4.45 p.m. as Corps Reserve. At 4.45 p.m. we got a message from the Division stating that the 21st Brigade had moved at 3.30 p.m. to attack MOULIN DU PIETRE to clear trenches in front of the 22nd Brigade now holding our old trenches to the East.
6.45 p.m. At 6.45 p.m. we received orders to billet the men but to be ready to turn out at a moments notice as a German counter attack was expected. So far as we could ascertain many Germans had been killed and 400 prisoners had been captured in the days fighting, many of whom had passed by us during the day. One very regrettable instance occurred during the day, one of our aeroplanes suddenly collapsed and fell from a height of 2,000 feet into a field by CAMERON LANE, both airmen being killed.

p.m. At 10 p.m. we got orders to move into the 8th Division old support trenches RUE TILLELOY before daylight.

Nothing of importance occurred during the night.
9 p.m. We were informed that the 21st Brigade were holding a position with their left resting on the German trenches some 200 yards East of Moated Grange, thence due East to elbow of road at MOULIN DU PIETRE, thence southward to the road and joining up there with the left of the 24th Brigade. Subsequent events the following day proved this to be incorrect and their position was not nearly so far forward.
2 a.m. March 11th. At 2 a.m. the following extract of orders was received. "Fourth Corps moves to-day to LA CLIQUERIE

LA PLOUICH/

Sheet 3.

LA PLOUICH - AUBERS. Objective - 21st, RUE D'ENFER - LES MOTTES FARM - TRIVILET. Artillery will bombard houses immediately in front of this Brigade from 6.45 a.m. to 7 a.m. when Infantry will advance. 20th Brigade will be ready on the left of MOATED GRANGE and attack AUBERS from the S.W., right passing through PIETRE. Objective LE PLOUICH.- East end of AUBERS to last L in RUE DELEVAL. 22nd Brigade will assist advance with its fire. Some Batteries will be ready to move to AUBERS ridge when captured. 20th Brigade will maintain touch with left of 8th Division as latter advance to LA CLIQUETERIE

3.30 a.m. At 3.30 a.m. the Brigade moved off from CAMERON LANE in the following order, 1st Grenadier Guards, 2nd Scots Guards, 2nd Border Regiment, 6th Gordon Highlanders. (The 2nd Batt: Gordon Highlanders having been transferred temporarily yesterday to the 21st Brigade). The route we followed was along the light railway, odd rifle shots were sweeping the ground and the Germans burst some shells over us causing a few casualties. Much to our disgust we found every available fire shelter occupied by the 8th Division Reserve on arrival, but after a deal of pushing and shoving we managed to squeeze the Brigade in to trenches and breastworks already occupied, making the men lie down three deep. The only place we could find for Brigade Headquarters was a small sandbag breastwork up against a shrine, the latter had to be used as a telephone box. Reports came in to say the Germans had brought up a re-inforcement of 1 Division.

It was now discovered at 6.30 a.m. that the 21st Brigade did not extend so much to the right as they had imagined and the 20th Brigade were ordered to prolong the line on the right of the 21st Brigade joining up with the left of the 8th Division with its objective MOULIN DU PIETRE

PIETRE/

Sheet 4.

PIETRE and attack AUBERS.

The attack was launched at 7 a.m., Grenadiers on the right and 2nd Gordon Highlanders on the left, supported by the Scots Guards and Border Regiment. The 6th Gordon Highlanders being retained in Reserve. The moment the attack began to advance beyond the line gained on the previous day, it came under a very severe enfilade fire from the left. 8:45 a.m. The Grenadiers reported they were on as far as R.LAYES, some 800 yards W. of PIETRE (this subsequently turning out to be an error and they were really astride a small stream, which they mistook for the LAYES, some 600 yards S.W. of the elbow on the MIN DU PIETRE road). The 21st Brigade reported that they were on the line as follows, their left resting on our old trenches to the elbow in the road. The situation as reported was obviously incorrect, as had they been on that line our Brigade would have been echeloned back on their right rear and could not possibly have been enfiladed from the left. At any rate so severe was the fire that the attack could not advance and were hung up holding the ground on which they were on all day, suffering somewhat heavy casualties. Late in the day it was discovered that the 21st Brigade were facing S.E. instead of N.E. and the 20th (our) Brigade were facing N.E. but were not so far forward as they supposed. The position being roughly as in sketch.

At 8 p.m. the Grenadiers were relieved by the 8th Division and at 10 o'clock the Scots Guards were brought back in support, leaving the Borders and 2nd Gordons on their positions in front.

The/

Sheet 5.

The rest of the night spent in straightening out and consolidating the line with the assistance of the R.E. Towards evening a great increase in the German Artillery Fire was noticeable and it was obvious that their guns had been strongly reinforced by fresh batteries. At 9 p.m. orders came in that the 20th Brigade were to attack a line of redoubts near "A" just W of the ~~005545~~ PIETRE road. The attack to be carried out by the two Battalions and to be preceded by an Artillery Bombardment of half an hour commencing at 7 a.m., but if the mroning was too misty the bombardment would be deferred and the Division would notify us. The bombardment would end at 7.30 a.m. precisely, but if postponed 30 minutes after its commencement, the Infantry to assult immediately bombardment had ceased before the enemy had time to recover. The Infantry with the help of the R.E. to consolidate their captured positions immediately gained.

Casualties had been fairly severe this day, particularly amongst the Officers.

The Grenadiers lost Captain Hon. H. Douglas Pennant, Lieutenant Darby, Lieutenant Lord Bradborne, Lieutenant Burnand, killed, Lieutenant Foster (since died of wounds) 2nd Lieutenant Mildmay, Captain Sartorious, wounded.

Scots Guards. Lieutenant C. Seymour and Ewart wounded.

2nd Gordon Highlanders. Lieutenant W.H. Ross, 2nd Lieutenant E.R. Mulloch, 2nd Lieutenant Pender, killed, Major Crauford, C.I.E., D.S.O., Lieutenant H.M. Sprott, Lieutenant D.M. Bain and 2nd Lieutenant A.W. Chaytor, wounded. The 6th Battalion Gordon Highlanders in reserve near Brigade Headquarters had 2 Officers killed and 2 wounded by shell fire.

March 12th. Battalions were detailed for the attack as follows, Scots Guards on the right, objective, German

trenches/

Sheet 6.

trenches in front of MIN DU PIETRE. Border Regiment on the left, objective, "A" Redoubt. The morning being misty the attack was postponed at first till 8 a.m. and subsequently, the mist not clearing, till 10.30 a.m. a message to this latter effect informing us that the Artillery bombardment would commence at 9.50 a.m. AT 9.45 a.m. however, a message came to the effect that owing to fog this attack would be postponed a further two hours. This message did not reach the firing line and they had already advanced about 100 yards under a heavy fire before they were stopped. At 9.45 a.m. General Watts reported the enemy to be pressing his left down one of the many OLD communication trenches and requested the loan of bombers to meet this counter move on the part of the enemy. Accordingly we sent him 20 from our Brigade Bomber Reserve, this party subsequently doing some very fine work. On arrival on the left of the 21st Brigade they found the Wiltshires being hard pressed by the enemy who was endeavouring to turn their left flank sending down strong parties by a communication trench. The Bombers immediately advanced up the trench to meet them Private Barber of the Grenadiers getting forward 100 yards ahead and put in such good work with his bombs that 200 of them surrendered. This man has unfortunately been reported missing but has been recommended for the V.C.

At 10.30 a.m. the Division reported that a German Officer now prisoner stated that their authorities had ordered NEUVE CHAPELLE to be re-taken to-day.

At 10.40 a.m. Division requested us to send two Battalions into Divisional Reserve in CAMERON LANE, 2 Companies 2nd Gordon Highlanders and 6th Battalion Gordons detailed. At 11.50 a.m. the bombardment commenced which lasted till 12.30 p.m. The Scots Guards and Border Regiment then advancing with little opposition captured the
redoubt/

Sheet 7.

the redoubt and trench West of MIN DU PIETRE road, capturing some further 400 prisoners. The bombardment had been appalling and had completely reduced the Germans to a state of abject terror, a captured German Officer remarking "it was is'nt war, its carnage". Meanwhile at 12.30 p.m. the 1st Battalion Grenadier Guards in Brigade Reserve had been ordered to push out and advance on MIN DU PIETRE on the right of the Scots Guards. There was a tremendously heavy shell fire at the time from the Germans, which made progress for them slow and difficult, as they had to keep under cover as much as possible. Major G.Trotter, D.S.O. was wounded in the head (slightly) just as they commenced to advance. Shortly afterwards their Commanding Officer, Lieut: Colonel L.Fisher-Rowe was killed by a bullet. Whether these two Officers alone knew the objective or not has not been ascertained, but the Grenadiers lost their direction and eventually found themselves in the old British Trench opposite "A".

1.50 p.m. At 1.50 p.m. a report was received that 600 prisoners were coming in to the MOATED GRANGE. During the remainder of the day, Battalions occupied their time in re-organizing and making their position gained as strongly as possible. 600 prisoners captured during the day by our Brigade. The Germans brought a terrific shell fire to bear on the newly captured positions and any movement above ground was difficult. They had been very busy all the morning, devoting their attention with Jack Johnson's, White Hopes and Shrapnel on the Brigade Reserve, though fortunately doing very little damage. One Jack Johnson however burst on four men cooking their breakfast ten yards from Brigade Headquarters, two men were blown to atoms and could not be found, one cut in half and one blown up a tree, his clothing and portions of him hanging on the boughs 30 feet

up the/

Sheet 8.

8 p.m. up the tree. At 8 p.m. the General Officer Commanding 7th Division arrived to have a Conference, his orders were to shift the Grenadiers from their present position in the old British Trenches opposite "A" to relieve the Royal Scots Fusiliers opposite MIN DU PIETRE, push the 2nd Gordon Highlanders up on their left and join up with the Border Regiment now at "A" in the German old trenches. The Conference lasted till 11 p.m. and it was pointed out that it would be difficult to re-sort the line as the night was very dark and the country was closely intersected by numerous trenches and barbed wire and extremely heavy and wet. Being anxious to continue the advance and capture AUBERS, the G.O.C. decided that the line must be re-sorted. Knowing it would take best part of the whole night to get this accomplished, the Brigadier with a Staff Officer set off at once to personally take an Officer of each Battalion and point out on the ground the positions they were to occupy before daylight. Setting off at 11 p.m. it was two hous before he actually got to the Grenadiers. The night was pitch black and the country indescribably difficult to traverse in the dark, progress could only be made by a few yards at a time the guides losing their way.

By 3 a.m. the Grenadiers were ordered to move into their new positions which were some thousand yards away. Daylight found them with only one company in the Royal Scots Fusiliers trenches whom they were to relieve and the remainder of the Battalion stretched out across the open. Meanwhile the 6th Battalion Gordon Highlanders had been ordered up to relieve the 2nd Battalion Gordon Highlanders, the intention being that after a heavy bombardment the line consisting of the Grenadiers, 6th Gordons and Border Regiment was to advance to take the houses along the MIN DU PIETRE road.

The 8th/

Sheet 9.

The 8th Division having been ordered to capture during the night the houses along the Road "C". The attack failed. The 6th Battalion Gordon Highlanders lost their way in the dark and arrived to relieve the 2nd Gordon Highlanders after daylight. To move Battalions out of their positions in daylight was out of the question, so both the 2nd Gordon Highlanders and Royal Scots Fusiliers remained in their trenches. The bombardment commenced shortly after daylight on the house on the MIN DU PIETRE road, unfortunately the shells of the Heavy Howitzer Batteries falling short and inflicting some damage to our own troops. The Grenadiers were straggled out all over the country and it was impossible to re-organise them under the heavy fire and form them up for attack. The Border Regiment, 6th Gordon Highlanders and 2nd Gordon Highlanders were being enfiladed from the right and vainly tried to attack. The enemy brought a very heavy shell fire to bear on them. The attack was hung up for a whole day and no ground was gained. This attack would probably have been successful had the 23rd Brigade captured the house on the road "C" over night. As it was from here the enemy were enfilading us. At night it was decided to re-organise the troops and consolidate the position. The Grenadiers and 6th Gordon Highlanders were withdrawn and the 2nd Gordon Highlanders were to be relieved by the South Staffords before daylight. The latter losing their way did not relieve the 2nd Gordon Highlanders at all and returned to us to Brigade Reserve at 7 a.m. March 14th. The Brigade remained in the captured positions all day and no further advance being attempted. The enemy was inactive and except for heavy shelling at intervals attempted no offensive movement. On the night of the 14th the Brigade was relieved by the 24th Brigade

and/

Sheet 10.

retired into billets at LAVENTIE to rest, last Unit arriving at 4 a.m. the 15th.

The following are the Casualties for the four days fighting in the Brigade:-

	Officers	Other Ranks.
1st Bn. Grenadier Guards	14	328
2nd Bn. Scots Guards	6	189
2nd Border Regiment	14	266
2nd Gordon Highlanders	16	235
6th Gordon Highlanders	16	289
Total.	66	1307

The following were the casualties amongst the Commanding Officers:-

Lieutenant Colonel Fisher Rowe.   Grenadiers.   Killed
Major Paynter, D.S.O.   Scots Guards.   Wounded.
Lieutenant Colonel Uniacke.   2nd Gordons.   Killed
Lieutenant Colonel MacLean   6th Gordons.   Killed.

General Headquarters reported nearly 2,000 prisoners taken and the enemy casualties at 18,000.

(sd) F.S.Heyworth, Brigadier General,
Commanding 20th Infantry Brigade.

7th Division.

Reference to the 20th Brigade report on operations sent you last night. The report stated that the 6th Bn. Gordon Highlanders were to relieve the 2nd Bn. Gordon Highlanders and did not arrive in time.

This was an error. The 6th Bn. Gordon Highlanders relieved the Scots Guards before daylight. Attached is the correction.

                                              (sd) A.W.E.Cator, Major,

20/3/15.   Brigade Major 20th Inf. Brigade.

Amendments to Report on Operations of 20th Brigade
10th - 14th instant.

Substitute the following for the last 11 lines on page 8.

"By 3 a.m. the Grenadiers were ordered to move into their new positions which were some thousand yards away. Daylight found them with only one company in the Royal Scots Fusiliers' Trenches whom they were to relieve and the remainder of the battalion stretched out across the open. Meanwhile the 6th Battalion Gordon Highlanders had been ordered up to relieve the 2nd Battalion Scots Guards the intention being that after a heavy bombardment the line consisting of the Grenadiers, 2nd and 6th Battalions Gordon Highlanders and Border regiment was to advance and take the houses along the MIN DU PIETRE road".

Substitute the following for the first 8 lines on page 9.

"The 8th Division having been ordered to capture during the night the houses along the road "C". The attack failed. To move a battalion out of its position in daylight was out of the question, so the Royal Scots Fusiliers remained in their trenches".

Sd.A.W.E.Cator. Brigade Major.
20th March, 1915.   20th Infantry Brigade.

1st Grenadier Guards

CONFIDENTIAL.
=============================

Headquarters,

    IVth Corps.

    I forward herewith report from Officer Commanding 1st Battalion Grenadier Guards on the operations in the neighbourhood of NEUVE CHAPELLE between the 10th and 14th March, 1915, which was inadvertently omitted from my 7/D/G/83 forwarded this day.

Div. H.Q.   (sd) Ian Stewart. Major,
24th March, 1915.   for Major General,
                                             Commanding 7th Division.

Headquarters,
    20th Brigade.

    Forwarded.

    I am informed from many different sources that the work done by Major G.F.Trotter up to the time of his being knocked out was of the greatest possible assistance to his Commanding Officer and the Battalion.

21-3-15.   (sd) Charles Corkran. Lt-Col.
                             Commanding 1st Bn. Grenadier Guards.

To:-   O.C. 1st Bn. Grenadier Guards.

From:-   Major G.F.Trotter, 1st Bn. Grenadier Guards.

21st March, 1915.

Sir,

In accordance with Brigade Order No. 13 M 142 of the 21st March, 1915, requiring an account of the operations in which the battalion was engaged from 10th to 14th inst. I beg to submit the following:-

On the 10th March, the Brigade of which this battalion formed part was in Corps Reserve south of ESTAIRES and moved to CAMERON LANE, this battalion arriving there at 3 p.m., and occupied support trenches until moved into billets at 7-30 p.m. At 4-15 a.m. the 11th March the battalion was moved from CAMERON LANE to occupy a line of our trenches from which they were to attack with the 2nd Bn. Gordon High-:landers the line PIETRE - MOULIN DE PIETRE, this battalion on the right, Gordon Highlanders on the left. The order for attack was issued immediately battalion had got into the trenches. The attack commenced at 7 a.m. punctually, King's Coy and No.2 Coy in firing line, Nos 3 & 4 Coys in support, and Scots Guards in reserve to this battalion. The attack opened under shell and rifle fire and proceeded across the line of abandoned German trenches and through some companies of the Devon Regiment and across the road in M.35 b. The Commanding Officer seeing heavy losses going on then went forward and found the leading companies were under enfilade fire from machine gun and rifle fire, and the battalion was put under cover in a disused and wet German trench. Major Duborty then came back and reported that he had two platoons in advance of this trench but that they were also enfiladed and in rear of a trench held by men of the Northamptonshire Regiment who, he thought, were some 200 yards from the main
                                                              German

main German line. The C.O. then sent back a message to Brigade Headquarters to the effect that he was enfiladed and casualties were severe, and stated he wished support on his left. He received a reply to hold on where he was. This was easily done despite a heavy shell fire until dark, when the battalion was withdrawn to support trenches in M.34.b., and remained there during the night of 11th/12th. At about 12-30 p.m. 12th March, the battalion was ordered to support Scots Guards and Border Regiment, and Nos 3 & 4 Coys proceeded to do so supported by the remaining Company of the battalion. The leading Company advanced from the breastworks at about 1-30 pm. From this moment I am only able to speak from hearsay and what Captain Hon. R.Lygon reported to me the following evening. I regret to say Lt-Colonel Fisher Rowe was mortally wounded at about 4 p.m. that evening and the command of the battalion devolved on Major G.W. Daberty. The battalion was moved to a new position in the late hours of the 12th/13th, and the battalion had hardly completed the movement when an attack order was received and Major Daberty was killed in leading it. The attack then came to a standstill owing to our heavy guns shelling both firing line and supports.

Captain Hon. R.Lygon was now in command of the battalion and determined to remain where he was. The battalion came out of action that evening 13th/14th and went into billets at LAVENTIE where I assumed temporary command.

I would, in conclusion, submit to your notice the good work done by the following Officers, N.C.O.s, and men, on the days mentioned above.

        Major G.W.Duberty. Killed.
        Capt. Hon. R.Lygon M.V.O.
          "   " G.H.Douglas Pennant. Killed
        Lt. & A/Adjt. C.Fisher Rowe. Wounded.
        2/Lt. G.Westmacott. Wounded and shaken by a bomb remained in command of his Company all day the 13th and was of great assistance to Captain Lygon whilst in command of the battalion on that date.

I would also like to mention Lieut & Quartermaster Tenn for his endeavours to get rations etc to the battalion under, at times, very difficult circumstances.

The work of the stretcher-bearers under command of Captain Petit R.A.M.C., is deserving of special recognition, and I would bring his name to your notice.

The following N.C.O.s and men I would respectfully submit as having done very well:-

    C.Q.M.S. Hughes, Kings Co.
    C.S.M. J.Yong   No. 2 Coy.
    C.S.M. T.Wall.   No. 3 Coy. Wounded.
    C.S.M. Jones,   No. 4 Coy.
    Sergt. Smith,   Stretcher-bearer. Wounded.
    Sergt. Langley, No. 3 Coy.
    Private Mactim, Battalion Orderly.
      "   Lund.   Stretcher-bearer.
      "   Sambourne,   "

I regret to say that the losses in the battalion amongst the officers were very heavy, as including the Commanding Officer, nine were killed or died of their wounds, and six were wounded. The casualties as far as can be gathered in other ranks amount to, I believe, 342 killed and wounded.

        I have the honour to be,
            Sir,
                (sd) Gerald F. Trotter. Major, 1st Gren:Gds

2nd Scots Guards

Account of recent operations.
2nd Battalion Scots Guards.
-----------:-:-:-:-:-:-:-:-:-:-:-:-:----------

On 10th March the battalion remained at CAMERON LANE in Corps Reserve.

At 4 a,m, on 11th March the battalion left CAMERON LANE and moved into breastworks on the PONT LOGY - FAUQUISSART road close to the 20th Brigade Headquarters, with orders to attack in support of 1st Battalion Grenadier Guards in the direction of MOULIN DU PIETRE, PIETRE, and AUBERS. At 7 a.m. having lost a few men from shells bursting in the breastwork the battalion advanced at 7-10 am in lines of half companies, R.F. Coy leading. After advancing for about 1,000 yards under fire over several lines of trenches and some wide and deep ditches rather difficult to negotiate, the attack was held up, and the battalion halted with its first line close up to, and intermingled with, the last line of the Grenadier Guards. The battalion remained in this position for the rest of the day, the men digging themselves in as well as they were able to under a fairly heavy shell fire. Some men were also lost owing to rifle fire, i.e., overs fired at the Grenadier Guards, and an intermittent enfilade fire from the right. The battalions losses during the day were two Officers - Lieut. Seymour and 2/Lieut Ewart - and about 50 men.

The last line of the battalion halted in the first line of the German trenches captured the day before. As soon as it was dark, companies dug themselves in.

At about 10-30 pm orders were received for the battalion to attack a fort and a house held by the enemy near MOULIN DU PIETRE at 7 a.m. An intermittent shell fire was kept up by the enemy during the night and became rather heavy about 4 a.m. 12th March. At 4-15 am the battalion moved off along the NEUVE CHAPELLE - FAUQUISSART road to a point where a captured communication trench reached the road, and halted in some and halted in some shallow trenches on either side of the road about 5-30 am. Captain G.H.Loder was injured and 2/Lieut. Bullock wounded during the night. Orders were received postponing the attack until 10-30 am. The enemy's shell fire was heavy between 5 am and 8 am.

About 8-30 am the battalion moved up the communication trench, which was in places waist deep in water, and into some shallow trenches which had been dug at right angles to it the night before. The formation was lines of half companies, L.F. Company in the leading lines.

The 2nd Bn. Border Regiment was in similar trenches and formation in front, and the battalion's orders were to come up on their right when the attack commenced and to take the defended house while the Border Regiment captured the fort.

It subsequently became apparent that the two assaults could not be simultaneous, as the house was 300 yards beyond the fort, and the latter had first to be reduced.

A message from the Brigade postponing the attack until 12-30 pm was not received owing to the orderlies who carried it being killed, and the attack was launched at 10-30 am without artillery preparation.

The battalion got up on the right of the Border Regiment after some difficulty had been caused by a deep ditch which had to be crossed, and after advancing about 150 yards was compelled to stop by very heavy machine gun and rifle fire.

Three Officers and about 100 men were lost during the advance.

At about 11-30 am the artillery opened and shelled the enemy's first position very heavily and with great accuracy for about two hours, after which white flags began to appear and some of the enemy emerged from their trench with their hands up. An immediate advance was made and the first pos:ition captured without difficulty. The battalion's first three lines arrived in the fort intermingled with Officers and men and men of the Border Regiment, and 300 prisoners and a machine gun were captured.

Lieut. Swinton led the L.F. Coy with great gallantry and success in the attack. The battalion's casualties were 3 Officers - Capt. Sir E.Hulse, killed, Major Paynter and 2/Lieut.Barry wounded - and over 100 N.C.O.s and men.

A communication trench leading back to the PIETRE - RUE DE BACQUEROT road was next attacked by men of the battalion and the Border Regiment, and some progress made, but enfilade fire from the right and machine gun fire from the houses on the road was sufficiently heavy to frustrate all attempts to advance on to the road across the open, so that no further advantage could be obtained.

The position was now consolidated and the battalion remained in the fort and in the trenches in rear of it until dark.

The battalion was withdrawn before daylight on 13th March to CAMERON LANE.

At 4 am on the 14th March the battalion marched up to Brigade Headquarters with orders to man the breastworks near there in support of the firing line. On arrival it was found that there was no room and the battalion returned to CAMERON LANE except R.F. Coy which remained in the breastworks until dark. At 8 am the battalion went into billets in LEVANTIE.

The battalion's losses during the operations were 6 Officers and 192 other ranks.

During the period when the attack was held up on 12th March, No. 9522 Lce Cpl. McVean displayed great gallantry in leaving the cover of a trench under a heavy machine gun and rifle fire to give water to a wounded man.

A notable/

A notable feature of the operations was the great gallantry displayed by those responsible for attending to the wounded. Captain Houston, the R.A.M.C. Officer attached to the battalion, assisted by two of the battalion stretcher-bearers No. 414 Corporal S.Lemen and 6608 Pte J.Litster were conspicuous in this respect, working day and night, often under a heavy fire.

      (sd) F.D.FitzWygram. Captain,
         Commanding 2nd Bn. Scots Guards.

2nd Gordon Highlanders

Account of the operations 10th to 14th March, 1915

Reference sheet 36 S.W..   2nd Bn. Gordon Highlanders.

10th.

The battalion arrived from ESTAIRES at shelters near PONT DU HEM at about 5 a.m. During the bombardment shells were falling fairly close all round, but the battalion escaped unhurt.

About 3 pm we were ordered to move up into support trenches on the RUE TILLELOY (square M.28.d.). We came under shrapnel fire crossing from the RUE DU BACQUEROT but had no casualties. We remained in these trenches until dusk.

About 6 pm "A" Coy was moved up into a line of trenches in front and slightly to the right in touch with the Middlesex Regiment, withdrawing after daylight next morning.

About 7-35 pm "B" Coy was ordered to move up in support of the Wiltshire Regiment. After much difficulty they found them in the German trenches not far from the big farm (square M.29.a.). Under instructions from O.C. Wiltshire Regiment this company spent the night digging a fire trench joining the old British and German trenches facing N.E. On the left were the 4th Bn. Caerom Highlanders holding the old line. At dawn this company had orders to retire and join battalion Headquarters in the support trenches of the night before. This company had about 6 casualties during the night.

11th March.

At 6-30 a.m. all company Commanders were sent for by the Colonel, and the operations explained, viz., that the 20th Brigade would attack with the Grenadier Guards on the right and 2nd Gordon Highlanders on the left of the front line: and the Scots Guards and Border Regiment in the second line. The Grenadier Guards to direct starting in an easterly direction and swinging round on to the MOULIN DU PIETRE

MOULIN DU PIETRE. The attack started about 7 am when we immediately came under shell fire. The battalion was in artillery formation with "A" Company on the right and "C" Company on the left of the first line, and "B" and "D" Coys in the second line.

Continuing the advance towards small house with orchard (sq.M.29.c.S.E.) we soon came under rifle fire from our left front. On coming to the orchard "C" and "D" Companies swung slightly to their left, "A" and "B" going through the orchard keeping touch with the Grenadier Guards. Coming out of the orchard they also swung round half left. From this point we came under very heavy rifle and machine gun fire from our left front, losing many casualties.

The Colonel and the Adjutant were with "C" Coy on the left. All very soon moved forward and got into an old trench under cover. It was in this advance that we lost Lieut. Ross and 2/Lieuts Pender and Mallock. The Grenadier Guards were directly on our right all the time. The battalion remained in these trenches the rest of the day, not being bothered much by shells or rifle fire. It was during this afternoon that Lieut. Letters went to try and get across a slight gap to "D" Company and was not seen again.

Lieut. J.G.Priestley - our Medical Officer - was wounded quite early in the day when we first deployed, and continued to dress the wounded the whole day until relieved in the evening, when he was quite exhausted.

There were wounded also Major Craufurd C.I.E.,D.S.O., Lieuts Sprot, Boyd, Bain, and Chater, during this morning.

At dusk, "A" and "B" Companies and the machine gun were ordered to dig a line of trench facing N.E. and in a line with the front hedge of the orchard. "C" and "D" Companies dug themselves in near the position they had occupied all day.

12th March.

12th March.

About 4 am the Companies received the order to move back to the shelters at PONT DU HEM before daylight. It was necessary to make a detour to the right as the Germans were shelling all the ground to the S.W. and S, of the light railway running between the Rue Du Bacquerot and the Rue Tilleloy. Battalion Headquarters remained where they had been all night, as it was considered that the line was rather weak there. The four companies remained at the shelters at PONT DU HEM until about 2 pm when General Capper ordered us up to report to our Brigade. We moved up to the same place in the shelter trenches as on the 10th. We again got shelled on the way but came through without much loss. On reporting to the 20th Brigade Headquarters we were ordered to move up in support of the Border Regiment. The battalion moved along the trench to the left and in behind the old British first line trenches with the intention of crossing to the German trenches by the fire trench dug by "B" Company on the night of the 10th, joining the two lines.

While in the British trench we were shelled very heavily for some time, and as it was getting late, it was thought advisable to wait there until dark, being quite close to the Border Regiment at the time.

At dark Regimental Headquarters joined under Major J.R.E Stansfield D.S.O., Colonel Uniacke having gone sick. We remained all night behind the British old line of trenches.

13th March.

About 3 am orders were received that the battalion would relieve the Yorks in the front line of trenches, and that at 9-30 am after an artillery bombardment we should charge the German trenches and the houses at MOULIN DU PIETRE on the road near "3" in M.30.

The battalion/

The battalion moved up and took over the trenches just before daylight. The trenches were very low and afforded very little cover: they also had a good many dead and wounded in them. Lieut-Colonel H.P.Uniacke suddenly arrived up with us although he had gone sick the previous night. He crawled along behind the trench up towards the right of our line and started looking over the trench every few seconds, and exposing himself very much while arranging the charge. He was killed outright - a very great loss to us.

At about 9-10 am during the bombardment some of our shells began falling very close to "A" Coy on the right, one going into the trench and killing one man. This was not encouraging for a charge, and as the enemy's rifle fire was very heavy, Major Stansfeld decided not to advance, but that he would go in to explain matters to the Brigade.

On our left the 6th Battalion Gordon Highlanders were being brought up in support, and some of them getting to our trench, Acting C.S.M. Munroe gathered a few of our men and joined up with the men of the 6th Battalion, went forward to an unoccupied line of trench about 50 yards in front where they remained all day.

Major Stansfeld, though himself wounded, was indefat-:igable in moving up and down the line - only possible on hands and knees - organising the attack, until he saw that it was out of the question.

That left Major J.F,Hamilton in command.

The battalion remained there all that day, losing Captain Hay and 2/Lieut. Mitchell wounded, and a certain number of other casualties from shell fire. In the evening we were told that we would be relieved during the night, and so the Quartermaster Captain Mackie, who came up to our trenches, did not bring rations, but had them ready in billets in LAVENTIE.

That night/

That night the body of Lt-Colonel Uniacke C.B. was taken back and buried next day in ESTAIRES. Our relief never arrived during the night, it having marched most of the night looking for us.

14th March.

In the early morning General Heyworth came up and looked at the line. We remained in the same trenches all day, suffering only a few losses.

At about 11 pm the Worcesters, 24th Brigade, arrived to take over our trenches which we had managed to clear of dead and wounded - some of the latter, including 3 Germans, having been there for some days.

We marched into billets in LAVENTIE.

During all these days Private Chalk, who was with Regimental Headquarters, was continually running messages under fire, and well deserves to be mentioned for his good work. Lance Corporal Stewart also did very good work with Regimental Headquarters.

(sd) J.F.Hamilton. Major,
2nd Bn. Gordon Highlanders.

6th Gordon Highlanders

Report as to the part taken by 1/6th Gordon Highlanders in operations from 10th - 14th March, 1915.

-----:-:-:-:-:-:-:-:-:-:-:-:-:-:-:-:-:-:-----

10th March.

Reveille 4 am. Marched at 6 am from ESTAIRES to reserve trenches in CAMERON LANE (M.21.b.) - occasional shrapnel.

11th March.

The battalion fell in at 4-15 am and marched in artillery formation by way of light railway to near Brigade Headquarters (M.29.c.) under considerable shrapnel fire, which continued all day. Eight casualties. "C" Coy on Brigade ration fatigue during night.

12th March.

Battalion subjected to heavy artillery fire from 4-30 am About noon we were retired to reserve trenches. Captain H.D.Laing and 2/Lieut. H.M.Inglis were killed, and Captain J.Dawson and 2/Lieut. R.R.Bisset were wounded before noon. Returned from reserve trenches about 2 pm to position held in morning.

Shell fire still continuing.

Officer and 50 N.C.O.s and men ammunition fatigue to 2nd Gordons in firing line.

Brigade fatigue parties of practically every man available for duty required for rations during night.

Casualties on the 12th, besides above-mentioned Officers 2 men killed, 23 wounded.

13th March.

Battalion moved off at 4-15 am to attack which was ordered to commence at 9-30 am. While moving forward to take up position before daybreak, subjected to heavy artillery fire and lost several men. The position to be attacked was
pointed

pointed out to Company Officers by the C.O. and the Adjutant.

Colonel McLean who had gone out in front to obtain information, was killed when about to enter a trench occupied by the 2nd Gordons. This would be about 7-30 am, and about the same time the Adjutant (Captain J.A.L.Campbell) was wounded.

On the loss of the Colonel the Command of the battalion devolved upon me. I at once sent Captain Smith to Brigade Headquarters to verify the order re the attack and to report the death of the Commanding Officer. He returned with instructions that everything was in order and that the 6th Gordons were to attack at 9-30 am after bombardment. I then issued orders to Company Commanders to advance in lines of half companies in the following order, "A" on the left, "B" on the right, "C" on the right supporting "B", and "D" on the left supporting "A", at 200 yards distance.

The battalion advanced to attack at 9-30 am in face of very heavy artillery, machine gun, and rifle fire, principally from our right flank. Both Officers and men did exceedingly well, advancing with good order and with good speed. Our front line went forward till in touch with the 2nd Gordons. It then occupied a shallow trench about 100 yards from left front of 2nd Gordons. Germans were noticed retiring - rapid fire was opened on them.

It was found, however, to be impossible owing to the fierceness of the fire to advance further, and I reported this to Headquarters 20th Brigade, pointing out that there was also a heavy enfilade fire. Reply was received at noon that howitzers and heavies were being turned on houses at MIN DU MOULIN to enable us to proceed. In spite of this the enemy's fire continued to be very heavy, and on that account, and looking to the loss the battalion had already
sustained.

sustained, I reported to Headquarters for instructions. I reorganised as well as possible, and selected positions for machine guns along with the machine gun Officer in case of counter attack from the right, which appeared to be imminent.

At 5-45 pm received instructions to hold present line, which was done.

About 9-30 pm I received intimation that the battalion would be relieved during the night and I continued to get in all wounded men and despatch them to the dressing station.

At 4-30 am Sunday 14th I received intimation that the 2nd Border Regiment had relieved us and I then marched the battalion on LEVANTIE, reporting same to Brigade Headquarters.

Casualties on the 13th were as follows:-

Officers:- Killed 3 Wounded 9
Other ranks:- " 29   " 217 Missing 12

General,

I have already reported as to the conduct of the Officers during the action, but I would again mention that Colonel McLean's bravery was quite outstanding, and I would also mention the conduct of 2/Lieut. P.K.Shand, who, though wounded, continued to cheer and organise his men.

The total casualties during the four days were:-

	Killed	Wounded	Missing
Officers	5	11	
Other ranks.	31	248	12

Total 307

Rue De Bacquerot. (M.6.d)   (sd) James M.Cook. Captain,
                                Commanding 1/6th Gordon Highlanders.

2nd Border Regiment

21. 3. 15.

To :-

    Headquarters,

        XXth Brigade.

      In forwarding the attached I would like to state how willingly everyone did his allotted task right from the senior downwards, all having had very little sleep for several days, and the greater proportion being very young Officers, N.C.O's and Men who had never been under heavy Artillery, Infantry & Machine Gun fire before.

                        Sd. H.Wood. Lieut: Colonel.
        Commanding 2/Border Regiment.

Account of operations 10th to 14th March, 1915.

Headquarters,
    20th Brigade.

On the morning of 10th March we paraded close to ESTAIRES Bridge and moved off at about 8 a.m. and went into dugouts occupied by 21st Infantry Brigade. We remained there all night and paraded early next morning, 11th, at 4.15 a.m. and moved in support of Gordon Highlanders. The attack commenced at 7.30 a.m., Gordon Highlanders and Grenadiers in front line, Border Regiment and Scots Guards in support. Whilst waiting for the Gordon Highlanders to advance the Battalion was subjected to very heavy shell fire, both high explosive and shrapnel, and had many casualties. Our objective was line DU PEETRE. On the advance of the Gordons being checked we came up in line and with the greater portion of our front line on their left. - "A" and "B" companies under Major A.S.W.Moffat with "C" and "D" companies in support.

A lot of casualties occurred in A and B Companies from enfilade fire and in two Platoons of "B" company when ordered to move round to the left flank.

The companies remained more or less in their positions that night but straightened the line and dug themselves in.

In the early morning of the 12th C and D Companies moved forward and took up positions in trenches dug during the night in advance of A & B Companies, whilst the Gordons withdrew into Reserve. The Scots Guards were to take up a position on our right. We were ordered to attack at 8.30 a.m. objective being breastwork and trenches about 600 yards to N.E. The advance at 8.30 a.m. was cancelled owing to fog, till 10.30 a.m. The attack was then ordered to take place at 10.30 a.m. precisely. At 10.30 a.m. "C" Company moved forward and immediately came under heavy rifle & M.G.fire

with/

with a Company of Scots Guards on their right. The attack continued for about 15 minutes but the casualties in both Regiments were so heavy that I ordered the advance to stop until strong artillery fire or covering fire could be brought to bear. At this critical time, 20 minutes after the attack had been launched, an order arrived to say the attack would be postponed till 12.30 p.m. As this did not arrive till 10.50 a.m. nothing could be done, except wait in their present position for the Artillery bombardment. At 12 midday the Artillery commenced their bombardment. At about 12.20 p.m. I again gave the order to advance although still enfiladed. The Battalion pushed on and got close up to the position and rushed it just as the guns ceased firing. The Germans came out holding up their hands and waving handkerchiefs some 400 prisoners were taken and large quantities of rifles, bayonets and ammunition &c. We then reorganised as quickly as possible and pushed forward in direction of red house on road - but we again came under heavy enfilade fire from our right flank; and having no Battalion on my right I had to stop and withdraw into the German trenches, which I held - sending a message back to that effect.

On G.O.C's order to consolidate position and ground captured the Companies were re-organised and told off to different positions of the German trenches which were greatly strengthened that night to provide against a counter attack. Some men of the Wilts Regt. who got mixed up with my Regiment took a small portion on the left of our line. The Machine Guns were brought up by hand under 2/Lieut: A.V.H.Wood, but had many hit - the two guns that did get up did very good work.

All the Companies did equally well and considering they were led by very young Officers, mostly all 2nd Lieuts, they showed great gallantry.

13th. We were under orders to remain in the trenches we now occupied and to be in reserve, ready to move forward if necessary to support the Grenadiers and Gordons should/

should they be in need of it. Owing to some mistake the attack was never launched. We came under exceptionally heavy shell fire but had few casualties. The night of the 13th was spent strengthening the position and parapets.

We were again shelled all the morning of the 14th and at 12 mid-night we were relieved by the Worcester Regiment.

I attach a separate report of Officers and Other Ranks whom I consider worthy of mention.

Total number of casualties of Officers and other ranks during the fighting attached.

Sd. H.Wood. Lieut:Colonel.
21st March, 1915. Commanding 2nd Bn.The Border Regiment.

Headquarters,
      XXth Brigade.

　　　　Re your B M 142 of 21st I beg to forward the names of Officers, N.C.O's and Men whom I consider worthy of recommendation in connection with the recent operations 10th to 14th March.

(1)　Major A.S.W.Moffat - He was continually up in the firing line both on 11th and 12th giving assistance and encouragement to the young Company Commanders and Platoon leaders at times under heavy fire and assisted me greatly on the 12th in reorganising the different units that had got mixed up after taking the German trenches.

(2)　2nd Lieut: W.Kerr, in command of "B" Company - He did exceptionally well in both attacks on 11th and 12th and it was in a great measure due to him for the steady way in which the men moved forward to the attack, under heavy rifle and machine gun fire.

　　He is a very capable leader under fire and a fine example to the men.

(3)　Lieut: G.P.L.Drake-Brockman - Although a very young Officer he did exceptionally well in handling his Company under heavy fire and shewed good judgment.

(4)　Lieut: T.H.Beves (twice wounded).

　　He did exceptionally well on the 12th in leading and encouraging his men in the attack and he shewed a splendid example to his men.

(5)　No.5180 Regtl. Sergt.Major V.H.S.Davenport - This N.C.O. gave me great assistance on both days of the attack, taking messages under fire to the Company Commanders and

　　　　　　　　　　　　　　　　　　　　　　　　helping/

helping to reorganise the Battalion and units of other Corps that had got mixed up with my Battalion after taking the German trenches.

(6) No.9284 Coy. Sergt Major T.Groggins (wounded) - This N.C.O., after his Officers had been wounded handled his Company exceptionally well. I especially noticed this N.C.O. He also got his men well together against a counter attack and showed good leadership.

(7) No.9426 L.Corpl W.Hodgson - In continually taking messages for me under heavy fire.

(8) No.10340 L.Corpl J.Robinson and No.9392 Private W.Corkish - Bringing Machine Gun into action under fire and continuing to work the gun after the former had been wounded.

(9) No.6684 Sergt T.Touer.
    Company Officers statement attached.

(10) No.4565 Private H.McDowell - D Coy. (killed).
    Company Officers statement attached.

                      Sd. H.Wood. Lieut:Colonel.
                Commanding 2nd Border Regiment.

(no date shewn)

2nd Bn. Border Regiment.

Total number of casualties - Officers & Other Ranks - during operations 10th 14th March, 1915.

::::::::::::

	Officers.		Other Ranks.
Killed	2.	Killed	58.
Wounded	13.	Wounded	180.
		Missing	41.
		Died of wounds	7.
Total:-	15.		286.

Reports on Battalions

7th Division.

Herewith my report on the Battalions in my Command in the operations of the 10th to 14th March, 1915.

Lavantie.   Brigadier-General.
19th March, 1915.   Commanding, 20th Infantry Brigade.

1st Battalion Grenadier Guards.

This Battalion on the morning of the of the 11th inst, was ordered to advance to the attack on AUBERS from the South West, their primary objective being PIETRE. Owing to a heavy enfilade firefrom the left the attack of the whole line was held up some 800 yards East of NEUVE CHAP-ELLE.   The Battalion suffered heavy casualties this day but not withstanding acted with great steadiness.

On the 12th instant they were ordered to advance on MIN DU PIETRE, unfortunately their Commanding Officer was killed and the Battalion lost direction finishing up their advance in the old British line near the MIN DU PIETRE road, this necessitated a reshifting of the Brigade at night, which owing to the difficult nature of the country and the darkness of the night took longer than was calculat-ed on, with the result that daylight found three companies in the open and it was impossible to organise them for the attack.   A heavy fire both of Artillery and Rifle fire opened on them causing many casualties, but notwithstanding this they acted the greatest gallantry and continued to hold their ground.

In these operations the Grenadiers lost 14 Officers and 328 other ranks.

Sheet 2.

2nd Battalion Scots Guards.

On the 11th instant this Battalion was supporting the 1st Grenadier Guards in their attack, two companies reaching the firing line suffered some casualties.

On the 12th instant the Scots Guards and Border Regiment attacked the enemy's line of works just West of the MIN DU PIETRE, this attack was carried out with great gallantry and dash and resulted in the capture of some 500 prisoners. In this attack their Commanding Officer Major G. Paynter. D.S.O. was wounded.

Casualties for the operations, 6 Officers, 189 Other Ranks.

2nd Battalion Border Regiment.

On the 11th instant this Battalion supported the 2nd Battalion Gordon Highlanders.

On the 12th instant this Battalion took part in the successful attack on the enemy's redoubt just West of the MIN DU PIETRE road, and was also instrumental in helping to capture the 500 prisoners.

Casualties for the operations. 14 Officers and 266 other ranks.

2nd Battalion Gordon Highlanders.

On the 11th instant this Battalion took part in the attack on PIETRE but like the Grenadiers on their right were unable to advance further than some 800 yards East of NEUVE CHAPPELLE owing to a heavy enfilade fire from the left. In this attack they suffered somewhat severely.

On the 12th instant they supported the Border Regiment in their attack prolonging the line to the Borders right at night.

On the 13th instant the line failed to advance on the MIN DU PIETRE road owing to heavy frontal and enfilade fire. Early in the attempt to advance their Commanding Officer, Lieutenant Colonel H. Uniacke. C.B. was killed, and the Adjutant, Major J. Stansfield, D.S.O. wounded. This Battalion acted with great steadiness throughout the operations.

Casualties for the operations. 16 Officers, 235 Other ranks

6th (Territorial) Battalion Gordon Highlanders.

This Battalion was in Brigade Reserve on the 11th and 12th instant, on both mornings they suffered somewhat from the heavy bombardment of the enemy. On the 13th instant they took part in the attempt to advance on the MIN DU PIETRE. All Battalions present there testify to the gallant manner in which they repeatedly tried to advance under a very heavy fire. Early in the morning their Commanding Officer, Lieutenant Colonel MacLean was killed and their Adjutant, Captain Campbell wounded, which makes their conduct all the more praise worthy. This was practically the first occasion in which they had been

called....

Sheet. 3.

called upon to advance under a heavy fire.

Casualties for the operations. 16 Officers. 289 Other ranks.

Confidential

20th Inf. Bde.

Reference Confidential Circular Memorandum No.14 of 24th. March, 1915, paragraph (b), the responsibility of the 7th. Division will only include defended localities 10.11-12-13.14.and 17.

Localities 18 and 19 are outside the area.

Please amend accordingly.

Div.H.Q.
30th. March, 1915.

Ian Stewart Major
for Lt.Colonel,
General Staff, 7th.Divn.

Confidential

CIRCULAR MEMORANDUM No.14.

Defensive arrangements for present Phase.

The following will be the arrangements in the event of a hostile attack while the 7th Division is distributed as at present.

(a). The Brigade in occupation of E and F lines will Retain such portion as the Brigadier considers advisable in Brigade reserve, to be employed in counter offensive action as circumstances dictate.

(b). Of the 3 Battalions of the 22nd Brigade billeted in LAVENTIE, one battalion will be detailed for the occupation of defended localities 10-11-12-13-14-17-18-19. The Brigadier General Commanding 22nd Brigade will ensure that the officers of the battalion detailed for this duty make themselves thoroughly acquainted with the localities they may be called upon to occupy; that the method of occupation of each is thought out so that the troops may be moved in to them without confusion by day or night; and that the methods of mutual support by cross fire is studied and understood.
He will also be responsible that these localities are kept clean and in a thorough state of repair, and that arrangements are made for supplying them with water, ammunition and rations.

(c). The remaining battalions of the 22nd Brigade billeted in LAVENTIE, together with the two battalions in ESTAIRES, will be held in Divisional Reserve.

(d). The Northumberland Hussars, Cyclist Company and Motor Machine Gun Battery (less 1 section in the trenches) will form a Mobile Divisional Reserve, and will assemble at road junction G.27.c. when called out.

(e). Arrangements for the Artillery in connection with the foregoing will be made by the Brigadier General Commanding, Royal Artillery.

(f). The Infantry Brigade billeted in LA GORGUE will be in Corps and Army Reserve.

Div.H.Q.

24th. March, 1915.

A.R.HOSKINS, Colonel,
General Staff, 7th. Division.

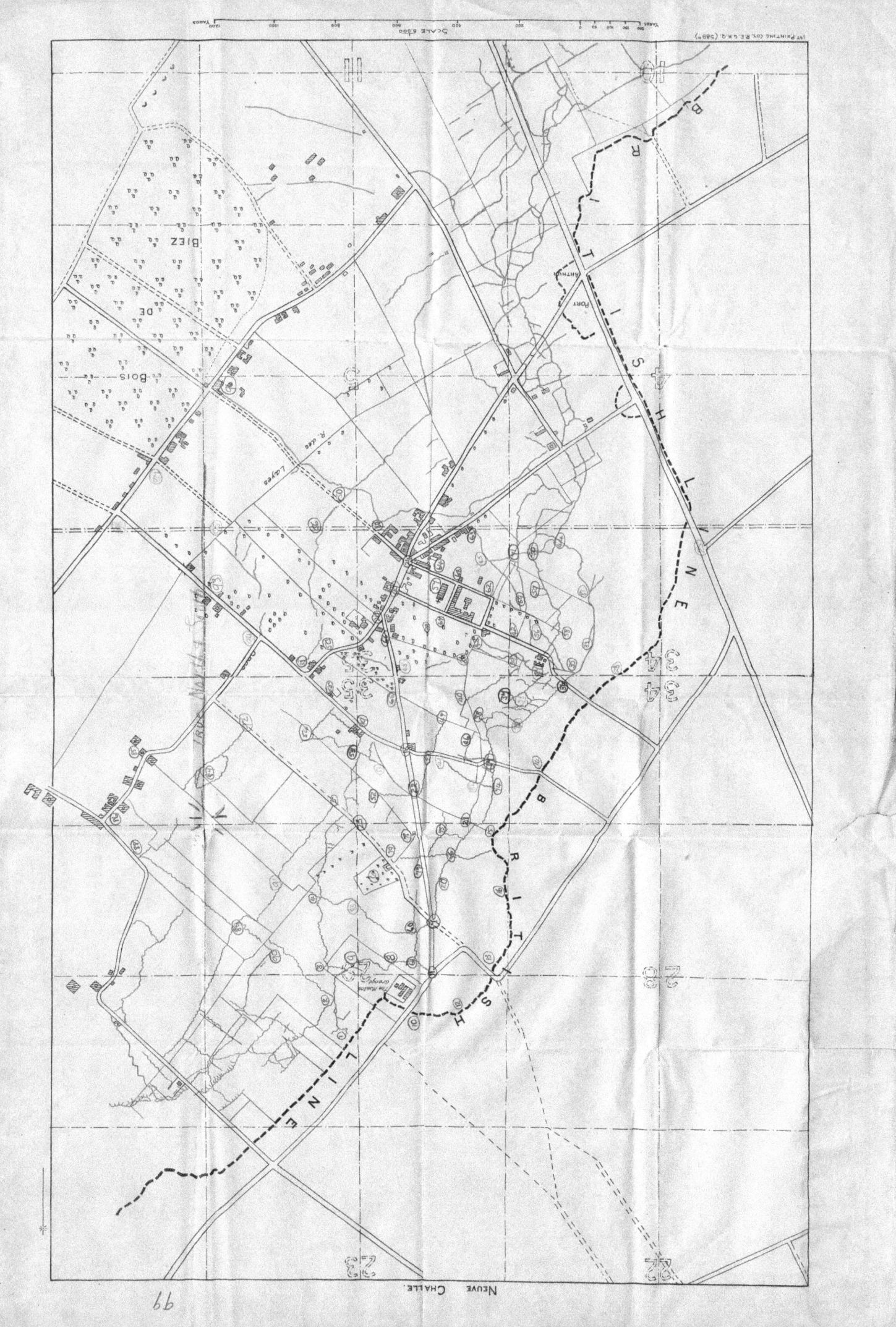

Army Form C. 2118.

WAR DIARY
or
INTELLIGENCE SUMMARY.
(Erase heading not required.) (epic for previous month)

Hour, Date, Place	Summary of Events and Information	Remarks and References to Appendices
March 3rd	On March 3rd the 13th Canadian Brigade relieved us. The Brigade proceeded to VIEUX BERQUIN into billets. Remained at VIEUX BERQUIN till Sunday, March 7th, when the Brigade proceeded to ESTAIRES, here were the 21st Brigade already billetted.	
March 7th		

Army Form C. 2118.

WAR DIARY
or
INTELLIGENCE SUMMARY.
(Erase heading not required.)

Instructions regarding War Diaries and Intelligence Summaries are contained in F.S. Regs., Part II. and the Staff Manual respectively. Title pages will be prepared in manuscript.

Hour, Date, Place	Summary of Events and Information	Remarks and references to Appendices
March 15th.	The day spent in re-organising and refitting.	
March 16th.	LAVENTIE considered too exposed to shell fire. The Grenadier Guards and 2nd Border Regiment and 2nd Gordon Highlanders accordingly sent to ESTAIRES. The Brigade Headquarters remaining at LAVENTIE.	
March 17th.	The good work performed by the Grenade Companies during the recent operations has made it clear how important these companies in each Brigade are. Our Company which has been reduced from 150 strong to 105 was accordingly made up to strength and an additional 20 men per Battalion were called for to be trained in Bomb throwing and tactics. The whole under Captain Nicol, Grenadier Guards. Captains Lord H.Seymour and J. Hughes, Grenadier Guards arrived from the 2nd Battalion to duty with the 1st Battalions	
March 18th.	The Brigade takes over the trenches of the 22nd Brigade at FAUQUISSART, the portion taken over about 2,700 yards long N.E. of AUBERS owing to the Brigade being so weak. Every battalion had to be put in with the exception of the 6th battalion Gordon Highlanders - who were placed in Reserve near PICANTIN.	
March 19th.	The following drafts arrived for the Grenadier Guards and the Scots Guards. Grenadier Guards. 6 Officers. 350 men. Scots Guards. 1 Officer. 70 men.	
March 20th.	Scots Guards come out of the trenches, the Grenadier Guards being now strong enough to hold that portion alone. Lieutenant-Colonel C. Corkran, C.M.G. arrived to take over command of the 1st Battalion Grenadier Guards. The following now command the Battalions of the Brigade.:- 1st Grenadier Guards.	

Army Form C. 2118.

WAR DIARY
or
INTELLIGENCE SUMMARY.
(Erase heading not required.)

Instructions regarding War Diaries and Intelligence Summaries are contained in F.S. Regs., Part II. and the Staff Manual respectively. Title pages will be prepared in manuscript.

Hour, Date, Place	Summary of Events and Information	Remarks and references to Appendices
March 20th continued.	1st Battalion Grenadier Guards. Lieut-Colonel C. Corkran. C.M.G. 2nd Battalion Scots Guards. Captain Sir F. Fitzwygram. 2nd Battalion Border Regiment. Lieut-Colonel Wood. C.M.G. 2nd Battalion Gordon Highlanders. Major Hamilton. 6th Battalion Gordon Highlanders. Captain Cook.	
March 21st.	Nothing worth recording.	
March 22nd.	Nothing worth recording.	
March 23rd.	Grenadier Guards relieved by the 2nd Scots Guards and 6th Battalion Gordon Highlanders in the trenches. Germans shell LAVENTIE and one of their aeroplanes dropped two bombs in ESTAIRES. Beyond putting the gas of the town out little damage was done.	
March 24th.	Nothing worth recording.	
March 25th.	Trenches relieved by the 21st Infantry Brigade, our Brigade going into Billets in LA GORGUE.	
March 26th.	Brigade Headquarters moved from LAVENTIE to LA GORGUE.	
March 31st.	The Brigade relieved the 21st Infantry Brigade in the trenches near FOUQUISSART.	

F.J. Heyworth
Brig.-General.
Commanding 20th Infantry Brigade.

Operation Orders

... arrangements for the control of Traffic

D

Note.

... of ... ... road ...

(1) In event of LAVENTIE becoming impassible ... ... FROMELLES road will be used for rearward traffic.

Divisional Orders.
Sketch of trenches Cameron Lane.

20th Infantry Brigade

Cases have occurred in the past where subordinate commanders have in action appealed for assistance to units outside our own Divisional Command.

Such appeals are generally misunderstood, and lead to the impression that we cannot carry out our own business.

Furthermore, if the appeal is responded to, it may mean that other troops have to turn aside from their business to help us.

In this way, the whole operations may become prejudiced.

The Divisional General desires that the general feeling should be to help others as much as we can, but demand as little assistance from others as possible.

If a subordinate commander considers that a great success can be obtained by combined action with troops of other units, he has a perfect right to point this out and suggest co-operation. Even here, he must allot himself the principal and most hazardous role, and not suggest that for the other party.

All reports and messages during action must be stated in the most temperate and calm language, and without any appearance of anxiety or alarm.

Div.H.Q.
7th.March,1915.

Colonel,
General Staff, 7th.Division.

2v Bde.

Copy No. 7

Note. Operation Orders are to be thoroughly studied, and memorized. Copies are not to be taken into the field.

Ref: Map 1/40,000.
Sheet No 36.

7th Division Operation Order No 46.

8th March, 1915.

1. The enemy before us appears to be situated as follows :-

   Their VII Corps hold a front from beyond our late left near BRIDOUX to the LA BASSEE Canal.

   Their 13th Division extends from the right of their VII Corps to North of NEUVE CHAPELLE.

   Their 14th Division holds the remainder of their Corps front.

   Their 25th Brigade holds from about ROUGE BANCS on their right to third E of NEUVE CHAPELLE: this Brigade has the 158th Regiment on its right, and the 13th Regiment on its left. The point of junction between these regiments is about the TRIVELET - FAUQUISSART road.

   Their 27th Brigade holds from third E of NEUVE CHAPELLE Southwards. This Brigade consists of the 58th Regiment on their right and the 16th Regiment on their left.

   Besides these the 7th Pioneer Regiment is available for general use in the Corps area.

   It is believed that there are a few reserves in LILLE.

2. The intention is :-

   (i) To capture NEUVE CHAPELLE.

   (ii) To advance to the line, road junction 400 yards South West of LIGNY LE PETIT - Eastern Corner of BOIS DU BIEZ - Cross roads West of PIETRE to enemy's front line trenches East of the PIETRE - RUE DU BACQUEROT road.

   (iii) To advance to the capture and occupation of the line, LE HUE - LIGNY LE GRAND - LA CLIQUETERIE - LE PLOUICH - ROUGES BANCS. This includes the complete capture of AUBERS.

2.

3. The plan for carrying out this intention is as follows :-

    (i) The 8th Division is attacking NEUVE CHAPELLE with 2 Brigades from the North West, starting from their trench line in M.34 and 28 as shown in sketch attached. (A) These troops have the task of capturing the trenches immediately beyond NEUVE CHAPELLE, resting their left flank on the house in M.29.c.9.5.

    (ii) Simultaneously the Indian Division is attacking NEUVE CHAPELLE from the South West, eventually resting its right flank on the BOIS DE BIEZ.

    (iii) The above attacks are covered by a concentration of Artillery fire from guns of all calibres, including very heavy guns.

    (iv) Meanwhile, 21st Brigade will, from a position of readiness in "CAMERON LANE", in M.15.d. and M.21.b., gradually occupy the 8th Division left support trenches in approximately M.28.d., as these become vacated by the 23rd Brigade moving to the attack.

*Sketch (B)

    (v) From these support trenches, the 21st Brigade will advance to the attack on the line, PIETRE (exclusive) to house in German first line trenches in M.30.a.; passing through the 8th Division line East of NEUVE CHAPELLE. A Divisional order will be issued for this Brigade to advance.

    (vi) Simultaneously, the reserve brigade of the 8th Division, which will have occupied the 8th Division right support trenches in M.34.a. and b., from a position in readiness West of ROUGE CROIX, is going to advance to the attack of the line, copse at East corner of BOIS DU BIEZ - PIETRE (inclusive).

The Indian Division is also going to simultaneously make good the BOIS DU BIEZ.

(vii).

3.

(vii) The 21st Brigade will consolidate the line mentioned in (v) assisted by R.E. and "miners" already attached to it, and will prepare for the next advance.

(viii) The 20th Brigade will follow up the 21st Brigade by :—

(a) Occupying the shelters in "CAMERON LANE" as the 21st Brigade leaves these. It will remain (less 1 battalion) as Corps Reserve and not advance without direct orders of the Corps Commander.

(b) Sending forward 1 battalion to the support trenches N.W. of NEUVE CHAPELLE, as soon as the 21st Brigade have vacated sufficient cover there.

This battalion will come under the orders of the Brig: General Commanding 21st Brigade.

(ix) As soon as the 21st Brigade, strengthened by the battalion from the 20th Brigade, is consolidated on the line mentioned in (v), it will receive orders to advance through to PIETRE and capture AUBERS attacking it from the South and South West, and occupying and holding LE PLOUICH.

Simultaneously it will clear the enemy's trenches to its left and the RUE D'ENFERS and LES MOTTES farm.

(x) The 8th Division meanwhile will be attacking LA CLIQUETRIE and the Indian Division LIGNY LE GRAND and LE HUE.

(xi) The 22nd Brigade will, as soon as it is able to leave its trenches, advance through the RUE DELEVAL and FERME DELEVAL, supporting the left of the 21st Brigade and occupying ROUGES BANCS with its left flank.

The ultimate positions to be reached and held by the Brigades of the 7th Division is shown on attached sketch. (C)

(xii) The Canadian Division is being ordered to maintain its position, and open Artillery, rifle and maxim gun fire on the enemy's positions on their immediate front, and on FROMELLES village, in order to hold the enemy to his ground and prevent reinforcements being sent to AUBERS.

(xiii) The following batteries of Artillery have been detailed to cover this advance from positions on the left flank :—
7 Horse Artillery Batteries.
3 Siege Batteries.
1. 4·5" Howitzer Battery.
111th Heavy Battery.

In/

4.

In addition to these the 35th Brigade R.F.A. will have the immediate task of covering the 21st Brigade in the first instance.

1 Section of a Mountain Battery which will already have taken part in the capture of NEUVE CHAPELLE will be available to accompany the 21st Brigade in its onward march. The Brigadier General Commanding 21st Brigade will give orders to this Section.

The Brigadier General R.A. 7th Division will issue detailed orders to this Artillery.

In addition to the above, other Artillery, under the Corps and Army Commanders, is covering generally the advance.

(xii) Engineer Companies are allotted as follows :-
20th Brigade - 55th Coy. less 1 Section.
21st Brigade - Highland Coy.
22nd Brigade - 54 Coy. less 2 Sections.
Reserve under C.R.E. :-
    55th Coy. 1 Section.
    54th Coy. 2 Sections.

4. The 22nd Infantry Brigade will detail one battalion as Divisional Reserve under cover in RUE BACQUEROT.
Battalion and name of Officer Commanding to be notified to Divisional Head Quarters by the 9th instant.

5. Depots of Supplies and Ammunition have been established at the tram head in RUE BACQUEROT and at FAUQUISSART, and R.E. stores in the front line trenches about the same places. These are to be regarded as emergency stores, not to be used by troops in position, or waiting behind our own trenches, but by troops who are attacking the enemy, and who may find

it/

5.

it difficult to get such stores in the ordinary way.

6. The Northumberland Hussars, Cyclist Company and Battery of Mobile Machine Guns will remain under cover about NOUVEAU MONDE ready to move at the shortest notice. The above will detail 2 cyclist orderlies each (motor cycles if possible) to remain at Divisional Head Quarters for carrying orders.

7. Brigade Ammunition Columns, S.A.A.Sections, will park in the fields clear of the road alongside the ESTAIRES - NOUVEAU MONDE - RUE DE LA LYS road, in order of their Infantry Brigades viz. 20th Brigade on right, 21st in centre and 22nd on left.

8. Field Hospitals will remain in their present positions; Advanced Dressing Stations North of LAVENTIE.
The bearer Divisions of the Field Ambulances attached to the 20th and 21st Infantry Brigades will remain under cover in "CAMERON LANE" when their Brigades advance, and will seek the first opportunity of following their Brigades to bring in casualties.
The bearer Division of the 22nd Field Ambulance will remain under orders of the Brigade Commander 22nd Infantry Brigade.

9. Roads available for the rearward services of the troops engaged are as shown in the attached diagram. (D)

10. The non-fighting portion of the 1st line transport is not to go South of the Railway till permission is given by Divisional Head Quarters. Areas allotted to these are as follows :-
21st Brigade in square G.33.d. North of the LAVENTIE - ESTAIRES road.
20th Brigade in square G.33.c. North of the same road.
22nd Brigade in square G.34.

6.

11. All transport, or troops waiting to advance are to keep in the fields completely clear of roads so as to in no way obstruct traffic.

12. The operations referred to in these orders will commence at an hour and date to be notified later.

13. Divisional Head Quarters will remain as at present, in the first instance.

A.R.HOSKINS, Colonel,
General Staff, 7th. Division.

Issued at 10 a.m. to :-

A.D.C (for G.O.C.)	Copy No.1.
G.S.O.1.	" 2.
G.S.O.2.(office copy)	" 3.
A.A.& Q.M.G.	" 4.
B.G.C.,R.A.	" 5.
C.R.E.	" 6.
20th Inf.Bde.	" 7.
21st Inf.Bde.	" 8.
22nd Inf.Bde.	" 9.
IVth Corps.	" 10.
1/Canadian Division.	" 11.
8th Division.	" 12.
Mountain Battery.	" 13.
A.D.M.S.	" 14.

Officer Commanding,

....

Please cancel this morning's March Table issued with Operation Orders No. 10. The following will now be the March Table.

Unit.	Starting Point.	Time.	Time of arrival.
2nd Border Regiment.	Billets.	6. a.m.	6.15 a.m.
6th Gordon Highlanders.	Billets.	6.10. a.m.	6.30 a.m.
2nd Scots Guards.	Billets.	6.15 a.m.	6.45 a.m.
1st Grenadier Guards.	Billets.	6.30 a.m.	7. a.m.

23rd Field Ambulance Bearers Division to be at Brigade Headquarters at 6.30 a.m. and will follow the Grenadier Guards.

for Brigade Major.
20th Infantry Brigade.

9th March, 1915.

"A" Form. Army Form C. 2121.

MESSAGES AND SIGNALS.

Very Secret and Confidential.

TO: 20 Inf Bde.

G.A.886. Day of Month: Ninth. AAA

Following received from 4th Corps begins Reference 4th Corps Operation Order No.10 of 7.3.15 the Artillery will complete such registration as is necessary by 7.30.a.m., at which hour the preliminary bombardment will commence. At 8.5.a.m. the Infantry assaults on the enemy's trenches will be carried out simultaneously at all points.

The Artillery fire on NEUVE CHAPELLE will be maintained until 8.35.a.m. when the village will be assaulted. Should the present drying weather continue and unless otherwise ordered, the attack will take place on the 10th instant Ends. Acknowledge.

From: 7th Division.
Time: 1.20.p.m.

Major,
General Staff, 7th Division.

"A" Form. Army Form C. 2121.

MESSAGES AND SIGNALS.   No. of Message

Prefix	Code	m.	Words	Charge	This message is on a/c of:	Recd. at	m.
Office of Origin and Service Instructions.			Sent			Date	
			At ___ m.		Service.	From	
			To			By	
			By		(Signature of "Franking Officer.")		

TO { Battalions. and 55th Field Company R.E.
23rd Field Ambulance and Grenade Coy.

Sender's Number	Day of Month	In reply to Number	AAA
B.M.	9th.		

Reference to Operation Orders No.10. owing to the
~~AAAS~~ wet state of the ground on the left side of the
road at the preliminary position of assembly all troops
will form up on the right of the road in close
columns of half companies. 1st Line Transport (non-
fighting excepted will be immediately in rear of
Battalions.) A Staff Officer will be there to direct
each battalion where to go. The Brigade will form
up as follows facing South. On the right the
Grenadier Guards. Scots Guards. No. 2. Border
Regiment. No. 3. 6th Gordon Highlanders. No. 4.
The 55th Field Company R.E. and the 23rd Field Ambulance
will be on the right of the Grenadier Guards.

From: 20th Infantry Brigade.
Place:
Time: 11.20 a.m.

The above may be forwarded as now corrected.   (Z)   Staff Captain.
Censor. Signature of Addressor or person authorised to telegraph in his name
* This line should be erased if not required.

NEUVE CHAPELLE

Copy No. 1.

OPERATION ORDERS.

BY

Brigadier-General F.J. Heyworth. D.S.O. Commanding
20th Infantry Brigade.

9th March. 1915.

Reference Map $\frac{1}{40,000}$. Sheets 36.

Information. 1. With reference to the plans of operations communicated verbally to Officer's Commanding Battalions, the Brigade will act as Corps Reserve. The 21st Brigade will occupy the fire shelters at M.15.b. and M.15.d.

Intention. 2. The Brigade will form up by 5 a.m. in a preliminary position of assembly just N. of PT CROIX. G.32.a. The Grenadier Guards and 2nd Border Regiment will form up on the right of the road. The Scots Guards and 6th Battn Gordon Highlanders will be on the left of the road. The 55th Field Company R.E. and the Bearer Division, 23rd Field Ambulance will form up in rear of the Border Regiment on the right of the road. A Staff Officer will be there to direct them to their places. As units of the 21st Brigade advance from their fire shelters in M.15.b. and M.15.d. CAMERON LANE, their places will be filled by units of the 20th Brigade. Each unit proceeding there by the following route.:- LA BASSEE ROAD - M.2. - LE DRUMEZ Cross Roads - M.19.a. - M.15. Each Battalion will detail one Officer to go to the fire shelters in M.15.b. and M.15.d. while still occupied by the 21st Brigade who will guide their units into the trenches vacated by those of the 21st Brigade. The 55th Field Company R.E. and Miners will follow the rear Battalion. The Bearer Division of the 23rd Field Ambulance will follow the 55th Field Company R.E. to CAMERON LANE, but when the Brigade advances will remain under cover and will seek the first opportunity

of ....

Intention. of following the Brigade to bring in casualties.

March Order. 3. Battalions will march to the fire shelters in CAMERON LANE as per margin.

6th Gordon Hrs.
2nd Border Reg.
Scots Guards.
Grenadier Gds.

Battalions will receive orders when they are to advance.

4. The following will be carried on the man.:-

    2 Sandbags.   200 rounds.

25% of the men will carry shovels.

Great Coats will be worn looped up.

5. 20 Bombers will accompany each Battalion and be attached to them during operations. The remainder of the Hand Grenade Company will be attached to Brigade Headquarters in Reserve.

1st Line Transport. 6. The non-fighting portion of the 1st Line Transport is not to go South of the Railway till permission is given. They will remain in Square G.33.c., North of the LAVANTIE - ESTAIRES Road.

Two S.A.A. Carts per Battalion will be told off to form Brigade Ammunition Reserve and will form up in rear of the 23rd Field Ambulance. The remainder of 1st Line Transport (non-fighting excepted) will accompany units.

Order of March. 7. Order of march from billets to preliminary position of assembly will be as per attached March Table.

8. All transport, or troops waiting to advance are to keep in the fields completely clear of roads so as to in no way obstruct traffic.

Brigade Headquarters. 9. Brigade Headquarters will be at PT CROIX - G.32.a. after 4.30 a.m.

                                        Brigade Major,
                                  20th Infantry Brigade.

Sheet 3.

Issued at 10 a.m. to .:-

Brigade Major (for Brig-Gen Comdg).   Copy No. 1.
Staff Captain.   Copy No 2.
Grenadier Guards.   Copy No. 3.
Scots Guards.   Copy No. 4.
Border Regiment.   Copy No. 5.
2nd Gordon Highlanders.   Copy No. 6.
6th Gordon Highlanders.   Copy No. 7.
55th Field Company R.E.   Copy No. 8.
23rd Field Ambulance.   Copy. No. 9.
7th Division.   Copy No. 10.
Hand Grenade Company.   Copy No. 11.

MARCH TABLE.

Unit.	Starting Point from.	Time.	Time of arrival.
2nd Gordon Highdrs.	Billets.	2.30 a.m.	4 a.m. at CAMERON LANE.
2nd Border Regiment.	Billets.	4.a.m.	4.15.a.m. at PT CROIX G.32.a.
6th Gordon Highldrs.	Billets.	4.10.a.m.	4.30.a.m. at PT CROIX G.32.a.
Scots Guards.	Billets.	4.15.a.m.	4.35.a.m. at PT CROIX. G.32.a.
Grenadier Guards.	Billets.	4.30.a.m.	5 a.m. at PT CROIX. G.32.a.

9th March, 1915.

[signature] Brigade Major,
20th Infantry Brigade.

Supplementary to 7th.Division Operation Order No. 98.

ARRANGEMENTS FOR ARTILLERY SUPPORT OF 7th.DIVISION.

Reference numbered Trench Map $\frac{1}{10,000}$.   8th.March,1915.

1st.Objective.   Line of Road from PIETRE to German Trenches at Point 100.

(A). Siege Battery, road between points (85) and (86) and houses.

(4") Siege Battery, points (99) (100) (101).
Two communication trenches and breastwork.

(B) Siege Battery, points (102) (103) and houses along road.

31st.Howitzer Battery, communication trench (1) to (86) and two houses at bend of road N. of where communication trench runs into the road.

13 Pounder Batteries R.H.A.

2 Brigades (6 Batteries) (2) to (100) and search back to road (144) (143).

One Brigade, searching communication trench (106) to (142).

36th.Brigade R.F.A. covering advance on the line (100) to (144).

The batteries will open fire at a slow rate from the time they come under orders of B.G.C.,R.A., 7th.Division.

Fire will be continued for twenty minutes from the time the 21st.Infantry Brigade begins its advance.

This time will be notified by 7th.Divisional Artillery Head quarters. If the forward Observing Officer in observation post near MIR sees that the Infantry advance is not up to the road at the end of this twenty minutes he will communicate to 7th.Division Artillery Head quarters who will order fire to be kept up for further periods of five minutes at a time.

As soon as the F.O.O. is satisfied that no further fire is required he will notify 7th.Divisional Artillery Head

quarters/

quarters who will then order batteries to switch on to second objectives.

N.B. 31st.Howitzer Battery will fire for the first ten minutes after the Infantry advance begins on the communication trench (1) to (88), afterwards onto the houses just North of where communication trench runs into the road.

2nd.Objective.

A.Siege. LES MOTTES FARM.

4th Siege. Points (115) to (116) in AUBERS VILLAGE.

B.Siege. group of buildings about 800 yards S.W. of point (116) (hereafter called (200).).

31st.Howitzer communication trenches running from points (106) (107). (108).

111th.Heavy Battery. Houses on RUE D'ENFER from Point (113) to Point (115).

13 Pounder Batteries R.H.A. Search area from points (107) to (115).
back to AUBERS.

18 Pounders 35th.Brigade cross roads RUE D'ENFERS to Point (200).

Arrangements for timing as in case of first objective.

3rd.Objective.

A.Siege. TRIVELET area., and Point 125 and communication trenches to it

4th Siege N.road of AUBERS VILLAGE.

B.Siege South road of AUBERS VILLAGE up to the Church.

31st.Howitzer Battery AUBERS VILLAGE South and east of the South road (Church).

111th Heavy Battery Point 117.

18 and 13 Pounders RUE DELAVAL and AUBERS.

An officer from R.H.A. group, siege and howitzer group, and 35th. Brigade R.F.A. will report to Brigadier-Commanding 31st.Infantry Brigade at his temporary headquarters in N.20.d. and an officer of

the/

the R.H.A. group also to Brigadier General Commanding 22nd. Infantry Brigade at his Head Quarters at H.11.d.8.2 or H.18.c.8.7.

        (Sd) H.K.JACKSON,   Brigadier General,
                      Commanding R.A., 7th. Division.

20th Inf. Bde.

    In addition to the above artillery arrangements there will be 2 Armoured Trains (perhaps 3). These will carry at least two 6", three 4·7" and two 4" guns.

Div.H.Q.
8th.March,1915.
                            Colonel,
                        General Staff, 7th. Division.

20th Infantry Brigade.   I.G.366.

<u>AUBERS</u>.   The village consists of two parallel streets linked at either end, separated from each other by 800 yards, in which space practically the whole rise of 50 feet takes place.

In the lower street are but few houses, but seen from S.W. the crest is an unbroken line of houses. There is a large Church and three factories. The village has numerous gardens with trees and hedges, the latter not making serious obstacles.

The ridge slopes away S.E. of the village for about 1,800 yards rising again rapidly towards LE PLOUICH and HT POMMEREAU. This shallow valley is covered with trees and plantations, and the railway line runs through it.

According to information given by a German prisoner, AUBERS is ruined and not in a state of defence, but there are trenches to N.W. of it, and a strong line to the S.E. The question of its being ruined is, however, doubtful, and one prisoner stated that his regiment had billets there.

The village is commanded by LE PLOUICH and HT.POMMEREAU.

The road running from FROMELLES is embanked after passing S.E. of cross roads in N.25.b.

<u>HT.POMMEREAU</u>. A small village shielded from view from N. and N.E. by trees. Stands on high ground and overlooks AUBERS from S.W.

Houses (only some half-dozen) are brick with gardens.

S.E. of village ground rises for about 10 feet with a very gentle slope.

<u>LA PLOUICH</u>. Consists of two large farms, each with its own courtyard and a few small houses. The N.E. one is a very substantially built farm with a moat, and overlooks the country to N. and N.E.

The road from here to the AUBERS - FROMELLES road is fairly wooded on both sides.

                                                            20/

To the North there is a small wood about 300 yards from
N. to S. and 100 yards from E. to W.

LA CLIQUENNIE FM. A substantial building with large courtyard,
commanding the country E. and N.E.

LE RIEZ. A straggling village about ½ mile long of one storey
houses. The country Eastward is quite open, as far as the crest
of the hill at FOURNES.

FOURNES. is a long straggling village, with a considerable
number of trees. The road from AUBERS runs through a cut 15'
deep and about 300 to 400' long.

A large distillery with a high chimney, approximately
where "H" comes on $\frac{1}{20,000}$ map.

From the W. the houses are concealed by trees.

R.des LAIES. N.E. of the FAUQUISSART - TRIVELET - AUBERS road
the R.des LAIES is about 12 feet wide at present, and varies in
depth from 3 to 5 feet. The road crosses it on a brick arch
culvert.

S.W. of this road the LAIES is reported as not much of an
obstacle.

7th.March,1915.

Confidential.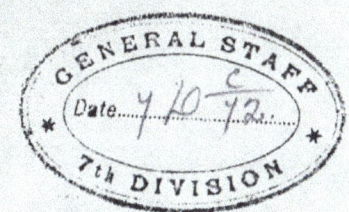

Notes on ground between NEUVE CHAPELLE and LILLE - LA BASSEE road from experience gained during fighting in October, 1914.

A. <u>Ground</u>.

1. Main ridge runs S.W. from HAUBOURDIN 2 miles S.W. of LILLE to FOURNES.

From FOURNES two spurs run out, one due West to HAUT POMMEREAU, the other follows roughly the line of the main road to ILLIES.

HAUT POMMEREAU spur is the most important feature of this area. Its highest point is near LA CLIQUETERIE Farm a strongly built brick farm with large dwelling house and yards. Ground here dominates AUBERS and PIETRE.

2. Ground between NEUVE CHAPELLE and BOIS du BIEZ open gentle slope. Between BOIS du BIEZ and AUBERS more enclosed; roads mostly lined with avenues of trees and number of small orchards. Approach to AUBERS from this side, i.e., by way PIETRE is covered from AUBERS itself, though more or less dominated by HAUT POMMEREAU. AUBERS was captured in October without difficulty from this side, a simultaneous advance being made against HAUT POMMEREAU. French Cavalry attempting to advance from FAUQUISSART on AUBERS were hung up until AUBERS was taken from direction of PIETRE. Ground between FAUQUISSART and AUBERS absolutely open.

3. Ground between AUBERS - LIGNY LE PETIT roads and the main LILLE - LA BASSEE road is enclosed with a good many scattered trees. Area between LIGNY LA PETIT and LORGIES very enclosed, chiefly allotment gardens with a good deal of wire, small fences and ditches. At LIGNY LE GRAND there is a small

circular/

2.

circular rise in the ground, an underfeature of main HAUT POMMEREAU Spur. There are a number of small fenced fields about L'AVENTURE and this part of ground requires careful treatment if it is proposed to hold a line through LA CLIQUETERIE Farm.

Best line of approach to HERLIES is from L'AVENTURE, provided LA CLIQUETERIE is held.

4. Ground in area AUBERS - LE RIEZ - FOURNES - FROMELLES is quite open and dominated on South by HAUT POMMEREAU, on the East by FOURNES.

FROMELLES is a shell trap being completely exposed to FOURNES ridge.

5. 2nd Corps line of defence ran just East of NEUVE CHAPELLE by CHAPIGNY to FAUQUISSART.

Portion between NEUVE CHAPELLE and BOIS du BIEZ is exposed to artillery from VIOLAINES and HAUT POMMEREAU.

A better line runs just N.E. of AUBERS by LE PLOUICH - LA CLIQUETERIE - LIGNY LE GRAND to LORGIES. This line was held for some days in October and was only given up because of pressure from the South.

A possible intermediate line runs from RUE d'ENFER by PIETRE to LIGNY LE PETIT.

B. Villages.

NEUVE CHAPELLE.

Main buildings are along RUE DU BOIS - FAUQUISSART road.

Most important feature is triangle of roads just North of village. Here Germans had number of machine guns in October, which flanked approaches to NEUVE CHAPELLE. This area consists of a few big houses with walled gardens,
orchards/

orchards etc. Approach to it from BOIS du BIEZ is fairly well covered.

From the gardens at the S.E. side of the main part of the village fire can be brought on to the BOIS du BIEZ.

PIETRE. Continuous rows of small cottages on both sides of the four cross roads.

AUBERS, has fine field of fire to N.E. and E. and many defensible buildings.

Is commanded on the South by the HAUT POMMEREAU spur. Best line of defence against attack from the East runs from East exit of village on FROMELLES road by LE PLOUICH to LA CLIQUETERIE.

FOURNES. Strongly built commanding village, which dominates ground to West as far as FROMELLES and LE PLOUICH and commands main LILLE roads as far as HERLIES - WICRES road.

The village is a conspicuous target and should be made untenable with sufficient artillery.

HERLIES. A long straggling village, defensible on the East side but easily approached from the South West (L'AVENTURE).

ILLIES. Is a strongly built village defensible against attack from the West, difficult to bring heavy artillery to bear upon the Western edge; best attacked from the direction of LA MOTTELETTE but WARNETON Farm and CHATEAU must be attacked simultaneously.

Reconnaisance of Counts
1
Positions of Artillery

General

S E C R E T.

20th Infantry Brigade.

Herewith two aeroplane photographs:-

(1) of country round PIETRE.

(2) of country to S.E. of AUBERS.

Please acknowledge receipt hereon.

                                   Major,

Div. H.Q.   for Colonel,

8th March, 1915.   General Staff, 7th Division.

2/7th Div

The above map received

         Major
         Brigade Major
         XX Inf Bde

9.3.15

CONFIDENTIAL. H.RWC.63.
7D/C/90.

Headquarters,
7th Division.

A correspondent of the "Daily Mail", Mr Valentine Williams, has the permission of the G.O.C., 1st Army to visit some of the units which took part in the fighting at NEUVE CHAPELLE to collect 'stories of human interest'. He will probably make his visit on April 1st.

All he writes will be censored at 1st Army Headquarters.

The Lieutenant General Commanding wishes his visit confined to such of the following battalions as may be convenient:-

    2nd Bn Gordon Highlanders.
    6th -------do-------
    2nd Bn Royal Scots Fusiliers.
    2nd Bn Border Regiment.

The information given to Mr Williams should be confined to "Stories of human interest" and the operations as a whole should not be discussed with him by Staff or Regimental Officers.

        Sd. P.Game, Major,
            for Brigadier-General,
31st March, 1915.   General Staff, IVth Corps.

3.

20th Infantry Brigade.

For information.

        Ian Steward Major
        for Lieut-Colonel,
31st March, 1915.   General Staff, 7th Division.

O.C. 2/ Borders
O.C. 2/ Gordons.
O.C. 6/ Gordons.

Please comply with the above orders initial & return to orderly.

A.W.Cabin Major
Brigade Major
20th Inf Brigade

2.4.15

Confidential.

20th Infantry Brigade.

With reference to attached.

When active operations are in progress the question of collecting equipment, arms, ammunition, tools, etc. whether belonging to our own men who are casualties or captured from the enemy, is an important one but extremely difficult to cope with.

If, however, the matter is thought out before-hand and some system organized, it is hoped that it may be possible to deal with the situation, at any rate, to some extent.

Will you kindly forward your views and suggestions on the matter and say what you consider to be practicable and feasible judging from experience during the recent fighting.

If articles collected on the battlefield could be sent under Brigade arrangements and "dumped" at the place where the rations are delivered at night they could be brought back in the empty wagons.

Is this practicable and if so to what extent?

Lt.Colonel

22/3/1915
A.A. & Q.M.G., 7th Division.

2nd E

2nd Echelon,
    4th Corps.

1st Army No: 565.A.   11th March 1915.

    With reference to this Office No: 565.A. dated 11/3/15, a notification has just been received from A.G., G.H.Q. that the instructions relative to clearing a battlefield contained in "Miscellaneous information published with Routine Orders" dated 23rd August 1914, are cancelled.

    The principles laid down therein will, however, be used for general guidance, but it is recognised that it is impossible to lay down hard and fast rules to meet all contingencies that may arise under such circumstances.

    Corps Commanders will therefore kindly make such arrangements as may be necessary to deal with that portion of the battlefield occupied or crossed by their troops, the Adjutant General's branch of Corps being in general charge.

    Particular care must be taken to ensure collection of all rifles &c. found lying about on the battlefield, and attention is invited to General Routine Order No: 624 (last para:) of February 11th 1915.

2nd Echelon.   (Signed) CHARLES TURNER, Lieut:Colonel,
1st Army.   A. A. G., 1st Army.

4th Corps No: 1748(a).   (2)

General Officer Commanding,
    7th Division.

    For information and necessary action.

              (Signed) J. DOYLE,   Major,
12/3/1915.   D. A. A. & Q. M. G., 4th Corps.

                    (3)

Headquarters,
    20th Infantry Brigade.

                    For information

                                Lieut:Colonel,
22/3/15.   A.A.& Q.M.G., 7th Divn:

CONFIDENTIAL.

Head Quarters.
7th Division.

With reference to your C/35/A.

It is difficult to lay down a hard and fast order for the clearance of the battlefield, either during the operations or immediately afterwards. From experience in the operations round NEUVE CHAPELLE on the 10th - 14th instant, frequent operations did occur during the operations for collecting equipment, arms, ammunition, tools, etc., from areas far back from the firing line. Under such circumstances might I suggest that parties small enough not to affect the Brigade Reserve tactically might be sent out and articles collected at a specified dumping centre. With regards to areas close up to the firing line, should there be a lull in the fighting and cover available, battalions might be ordered to collect all they were reasonably able to, and reporting where the articles were collected. These could be removed at a later period or under cover of darkness.

Laventie.
24th March, 1915.

Brigadier-General.
Commanding, 20th Infantry Brigade.

CIRCULAR MEMORANDUM No.10.

The projected forward movement is an offensive action which it is intended to carry out with the utmost vigour. No one is therefore authorised to order or sanction a retirement. If verbal orders containing any word of retirement are heard they are to be contradicted and suppressed at once, and are not to be obeyed. It is to be taken for granted that these have been circulated by the enemy in order to deceive us.
Any change of plans necessitated by the operations, will emanate from higher authority and will be conveyed <u>in writing</u> either by orderly or by written field signal message on proper form.
All that subordinate commanders have to think about is how best to get on, <u>making good at once all ground</u> captured.

2. The Divisional General is well aware that all ranks are imbued with the determined spirit to overcome the enemy before them, and to prove themselves the better men wherever and under whatever conditions the enemy may be met. He is quite certain that all realise that their duty to their country and their comrades demands the utmost devotion and self sacrifice.

3. It must be clearly understood that the business of attending to the wounded is the work <u>of the ambulance services and stretcher bearers only</u>. Combatant men have only to keep their attention fixed on beating the enemy; that is their sole duty.

4. Escorts to prisoners are to be reduced to what is strictly necessary - and the commander of the escort is to have a written order saying how many men he has in the escort, how many prisoners, and where he is to take them to.
Receipts will always be taken for prisoners when handed over by the commander of the escort.

5. The Divisional General desires to caution all ranks against repeating alarming reports or expressions. War cannot be made without casualties. Such things are the normal conditions of a battle, and are to be expected. Matters are not improved and helped by exaggerating these things. They must be accepted philosophically and all ranks are bound in honour and duty to maintain a cheerful and optimistic spirit at all times. This moral bravery is just as important as that physical bravery for which British Officers and men are justly celebrated.

6. The Divisional General only mentions these matters by way of instruction. He now looks to every one to show the world how the British soldier fights.

A.R.HOSKINS, Colonel,

9th.March,1915.　　　　　　　　　　　　General Staff, 7th. Division.

INSTRUCTIONS FOR CAVALRY OFFICERS WHO ARE MAKING A
RECONNAISSANCE OF THE GERMAN LINE.

Motor Cars are not to go beyond the Dressing Station at M.17. on the left of the road.

All horses are to be left at the road junction RUE DU BACQUEROT - FAUQUISSART and concealed behind farms.

Officers should not move down the FAUQUISSART Road more than three at a time, and on reaching the Danger Post on the left of the road will immediately turn in behind of the houses on the right of the road, until they reach the observing post.

Not more than two Officers should observe at the same time and great caution must be used not to show themselves. The remaining Officers staying behind.

Brigade Major.
20th Infantry Brigade.

MEMORANDUM No.11.

1. Before committing themselves to an attack over unknown ground Brigadiers and Officers Commanding units should endeavour to find out something of the ground they have to attack over. Reconnaissance is essential in order to know what to do. Scouts and patrols should also be employed. Reconnaissances to anticipate orders to advance are most useful.

2. Tactical advanced guards can be used with advantage, if touch with the enemy is not complete. Security detachments should <u>always</u> be used on a flank which is or which is likely to be exposed.

3. Leading over difficult ground where landmarks cannot be easily recognized, must be assisted by the use of the compass.

4. Wider extensions are required; and one unit should not be sent in if the preceding unit is already congested.

5. Frequent reports should be made to Divisional Headquarters regarding progress and information gained. Every endeavour should be made to check the accuracy of reports from the front line. If they are palpably improbable, they should either be retained for further verification or forwarded with a caution as to their accuracy.

6. At the close of a day's fighting, or at any period of liberty, a report with sketch of the disposition of the Brigade must be sent to Divisional Head Quarters.

7. After an action a short report <u>must</u> be sent without delay to Divisional Headquarters (F.S.Regulations Part II, Sec.138 (2).).

8. In the early evening after a day's fighting, or sooner if cover is good, or atmosphere hazy, units should be resorted and reorganized by the C.O. of the unit, and by the Staff of the Brigade, <u>as a matter of course.</u>

9. Bomb companies must be reorganized as quickly as possible, and as many men as possible trained to throw bombs. It is established beyond doubt that the hand grenade is the most effective weapon for fighting in trenches or very close country.
Brigadiers will notify Divisional Head Quarters by evening of 19th instant number of bombers they have now trained.

10. All officers should understand the necessity for reporting clearly any details as to the enemy's gun fire against them. What is the class of shell. Any indication as to range and direction. Without some information of this kind the reports are of little use to our Artillery for purposes of protecting the Infantry from such fire.

Div.H.Q.

17th, March, 1915.

Colonel,

<u>General Staff, 7th. Division.</u>

20th Infantry Brigade.

Herewith 2 copies of a Note on the country occupied by the VIIth German Corps, which has been compiled chiefly from information received from inhabitants and from aeroplane observations. They cannot be regarded as complete.

There are no more copies available.

Div, H.Q.
4-3-15.

Ian Stewart Major
for Colonel,
General Staff, 7th Division.

NOT TO BE TAKEN INTO THE TRENCHES.

AREA OCCUPIED BY VII GERMAN CORPS.

The country divides itself into three main areas:-
- (A) The low-lying area extending between the R.LAYES and approximately the line RADINGHEM - LE MAISNIL - FROMELLES - AUBERS - ILLIES.
- (B) The plateau lying S.E. of the above line and extending as far as HALLENES, SANTE, WAVRIN, HANTAY.
- (C) The low-lying area bounding the HAUTE DEULE.

(A) The low-lying area between R.LAYES, and the lower slope of the ascent to the plateau does not differ materially from the country immediately behind our own lines. The soil is said to be slightly more loamy and possibly a little drier on the right bank than on the left bank of the river.

The drainage system is also said to be slightly better owing to rather greater difference of level.

The area is plough land throughout, with the exception of the BOIS DU BIEZ, the orchards marked on the map and the immediate vicinity of the villages.

The fields are divided by irrigation cuts of a general width of from 2½ to 5'; the cuts lead to streams marked on the accompanying map in blue, the width of which varies from 3' to 5' with perpendicular banks.

The R.LAYES itself varies from 6' to 10' in breadth and has from 2½' to 5' of water in it.

The nature of the houses, so far as is known, is shown on the accompanying table.

The principal tactical features in the area are the villages of NEUVE CHAPELLE, the BOIS DU BIEZ and the marshy land lying in the road triangle between LIGNY LE PETIT and LORGIES.

NEUVE CHAPELLE.

The 1/20,000 map, sheet 36 S.W., is incorrect regarding the houses and the direction of the roads. These are correctly shown on the sketch map issued with this.

Almost all the houses are now in ruins, but the remains of the walls would still afford good cover.

The Germans are said to use the cellars of the houses on the east side of the village for sleeping places and there are also said to be numerous dug-outs just east of the houses.

The North side of the village is wooded. The triangle between the roads immediately North of the village is said to be surrounded by a wall and during the fighting in October was used by the Germans as a "keep".

South East of the village there are a few trees.

BOIS DU BIEZ.

The wood is formed of oaks from 40 to 50 years old and are about as thick as a man's thigh. It is not very thickly wooded and there is a very small amount of undergrowth.

Through the wood there runs a path, shown on the map, but unmetalled, which continues on the east side of the wood to a farm in the S.E. corner of square S.6.d.

At the N.W. corner of the wood, East of the houses marked, and up to the "L" of LA RUSSIE, there is a wood of large oaks covering an area of about 200 yards square.

In square S.6.b., on the N.E. corner of the BOIS DU BIEZ, there is a wood of fir trees covering an area of about 350 yards square.

On the S. and S.W. edges of the wood there is a ditch about 3' to 4' broad and with water in it at the present moment.

The houses marked on the West of the BOIS DU BIEZ are small cottages made of sun-dried bricks, a few only being of stout construction. Each of these cottages has a small garden with trees in it, but so far as is known, there are no wire fences.

Immediately West of PIETRE (square M.36.b.) there is a pond of about 200 square yards area and about 4' deep.

-2-

(B) THE PLATEAU.

The ascent to the plateau varies. Between RADINGHEM and PONT DE PIERRE (1 mile east of FROMELLES) it is a very gradual, scarcely noticeable, slope. Between FROMELLES and AUBERS, the ascent is sharper, about 20 feet in 300 yards. The crest line in this area is almost a straight line. AUBERS village is built on the slope.

Between AUBERS and ILLIES some slight spurs run out from the plateau. The ascent consequently varies near HT POMMEREAU which lies on the crest. It is steeper here than anywhere else in the area between LE MAISNIL and ILLIES.

Although the differences in level in the general area AUBERS - FROMELLES - LE RIEZ - ILLIES are so slight as to justify it being called a plateau, there are undulations, which from a tactical point of view, are of importance. The chief of these features are:-

(a) The slightly raised ground between HT POMMERAU & HERLIES with an off-shoot from LA CLIQUETERIE Farm to LE PLOUICH.
(b) A small round eminence at LIGNY LE GRAND, and
(c) The ascent up to FOURNES from the North.

Throughout the whole of the plateau area the soil is loam. The ground is plough land, the fields marked with small ditches about 1'6" to 2' broad. The villages are more substantially built and surrounded by trees and orchards, and a few small meadows.

The chief tactical features in the area are (i) the villages FROMELLES, AUBERS, HERLIES, HT POMMEREAU, FOURNES and LIGNY LE GRAND. (ii) The farms of LA PLOUICH and LA CLIQUETERIE.

ARTIFICIAL DEFENSIVE WORKS.

So far as is known the only defensive works constructed by the Germans are:-

(1) The front line of trenches shewn in 1:5,000 sketch issued by A. H. Q.

(2) The LILLE defences and the trenches made during the fighting in October and shewn on the accompanying 1:40,000 map (not received)

(3) The villages HERLIES, ILLIES, are known to have been prepared for defence during October and it is most probable that in addition the villages AUBERS, FROMELLES, HT POMMEREAU, LA CLIQUETERIE Farm and Le PLOUICH will be protected by defensive works.

APPENDIX I.

FROMELLES.
The village lies on a col on the crest of the ridge. It is surrounded by trees. The houses are substantially built, chiefly of brick with a garden. FROMELLES is defiladed from AUBERS by a rise in the ground. It is very exposed to fire from the south east.

AUBERS.
The main AUBERS, FROMELLES road is on the crest line at AUBERS. The village is substantially built with a large church. There are three factories in the village. The village has numerous gardens with trees and hedges. The latter are not sufficiently dense to form a serious obstacle. The village is commanded by LE PLOUICH and HT POMMEREAU.
South eastward of AUBERS there is a very gentle fall for about 1,200 yards.

HT POMMEREAU, is a small village of some half dozen houses. There are some trees immediately east of it which conceal it altogether from the east and north east. It stands on markedly high ground and overlooks the south west of AUBERS.
The houses are all brick with gardens.
South east of the village the ground rises for about ten feet with a very gentle slope.

HERLIES is a long straggling village, with a considerable number of trees.
The road from AUBERS to HERLIES runs through a cut 12' deep and about 300 to 400 yards long.
HERLIES has a large distillery with a high chimney, approximately where the letter "H" comes on the map 1:20,000.
From the west the houses are concealed by trees.

LIGNY LE GRAND is a village of only few houses and is noticeable by having a large number of small enclosures with thick hedges round it. The village itself stands out with a slight eminence about 10' above the level of the plateau.

LE PLOUICH. This consists of two large farms, each with its own courtyard and a few small houses. The N.E. one is a very substantially built farm with a moat and overlooks the country to N.& N.E.
The road from here to the AUBERS - FROMELLES road is fairly wooded on both sides.

LE RIEZ is a straggling village about ½ mile long only of one storey houses. The country to the eastward is quite open, as far as the crest of the hill at FOURNES.

LA PILLY is a small straggling village of four or five houses surrounded by trees.

LA CLIQUETERIE farm is a very substantial building with a large courtyard. It commands the country to the East and North east.

Intelligence

APPENDIX 1.

APPENDIX II.

NOTE ON VII GERMAN CORPS.

The formation of the Corps is normal (viz 2 divisions), each of two brigades, each of two regiments, each of three battalions with 150 guns and 50 - 75 machine guns.

The length of front held by the Corps is 22,000 yards; allowing 100 companies at 200 men per company, this gives us 20,000 rifles, that is to say approximately one rifle per yard.

All the regiments have been identified in the front line, with the exception of the Jaeger Battalion, that is to say, the Jaeger Battalion appears to form the Corps reserve.

The distribution of the units in the first line, supports and reserves, varies with different regiments, but in general it may be taken to be as follows:-

In the first line trenches	1/3rd.
In support 300-600 yards in rear	1/3rd.
In reserve 1½ to 3 miles in rear	1/3rd.

It seems probable that the regimental reserve are held so far back because there are no Corps reserves, so that the regimental reserve may be concentrated at any threatened point.

Behind the Corps holding the line we know of no organised army reserve. The nearest formed body of troops appears to be the XXVII Reserve Corps which is reported to be in the COMINES neighbourhood.

At LILLE there are some drafts and recruits undergoing training and some Landwehr formations.

APPENDIX III.

INFORMATION NOT SHEWN ON MAP.

Square "S".

The NEUVE CHAPELLE - LA BASSEE road is flanked on the Eastern edge of the road by a ditch 4' broad and 1½' deep. There are crossing places over this ditch at approximately every 200 yards.

The road is on an embankment 3' to 4' high between the cross roads S.W. of the BOIS DU BIEZ and LORGIES.

The tract shown as running from the Rue de Bois S. 10. a. South East of the road in S. 17. a. is a water cut about 10' broad.

The wood shewn at RICHEBOURG L'AVOUE does not exist.

The building shown at the southern end of S. 16. a., is a strong single storey farm enclosed by a wire fence.

The building shown at the N.E. corner of S. 21. b., is a farm surrounded by a moat, about 12' broad and 2' or 3' deep.

The building shown at the S.W. corner of S. 16. d., is a strongly built farmhouse, with a stone courtyard wall and with deep cellars.

The road shown in S. 18. b. and T. 13. a. do not exist.

The road shown in S. 22. c. running N.E. and S.W. and touching S. 16. d. does not exist.

In S. 27. a. North of LE PLOUICH there is a small wood about 300 yards from N. to S. and 100 yards from E. to W.

The track shown as running from ROUGES BANCS, N. 15. a., to near LE PLOUICH N. 28. c. is a water cut about 3' to 4' broad.

The track shown as running from FE DELEVAL to square N. 21. a., south east is a water cut.

APPENDIX IV.

FURTHER INFORMATION REGARDING AREA.

Note   These references refer to the 1/40,000 map beginning in
the Northern area and working South.

Square N.30.   MOULIN DU PIETRE.
The mill is a large windmill close to the road at the figure 5.
There is a small wood in square 30.b. south west.

Square N.26.   AUBERS.
The village consists of about 400 houses. There is one windmill, one steam mill, two distilleries, one brewery, a sugar factory and a weaving machine mill.

RUE D'ENFER is on an embankment from square 25.b. to square 26.a. In square 26.c. it runs through a small cutting.

The road running N.W. and N.E. through the corner of square 26.a. is bounded by a hedge. The line of the road after it turns due South in square 26.b. is continued for a short distance to the cemetery. This portion is an avenue with a line of trees, and this line of trees is continued beyond the end of the road, close to the RUE DE L'VAL in square 27.a.

Square N.27.d.
The principal building of LE PLOUICH is the FERME MARTIN shown on the map with a large courtyard. This farm is surrounded by meadow land with trees to the West and North of it. It is open to the east and south east. The farm has a moat round it.

In square 27.a. and 28.a. there is a wood of young trees about 20' to 30' high. A similar wood is in square 28.c. north west.

Square N.31.a.
The road shown by dotted lines on the map is a sunken road, six feet below the level of the ground.

The village of BAS POMEREAU consists of only five or six houses and lies low, below the crest of the ridge.

The area between the road and the railway in square N.32.a. and N.32.d. (north west of the railway) is pasture land enclosed by hedges.

Square T.3.a. LA CLIQUETERIE has a large farm solidly built, hidden from the west by gardens and a big hedge. It commands a good view towards the east and south east.

The railway in T.2.c. and T.2.d. is a small cutting about 2' deep.
At the road crossing L'ARMITURE there is a small orchard about 50 yards across.

Square T.8. LIGNY LE GRAND is a small village of some half dozen houses, built on the eastern side of a pronounced knoll, which, on the map, comes approximately where the figure 8 is, this only is meadow land with hedges farming out towards the east and north east.

The railway in T.9.c. and so far south as NEUVELLE is on an embankment varying from one to three feet high in height.

APPENDIX V.

(i) The ground between our lines and the enemy in the neighbourhood of PORT ARTHUR (and the advanced post) is plough and roots. It is very open and heavy going. As regards hostile obstacles on this front, there is a double line of chevaux-de-frise, with barbed wire entanglements through it all along the line, except for one gap of 50 yards where chevaux-de-frise is single. The chevaux-de-frise is about 4' high, made of wood, points sharpened. There also appears to be wire on and above the parapet. The parapet is reported fully manned. Chevaux-de-frise in many places, is some way from the parapet with wire entanglement between it and the parapet.

(ii) The hostile barricade, opposite the advanced post, is very conspicuous. There is no attempt at concealment. It must be 5' high at least and is built with red white and blue bags.

(iii) About 300 yards south down the LA BASSEE road from PORT ARTHUR there is one large red brick house and one or two smaller ones. The large house has never been shelled and is very probably used as an artillery observation station, as it almost looks into PORT ARTHUR.

APPENDIX VI.

REPORT ON THE DISTRICT BETWEEN FAUQUISSART AND AUBERS.

The road from FAUQUISSART to AUBERS is pavé. At a distance of 750 yards from FAUQUISSART the R.DES LAYES meets the road on the North side of the road. It runs along the road for 250 yards and then passes under it by a culvert. One hundred yards beyond this culvert on the North side of the road, there is a factory with a large chimney.

On the opposite side of the road, 50 yards back from the road, stands the chateau and farm of LE MOTTE.

Beyond the cross roads shewn on the map (Sq.N.25.b.) the road begins to ascend, at first very slightly, and on a short and slight embankment. This gradual ascent continues until the road junction in square N.26.a.c. From this point the descent is sharp up to the Church. North of the road, throughout this distance, the country is flat and unbroken.

South of the River DES LAYES there is only a few small cottages, which would present no serious difficulty.

EXPLANATION OF PANORAMA

(1) <u>To the right of the road FAUQUISSART - AUBERS.</u> The panorama is taken from the convent at the cross roads at FAUQUISSART.

The road to AUBERS leaves the cross roads on the extreme left of the panorama, runs along the farms of TRIVELET on its left and then turns sharply to the right, passing between the distillery and LA MOTTE farm on the extreme right of the sketch. It then turns to the left and goes fairly directly to AUBERS.

At TRIVELET there are two or three long farms and a clump of tall trees. These farms have apparently been placed in a state of defence. The large chimney of the beet distillery has been destroyed.

The chateau and farm of LE MOTTE have suffered from gun fire but are still standing. To the right of the road behind it in the sketch, the country slopes up to the ridge, and for at least a mile and a half the road to AUBERS is quite barren and devoid of trees or cover. Except for a few pollards the ascent TRIVELET to AUBERS is open, and so far as one can see, there is no dead ground.

To the left of AUBERS the ridge is covered with trees. Between the RUE TILLELOI and the R. DES LEYES the ground is flat and unbroken except for a few pollards.

(2) <u>To the left of the road FAUQUISSART - AUBERS.</u>

The village of AUBERS contains several large factories, chiefly for the manufacture of tiles.

The two principal obstacles in this area are the R. DES LAYES and the lower road in AUBERS (Squares N. 23. a.b.) which runs along the bottom of the ridge for a distance of about 600 yards. The line is continued beyond the ridge by a treble row of thin tall trees bounding the cemetery. Beyond these trees the ground is open for a hundred yards and then the same line is continued by a hedge which, on the extreme left runs into a small coppice.

On the other side of this line the country appears to be quite bare, and between the line and our trenches is flat.

There appears to be no dead ground.

The factories and the houses of AUBERS, and on the left, the house standing on the road AUBERS - FROMELLES, form an almost unbroken wall at the summit of the road for a distance of about a mile and have probably been placed into a state of defence.

Reference 1/40,000 or 1/20,000 Squared   INTELLIGENCE G.474.
Map.

Notes on Country N.E. of NEUVE CHAPELLE and area FROMELLES - AUBERS -
ILLIES - HERLIES.

1. The country up to the line LES MOTTES Fe - HT POMMEREAU - LIGNY LE GRAND, does not differ materially from that immediately behind our lines. East of the above line the ground commences to rise towards the AUBERS - LA CLIQUETERIE plateau; the villages are more substantially built and surrounded with trees and orchards.

2. Between NEUVE CHAPELLE and BOIS DU BEIZ it is very flat and open and the Riviere Des LAYES here is no great obstacle.
Between NEUVE CHAPELLE - LA RUSSIE and HT POMMEREAU - PIETRE - MIN DU PIETRE, it is generally flat and open plough land, the western part having fair sized fields with small hedges and shallow ditches, the eastern is mostly wire fenced, with a few hedges.

3. Between the road junction in M.30.c.7.1 and the M in MIN DU PIETRE there are houses with orchards and thick hedges. There are also orchards and clumps of trees roind the LES MOTTES Fe and at P of MIN DU PIETRE; just North of LES MOTTES Fe is a large distillery.

4. The road from PIETRE to the road junction to the S.E. is below the level of the ground on either side and has few trees; at the road junction itself is a farm "PANNEQUIN" with orchards with a small wood to the South of it.

5. From the above road, the country towards AUBERS is open with a few farms and trees along the road in N.31.b.

6. AUBERS consists of two pa&allel streets, linked at either end, in which space the whole rise of 50 feet takes place. It has a large church and three factories and substantially built houses. There are numerous gardens with trees and hedges but the latter are not serious obstacles. The North Western slope towards the RIVIERE DES LAYES is very open. The village is commanded by LE PLOUICH and HT POMMEREAU.
The road running from TRIVELET on the N.W. after passing S.E. of cross roads in N.25.b. is embanked.

7. From the road junction in N.31.c. (see para.4) southwards to HALPEGARBE there are farms and orchards along the road about every 300 yards. The rise to the LA CLIQUETERIE plateau begins about halfway between this road and the railway to the East of it; the ground up to the railway is open plough land.

8. HT POMMEREAU consists of a few brick houses in N.31.d. - S.E. with trees on the Eastern side, - it lies on the Southern end of the AUBERS ridge and overlooks AUBERS village.

9. In T.2.a and c. are a collection of farms and orchards and a good many trees, and in T.2.a. N.E. is a large three storied house, which viewed from FAUQUISSART has two prominent points on either side of the roof. The country from this locality towards AUBERS and LE PLOUICH to N. and N.E. is very open.

10. LE PLOUICH consists of 2 large farms and some small houses. The North Eastern farm is very substantially built, is surrounddd by a moat and overlooks the country to N. and N.E.; large trees are near both farms and there are trees on both sides of the road running up to the AUBERS - FROMELLES road.

11/

11. East of HT POMMEREAU is LA CLIQUETERIE Fe., a substantial building surrounded by orchards and trees: the building commands the country to the East and North East.

12. South of LA CLIQUETERIE Fe lies L'AVENTURE, a few houses lying on the Southern slope of the LA CLIQUETERIE Plateau. This slope is steep for this part of the country.

13. S.W. of L'AVENTURE is LIGNY LE GRAND (T.8.b.d.) a village of a few houses only, on a slight eminence 10 feet above the level of the surrounding ground; round it are numerous small enclosures with thick hedges.

14. S.W. of LIGNY LE GRAND, the area marked RUE DES TRONCBANI between LIGNY LE PETIT and LORGIES is reported to be marshy; it consists of gardens and small enclosures.

15. East of the line AUBERS - LA CLIQUETERIE - L'AVENTURE - LIGNY LE GRAND, lie the villages of FROMELLES - LE RIEZ - HERLIES - and WARNETON Fe.

16. FROMELLES is a large village surrounded by trees with substantially built brick houses and gardens- the village is very exposed to fire from the South East and is defiladed from AUBERS by a rise in the ground.

17. LE RIEZ is a straggling village of small houses along 400 yards of road. The country to the East is quite open as far as FOURNES.

18. HERLIES, which lies on the Eastern slope of LA CLIQUETERIE Fe plateau, is a long straggling village with many trees which hide the village from the West. From the road junction in T.4.d. for 400 yards towards AUBERS the road runs through a cutting 12 feet high. There is a large distillery with a high chimney immediately East of the village.

19. Further to the East there are a few houses surrounded by trees at le PILLY.

20. South West of HERLIES at WARNETON Fe just North of the Chateau is a small enclosed wood.

21. The villages HERLIES and ILLIES were prepared for defence last October and it is most probable that the villages of AUBERS, FROMELLES, HT POMMEREAU, LA CLIQUETERIE Fe and LE PLOUICH are now also protected by defensive works.

9th.March,1915.

(Sd) H.E.BRAINE, Captain,

General Staff, 8th. Division.

Information given by a resident of NEUVE CHAPELLE.

Reference map $\frac{1}{20,000}$. Sheet 36.S.W.

A wood of 100 square metres, thick but not high, in N.25.c.1.1.
Unmetalled road in N.31 is sunken and marked by a big tree.
Behind farm at North some bush - ground very wet.

A wood N.of HT in HT POMMEREAU - small trees, or rather bush -
on slope to POMMEREAU. Very abrupt slope then.
Good position for enemy artillery N.of second M in HT
POMMEREAU. A country wood runs back Eastward from there to
some farms.
Also good position in hollow road in T.10.a.1.9., more than
3 metres below level of road.

LE PLOUICH - grass all round farm - but small bush also there.

AUBERS - a chimney of brewery near church seen smoking
lately - probably being used by Germans for pumping out
water.
At corner of cemetary an electric station for transforming
electric current. Force enough to employ electricity - which
comes from LILLE or further off.
WASQUEHAL and LOMME are electric power stations near LILLE.

R.des LAYES varies from 4 metres to 5 - about 2 metres 25
deep. If a block occurs, may be deeper.

N.of LA RUSSIE (S.6.a.) another small wood not marked. About
100 square metres, with some big trees. The foundations and
ruins of an old windmill in the centre - about 25 metres
square, 10 metres high, of brick and earth.
Another small wood N.E. but ground there very wet.

The road through D of BOIS DU BIEZ is a rough unmetalled
road, but broad.

BOIS DU BIEZ divided into 9 parts from N.E. to S.W., cut in
different years.
    1st section from S.W. is 3 years old.
    2nd   do.   2   do.   2½ feet high.
    3rd   do.   1   do.   bare.
    4th   do.   9   do.   9 feet.
    5th   do   8   do.
                and so on.

On N.E.part ground bad - and very few trees. Wood very wet.

The white path on map 36 S.W. is divided from road to S.E. by
a ditch 3 feet deep and 3 feet broad.
The only two bridges are one at S.corner and one on road marked
in brown.
The best position for enemy guns on S.E. of wood is 100 metres
from exit by brown road, and 15 metres to N.
No natural bushes in T.12 outside BOIS DU BIEZ.

9th.March,1915.   A.R.HOSKINS, Colonel,
                                General Staff, 7th. Division.

CONFIDENTIAL.

20th Infantry Brigade.

With reference to the "Instructions for handing over to Canadian Division" of today's date, attaching Officers to each unit &c of the Canadian Division for four days, will you please give instructions to each of these Officers that 24 hours after rejoining his own unit he will submit a short report through this office, stating in what respects, in his opinion, the unit he was attached to required advice and improvement, in order that the necessary steps may be taken by the Corps Commander.

Ian Stewart Major
for Colonel,

1st March 1915.   General Staff, 7th. Division.

CONFIDENTIAL.

Instructions for handing over to Canadian Division.

1. Copies of instructions in 4th Corps Memorandum No.H.R.S.66 (G) of 28th February have been issued for information and compliance.

2. Machine Guns necessary for the defence of each section are to remain in the parapet with their detachments for 24 hours, when they will be withdrawn to their units, and replaced by guns of the Canadian Division.

3. Grenades and Reserve Ammunition already in the trenches will remain, and be taken over by the relieving formation.

4. Each Brigade will leave a detachment from their Grenade Company of 1 N.C.O. and 6 men who will remain behind for 7 days and act as instructors to the relieving formation.

5. The following, whether in the trenches or in reserve, will be left for 4 days after the transfer of duties is complete, to stay with the relieving unit of the Canadian Division and afford all possible assistance:-
   1 Officer per Battalion. *4 for first 24 hours, 1 Officer per company, 1 NCO per platoon*
   1 Officer per Brigade of Artillery.
   1 Officer per R.E.Field Company.

6. One half of the periscopes and Very's Lights of the Division are to be handed over to the Canadian Division.
   The 22nd Brigade will retain all theirs.
   The 21st Brigade will hand half of theirs over to the 22nd Brigade for use of the 1st Canadian Brigade, who go into the trenches tonight. These articles should therefore be handed in to 22nd Brigade Head quarters by 3.p.m. today.
   The 21st Brigade will hand over the remainder of their periscopes and Very's Lights to the 2nd Canadian Brigade relieving them.
   20th Brigade will hand over half their periscopes and Very's lights to the 3rd Canadian Brigade relieving them.
   The 20th and 21st Brigades will at once indent to replace articles handed over.

Ian Stewart [signature]
for Colonel,

1st March, 1915.   General Staff, 7th. Division.

Brigades will leave a sufficiency of all trench stores in the trenches to enable the relieving units to maintain them in a proper state of defence and will at once indent to make those good.
Such articles of which the Canadian Division has a sufficient supply must be withdrawn.

Equipment to be collected tomorrow.
Waistcoats. Central stores SAILLY
100 Tools in each subsection
Pumps.
1 NCO 6 men Grenade

The following will be the arrangements in
connection with handing over the trenches to the
3rd Canadian Brigade on the 2nd instant.
_____

Guides. Two Battalions of the 3rd Canadian Brigade will
relieve No 1 and 2 Subsections at 6.30 p.m. Representatives from each Company in the trenches will
meet the Canadian Battalions from No 1 Subsection
at No 1 H.Q. RUE PETILLON, from No 2 Subsection at
No 2 Subsection Dressing Station. In the case of the
Company which relieves the Northumberland Hussars,
a representative from the latter will meet them at
the SAILLY FROMELLES – RUE DU BOIS Cross Roads.
These representatives will conduct each company to its
respective place in the trenches.
The following personnel will be left behind in the
trenches by the Grenadier Guards and Border Regt.

Offrs & N.C.O. For the first 24 hours, 1 Officer per Company, 1 N.C.O
per platoon, 1 Officer per Battalion for 4 days.
The above will rejoin their units at the expiration
of these periods.

Machine Guns. Machine Guns necessary for the Defence of each
Section are to remain in the parapet with their
Detachments for 24 hours when they will be withdrawn to their units and replaced by guns of
the Canadian Division.

Tools 100 Tools per Subsection will be left behind and
handed over to the relieving Battalions.

Grenades & Ammunition Grenades and Reserve Ammunition already in the
trenches will remain, and be taken over by relieving
Battalions.

Pumps. Pumps will be left in all the reclaimed trenches
which require constant pumping and baling.

Periscopes Hay teats One half the Periscopes and Hay teats will
be handed over to the incoming Battalions.

Billets On being relieved the Grenadiers will Billet for
that night in the RUE DU BOIS. The Borders will
Billet in the central Billets now occupied by the
6th Bn Gordon Highlanders. These two Battns will
rejoin the Brigade at VIEUX BERQUIN, on the
evening of the 4th inst after dark. The billeting
parties preceding them to meet the Staff Captain at
that place at midday.
Further march orders are being sent out.

2/3/15
H.Q. Infantry Brigade
Brigade Major

20th Inf. Bde.   Confidential

As it is possible that the enemy may think that we have the intention of taking the offensive, and as it is sound, and moreover the teaching of the Germans to anticipate an offensive by attacking, it is the plan of the ~~Brigade~~ Army Commander that an offensive on the part of the enemy is to be vigorously countered by us, and moreover that we should roll him back and at once without pause pass to an extended forward movement ourselves.

It is therefore probable that troops which are at present some distance in rear of the front line will shortly receive orders to close further forward and it is especially necessaryv that all should be in readiness for a move at short notice, which may be anticipated at any time.

6=3=15.
                                                  J. R. Hutchison Major
                                                  for Colonel.
                                                  General Staff, 7th Division.

To O.C. 1/Grenadier Guards
    " 2/ Scots Guards
    " 2nd/ Border Regt
    " 2/ Gordon Highlanders
    " 6/ Gordon Highlanders

Passed to you for yr information & action
Please initial & return to bearer.

                          A W F Cator Major
                                  Brigade Major
6.3.15   XX I B

Officer Commanding,

....

Please cancel this morning's March Table issued with Operation Orders No. 10. The following will now be the March Table.

Unit.	Starting Point.	Time.	Time of arrival.
2nd Border Regiment.	Billets.	6. a.m.	6.15 a.m.
6th Gordon Highlanders.	Billets.	6.10. a.m.	6.30 a.m.
2nd Scots Guards.	Billets.	6.15 a.m.	6.35 a.m.
1st Grenadier Guards.	Billets.	6.30 a.m.	7. a.m.

23rd Field Ambulance Bearers Division to be at Brigade Headquarters at 6.30 a.m. and will follow the Grenadier Guards.

Brigade Major.

9th March, 1915.   20th Infantry Brigade.

BRIGADE ORDERS
BY

Brigadier-General F.J. Heyworth. D.S.O. Commanding,
20th Infantry Brigade.

18th March, 1915.

The Brigade will relieve the 22nd Brigade to-night in the Trenches.

the Grenadier Guards (on the right) will occupy half the Trenches now occupied by the 2nd Warwicks. The 2nd Scots Guards will occupy the remaining half of the Warwicks Trenches.

The 2nd warwicks are sending 1 N.C.O. per platoon tto M.17 CrossRoads at 6.45 p.m. at M.12.c. and Each guide will conduct two of our platoons - e.g., No. 1 Platoon Warwicks will conduct No. 1 and 2 Platoons of Grenadier Guards. etc.

The Border Regiment will occupy the trenches now held by the 2nd Queens. 1 N.C.O. per platoon will meet them at 6.45 p.m. at M.12.c. Cross Roads and conduct them to their trenches.

The 2nd Gordon Highlanders will occupy the trenches now held by the 1st South Staffords. 1. N.C.O. per platoon will meet them at the Road Junction M.6.d.

The 6th Gordon Highlanders will move into Brigade Reserve Billets in the RUE DU BACQUEROT about M.17.b, M.12.b. and c. and M.6.d, relieving the 8th Royal Scots. The Staff Captain will direct them to their Billets.

A certain number of tools and ammunition will be handed over by the 22nd Brigade.

Brigade Headquarters will remain where they are at present. Battalions will be in telephonic communication with them.

The 22nd Brigade are leaving 1 N.C.O. behind for 24 hours to point out details.

Brigade Major.
20th Infantry Brigade.

March Table.

Unit.	Starting Place and Time.	Route.	Place of arrival.
Grenadier Guards	Main Brigade at ESTAIRES. ~~4.35~~ 5.15 p.m.	G.32.b. LAVANTIE. Pt D'ESQUIN. M.10.d. Cross Roads. M.17.	M.17. Cross Roads.
Border Regiment.	Bridge at ESTAIRES. ~~4.50~~ 5.5 p.m.	G.32.b. LAVANTIE. M.12.c.	M.12.c.
2nd Gordon Highlanders.	at E. east end of their billets. ~~4.15~~ 4.55 p.m.	G.32.b. LAVANTIE. Road Junction M.6.d.	M.6.d.
2nd Scots Guards	H.Q. Scots Guards. 6 p.m.	Pt. D'ESQUIN. M.10.d. Cross Road M.17.	M.17 Cross Roads.
6th Gordon Highlanders.	H.Q. 6th Gordon Highlanders. 6.15 p.m.	M.5. M.6.b.	M.6.b. The Staff Captain will direct them to their billets.

signature
Brigade Major.

18th March, 1915.   20th Infantry Brigade.

Hd.Qrs.IV Army No.480 (G).

7th. Division.

The Lieutenant-General Commanding wishes your attention drawn to the fact that issues of R.E. stores appear in some cases to be excessive. Thus, during February seventy sand bags have been drawn per yard of front occupied by the First Army, and the rate during the current month has increased.

It is obvious that great difficulty will be met in continuing supplies on this scale, and all economy compatible with efficient work must therefore be exercised.

Present circumstances no doubt demand large issues of sandbags and other R.E. stores in the IVth Corps owing to the recent advance to the new line, but the Lieutenant-General Commanding wishes steps taken to ensure that such stores are neither unnecessarily demanded nor wasted when received. Every care must be taken to collect tools on the temporary cessation of work, otherwise much unnecessary loss is bound to occur.

H.Q. IVth Corps,	(Sd) P.Game, Major, for Brig:Genl:
19th. March, 1915.	General Staff, IVth Corps.

2.

20th Inf. Brigade

You must exercise all care in the use of these stores, compatible with ~~economy~~ efficiency.

Div.H.Q.
22.3.1915.

Colonel,
General Staff, 7th. Division.

Brigade Major

Herewith   copies of plan for road traffic.

In the event of active operations the following steps will be taken.

(a) All civilian traffic will be stopped. A Detachment Northumberland Hussars will be required for the N. & S Merville Roads.

(b) Traffic direction will be carried out by the M.M.P. assisted by Cyclists.

Stationary posts for traffic are shewn in plan marked T.

For traffic and collection of stragglers T.S.

(c) Prisoners of War collecting Stations will be established under an officer Northumberland Hussars at LAVENTIE Station.

Prisoners of War will be conducted along the Railway Line to the level crossing on the La BASSEE road thence along the road G.32 (a) to L.35 (a) to LA GORGUE (A.P.M's Guard Room). They will be conducted thence to MERVILLE by French Territorials and handed over to A.P.M., 4th Corps.

(d) These arrangements will be supplemented by Mounted Patrols where found necessary as far as numbers permit a patrol being kept   continually in readiness to go forward and direct traffic should the line make an appreciable advance.

(e) A Guard will be required on the bridge over the R.LYS and R.LAWE.

24/3/15

Lt.Colonel
A.A. & Q.M.G., 7th Division.

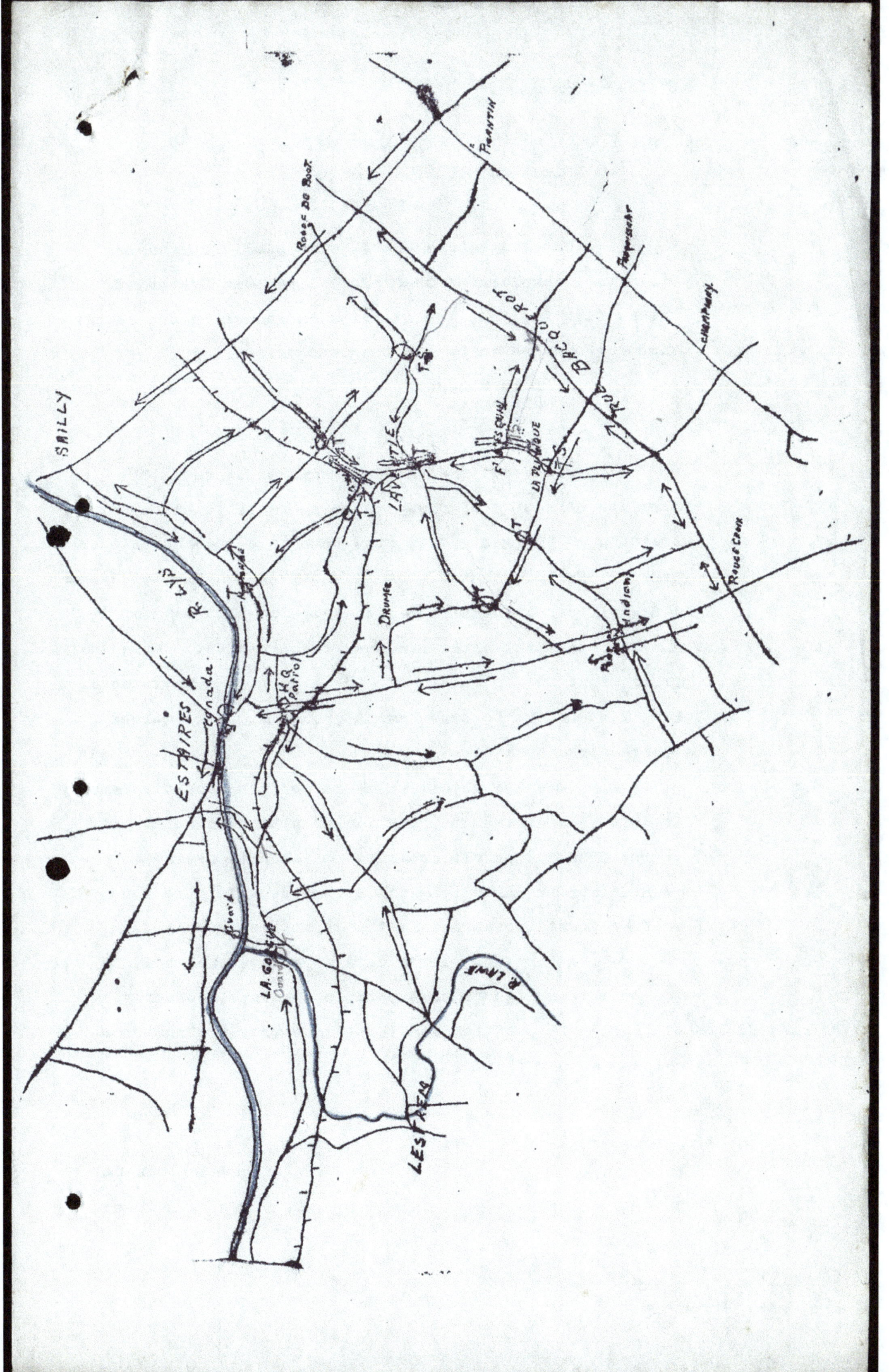

Officer Commanding

The Brigadier-General wishes all Commanding Officers to explain to their Battalions the System of Trench fighting from the experiences gained in the recent fighting, and to carry out the same, organising,

> Bomb Throwers.
> Riflemen.
> Sandbaggers.
> Working Parties.

Point out the value of bomb throwers. The absolute necessity of always pushing on till the objective has been gained and not to stop because a trench has been taken. Explain that if the Infantry are unable to advance and artillery support is called in - it will last for 10 minutes, the last three minutes being intense. When it ceases [clears] that is the moment for the troops to move forward, but even during the bombardment ground might be gained by creeping forward.

Once the objective is gained, the position must at once be consolidated, particular attention being paid to the flanks, and all precautions taken to resist a counter attack which is certain to come. Machine guns must be pushed forward once the objective is gained.

At the end of the days fighting, each body of troops without orders must send in a reliable orderly to Brigade Hd Qrs stating their position and the troops they are in touch with on either flanks.

Laventie. F.J. Heyworth Brigadier- General.
25th March, 1915. Commanding 20th Infantry Brigade.

Copy No. 5.

Instructions for Artillery support of the defences

Ref 1/40,000 Map.   28th March, 1915.

1.   The 106th Battery, R.F.A. withdraws temporarily into reserve at 4.45 a.m. to-morrow.
        The 3rd Canadian Artillery Brigade comes into action to-night (1 Battery 4.45 a.m. to-morrow) about squares M.1.a & B.

2.   The R.H.A. Batteries of No.2 Group will continue to cover the right-half of the 7th Division line from CHAPIGNY to a point opposite the junction of the RUE MASSELOT and the RUE TILLELOY.

3.   The 13th Brigade R.F.A. will continue to cover the front of the Indian Corps Battalion on the right of the 7th Divsion, while being ready to bring fire to bear at short notice on the trenches opposite the right half of the 7th Division line and on the approaches to them in case of need.

4.   No. 5 Group assisted by the 22nd F.A. Brigade (less 1 Battery) will cover the left half of the 7th Division line.
        O.C. No. 5 Group will establish communication with B.G.C. Infantry Brigade holding the trenches (21st Infantry Bde. at present; Hd Qrs. Laventie, M.4.b.4.4.) and arrange for the necessary F.O.O's with Infantry. One F.O.O. must be at night in close touch with the Hd.Qrs. of each Battalion in the trenche

5.   The above measures will take effect from 6.p.m. to-night.

28.3.1913.   (Sd)   S.W.H. Rawlins.   Major R.A.
                            Brigade Major, 7th Divisional Artillery.

B.G.44.

From O.C. 5th Group.

To Brigade Major R.A. 7th Divisional Artillery.

29.3.1915.

Reference your B.M. 205 of 28.3.1915. and in continuation of my B.G. 42 of 28.3.1915.

(1) The following arrangements have been made to cover the left half of the 7th Division Line.

(2) 104th and 105th Batteries of 22nd Brigade to cover "F" 1 and 2. (i.e., from 310 to 323.)

3rd Canadian Brigade R.F.A. to cover "F" 3 and 4. (i.e., from 321 to 370.)

"N2 "X" and "V" Batteries R.H.A. to cover "F" 5 and 6. (i.e., from 334 to 371.)

(3) The Brigadier-General Commanding 21st Infantry Brigade informs me that one battalion is at present holding the left front with Head Quarters at road junction at M.7.b. A Forward Observing Officer will be kept at this Head Quarters with telephone line to 5 Group Headquarters and 3rd Canadian Brigade Headquarters.

(Sd) H.F. Askwill. Lieutenant-Colonel. R.H.A.
Officer Commanding 5th Group.

To Brigade Major, 21st Infantry Brigade.
Copy forwarded for information.

(SD) A.F. Brook. Captain and Adjutant.
R.H.A. 5th Group.

Confidential

General Staff, 7th Division
Date 4/4/31

1st Canadian Division.

With reference to your G.826, there is no objection to your officers visiting trenches, but, in order to maintain secrecy, it is requested that the following rules may be strictly observed :-

(a) Not more than 6 officers should be in trenches at one time.
(b) Not more than 3 officers are to collect in one place.
(c) Artillery observation stations are not to be used by officers visiting the trenches.
(d) These parties should report at the Hd Qrs of the Brigade in the trenches for instructions before going down.

21st Brigade is in the trenches up to evening of 31st instant! (Hd Qrs LAVENTIE' M.4.b.3.5.)

20th Brigade relieves 21st Brigade on evening of 31st. (Hd Qrs now in LA GORGUE, but will move to LAVENTIE on morning of 1st April, Hd Qrs M.34.c.3.3.)

The early morning is the most peaceful time.

Div.H.Q.
30th March, 1915.

Ian Stewart Major
for Lieut-Colonel,
General Staff, 7th Division.

20th Infantry Brigade.
For your information.

30-3-15.

Ian Stewart Major / Lt-Colonel,
General Staff, 7th Division.

CIRCULAR MEMORANDUM No.15.

T.C. 131.   SECRET.

20th Inf Bde

1. It is most important for our general plans, and for the security of our Artillery observing stations and forward batteries, that the ground behind our lines, the RUE TILLELOY, as far back as the RUE BACQUEROT should resume the quiet atmosphere which prevailed there before the action at NEUVE CHAPELLE.

2. To stop promiscuous and unnecessary traffic, the following regulations have been made.

    (a). No motors or horses, or horse drawn vehicles are to proceed by daylight beyond (i.e. in direction of the enemy) the line of control posts established at or near the RUE DU BACQUEROT.

    > Secret.   7th Division No. C/37/A
    >
    > With reference to Corcular Memorandum No. 15 of 31st March, 1915. - para 2 (b) - Transport wagons may proceed S. of the Railway on the LA BASSEE and LE DRUMEZ roads only between 6 a.m. and 6 p.m. as far as the points where the line on map Sheet 36A, 1:40000, from PONT RIQUEILL to RUE de PARADIS cuts those roads in M.2.d. and M.3.c.

    General Commanding R.A., 7th Division, Officers Commanding Brigades of Artillery, or the C.R.E.
    Similarly, parties of men who have, of necessity to move between RUE DU BACQUEROT and the trench line by day, must have passes from one of the above authorities also.
    In the case of officers or others who have to go continually into the above mentioned area, the pass can be a permanent one.

    (f). Parties, whether of officers, or otherwise, proceeding South of the RUE DU BACQUEROT must keep as much as possible under cover from view, and must avoid using the roads leading towards the RUE TILLELOY, South of the stream running from M.18.c. to M.7.b.; or the roads leading from the RUE TILLELOY into the trenches.

CIRCULAR MEMORANDUM No.15.

20th Inf Bde   T.C. 161.   SECRET.

1. It is most important for our general plans, and for the security of our Artillery observing stations and forward batteries, that the ground behind our lines, the RUE TILLELOY, as far back as the RUE BACQUEROT should resume the quiet atmosphere which prevailed there before the action at NEUVE CHAPELLE.

2. To stop promiscuous and unnecessary traffic, the following regulations have been made.

   (a). No motors or horses, or horse drawn vehicles are to proceed by daylight beyond (i.e. in direction of the enemy) the line of control posts established at or near the RUE DU BACQUEROT.

   (b). Transport wagons, and wagons containing materiel, are not to proceed South of the railway between the hours of 6.A.M. - 6.P.M.

   (c). Working parties are not to work by daylight South of the RUE DU BACQUEROT, except working parties at or immediately in rear of our actual trench line.

   (d). Working parties, or bodies of troops sent to the trenches are to go both in and out under cover of night.

   (e). Parties of officers visiting the trenches must have passes emanating from Divisional or Brigade Head Quarters, Brigadier General Commanding R.A.,7th Division, Officers Commanding Brigades of Artillery, or the C.R.E.
   Similarly, parties of men who have, of necessity to move between RUE DU BACQUEROT and the trench line by day, must have passes from one of the above authorities also.
   In the case of officers or others who have to go continually into the above mentioned area, the pass can be a permanent one.

   (f). Parties, whether of officers, or otherwise, proceeding South of the RUE DU BACQUEROT must keep as much as possible under cover from view, and must avoid using the <u>roads</u> leading towards the RUE TILLELOY, South of the stream running from M.18.c. to M.7.b.; or the <u>roads</u> leading from the RUE TILLELOY into the trenches.

3. Naturally, these regulations are not intended to apply to actual tactical emergency.

4. The Divisional General desires that officers of all arms will assist him in securing a greater atmosphere of quiet in the portion of our area designated above : and is sure that all officers will see the importance of obtaining this object, and will help to produce it.

Div.H.Q. F.GATHORNE HARDY, Lieut-Colonel,
31st. March, 1915. General Staff, 7th. Division.

General Staff, 7th Division.
No. 7.D. 444.

20th Infantry Brigade.

In future a telegraphic report should be sent in each day, so as to reach this office by 5.30 p.m., giving a summary of information acquired during the preceding 24 hours. This should include such information as the location of hostile machine guns, alterations in wire entanglements, location of hostile batteries, and any hostile aeroplanes observed during the day.

            (Sd) G. Hutchinson. Major,
30th March, 1915.   General Staff, 7th Division.

--- 2 ---

Officer Commanding,

Reference the above minute, please include the information required for the 5.30 p.m. wire in your 10 a.m. and 4.30 p.m. daily report whilst in the trenches.

Brigade H.Qrs.   Staff Captain.
31st March, 1915.   20th Infantry Brigade.

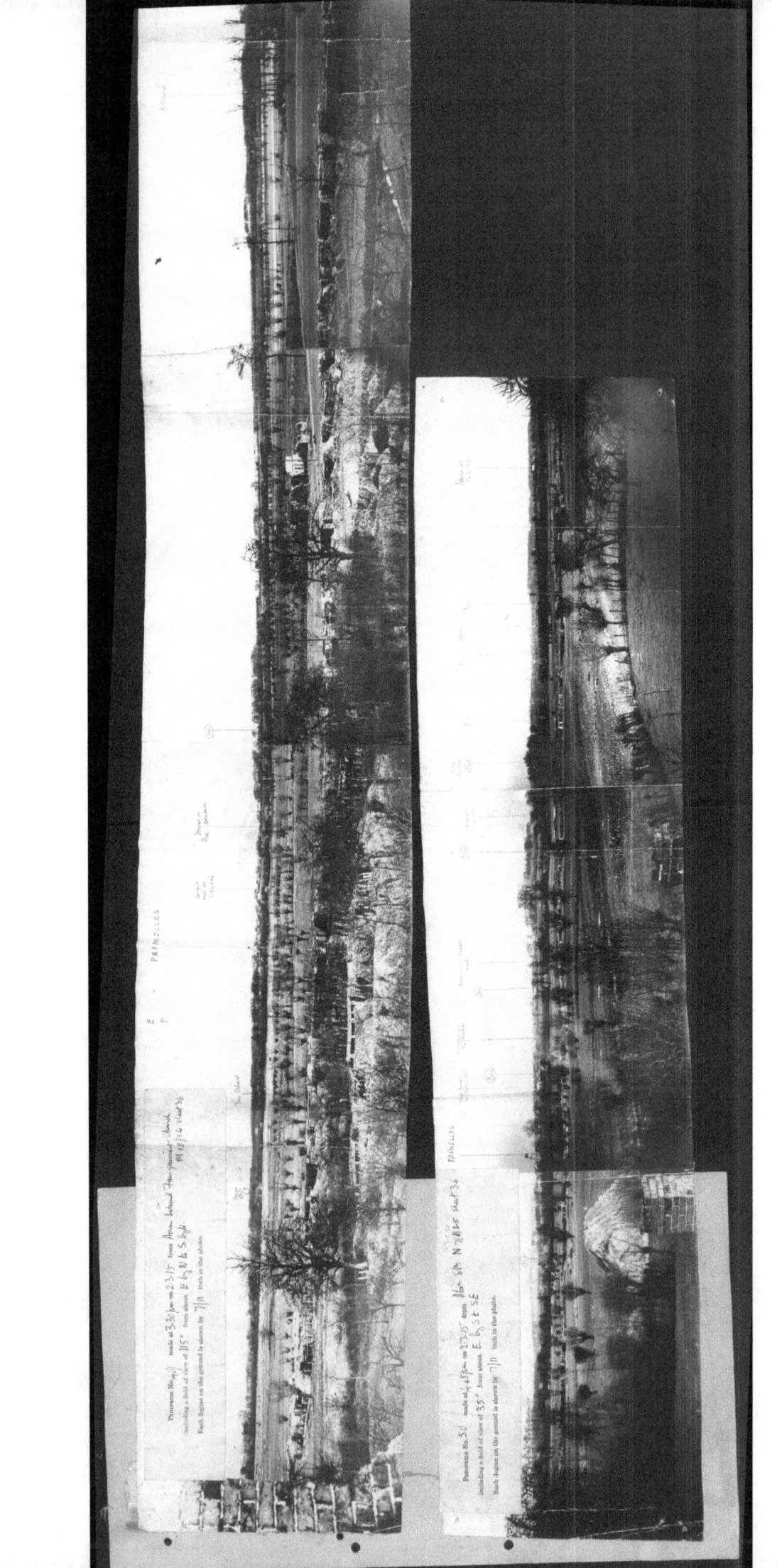

Confidential.

G.O.C. 7 Div.

The 2Bn Roy.Warwick Regt has suffered heavily on several occasions between Oct 19 and Nov 7 in the heavy fighting East of Ypres ,only 2 subalterns and 180 other ranks remaining. ON Nov 10 Maj Brewis took command and drafts joined on various dates , consisting chiefly of young officers and men of the special reserve .Early in Dec ,the battalion was nearly up to strenght but short of officers , the officers were young and inexperienced the N.C.Os mostly of little value having been made from the best men but not trained as N.C.Os. The Batt was framing well but heavy losses again on the 18 Dec again broke up its organisation. During the following 10 days the commanding officer was a revently promoted special reserve captain. Lt Col Poole took over command Dec 30 and Maj Hart joined a few days later. Drafts were received which made up the lower ranks. Lt Col Poole left the batt 19 Jan. The Batt thus suffered from frequent change of C.O. At present Maj Hart has 2 special reserve captains
      3 regular 2Lieuts
      11 special reserve 2Lieuts.

Maj Hart has not yet had sufficient opportunity to show his power of command , but from I have seen I do not think he is capable of dealing with the difficult situation. The behaviour of the Batt has ben normal except for the many cases of absence. These have un doubtdly been with the object of avoiding duty in the trenches or duty in the face of the enemy. These offences have been framed as desertion but some cases have failed as such owing to the inability to prove the actual warning of the accused for the duty in question. This has nesessitated the alteration of the charge. Notice was published a short time ago in orders pointing out certain serious offences, desertion and sleping on a post, explaining the full penalty and likeligood of this being enforced. Particular orders have been issued as regards warning men for duties and for posting or relieving sentries.

I feel sure that an example to the full penalty is required to stop men absenting themselves from duties above mentioned, as imprisonment and Field Punishment have no terrors for men who wish to commit these offences. I am quite sure that the only prospect of putting this batalion in an efficient state is a strong commanding officer, and supported by a few senior regular officers. These are all the more essential in view of the quality of N.C.Os at present available. I am giving the battalion all possible assistance.

          Brig.Gen.
          22 Inf Brigade.

Jan 30.1915

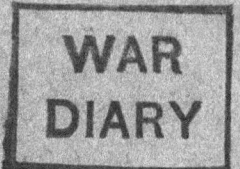

Headquarters,

20th INFANTRY BRIGADE.

(7th Division)

A P R I L

1 9 1 5

Div. Operation Orders.
Bde.   :   :
Appendices.

Army Form C. 2118.

WAR DIARY
or
INTELLIGENCE SUMMARY

(Erase heading not required.)

Instructions regarding War Diaries and Intelligence Summaries are contained in F.S. Regs., Part II. and the Staff Manual respectively. Title pages will be prepared in manuscript.

Hour, Date, Place	Summary of Events and Information	Remarks and references to Appendices
	A P R I L - 1915.	
April 1st to 4th.	Nothing to record.	
April 5th.	Prince of Wales visited 20th Infantry Brigade Headquarters. Major F.G. Alston. Scots Guards took over duties of Brigade Major from Major A.B. Cator. D.S.O. Scots Guards, appointed to command of 2nd Battalion Scots Guards.	
April 6th.	Army Commander visited 20th Infantry Brigade Headquarters at 3.45 p.m.	
April 7th.	The Brigade was relieved in the trenches at night by the 22nd Infantry Brigade, and went into Billets at LAVENTIE and ESTAIRES.	
April 8th.	Brigadier-General and Brigade Major visited Training Grounds and Billets at ESTAIRES. Forenoon. Brigadier-General inspected Scots Guards draft in the afternoon.	
April 9th.	Brigadier-General F.J. Heyworth, D.S.O. proceeded on leave to England. Lieutenant-Colonel L.I. Wood, Commanding 2nd Battalion Border Regiment taking over temporary command. Colonel Wood and Brigade Major visited the Defended Localities Nos 10. 11.12.13.14. and 17. in the RUE BACQUEROT this morning.	
April 10th.	Nothing to record.	
April 11th.	Nothing to record.	
April 12th.	Good deal of musketry fire at 4 a.m. 2 Prisoners were brought in by Royal Welsh Fusiliers. Lieutenant-Colonel Wood and Brigade Major watched experiments of messages being sent by the Very Pistols at the Headquarters, 6th Battalion Gordon Highlanders. At 5.30 p.m. Corps Commander inspected Bomber's Company.	
	April, 13th.	

Army Form C. 2118.

WAR DIARY
or
INTELLIGENCE SUMMARY

(Erase heading not required.)

Instructions regarding War Diaries and Intelligence Summaries are contained in F. S. Regs, Part II. and the Staff Manual respectively. Title pages will be prepared in manuscript.

Hour, Date, Place	Summary of Events and Information	Remarks and references to Appendices
April 13th.	Nothing to record.	
April 14th.	Nothing to record.	
April 15th.	Private Stewart, 2nd Battalion Gordon Highlanders was accidentally killed this afternoon during Bomb practice.	
April 16th.	Brigadier-General F.J. Heyworth. D.S.O. returned from leave.	
April 17th.	Brigadier-General Commanding and Brigade Major watched No.1. Trench Mortar Battery training with Infantry and experiments with sleighs.	
April 18th.	Nothing to record.	
April 19th.	Brigadier-General Commanding and Brigade Major went to the 105th Battery Headquarters to see new sleighs for Mortar Battery. New light pattern much more satisfactory. The Commander-in-Chief inspected the Brigade and addressed each Battalion in person at 2.30 p.m. at ESTAIRES. Brigadier-General Commanding attended a conference at Divisional Headquarters at 6.30 p.m.	
April 20th.	General MacFarlane visited Brigade Headquarters reference to 1st West Riding Brigade going to trenches under instruction.	
April 21st.	Brigadier-General Commanding and General Gough witnessed attack practice of 6th Battalion Gordon Highlanders and Mortar Battery. The Brigade went into the trenches to-night, 1st Battalion Grenadier Guards, 2nd Battalion Scots Guards and 6th Battalion Gordon Highlanders (half Battalion).	
April 22nd.	A conference of Commanding Officers was held at 4 p.m. April 23rd.	

Army Form C. 2118.

WAR DIARY
or
INTELLIGENCE SUMMARY

(Erase heading not required.)

Instructions regarding War Diaries and Intelligence Summaries are contained in F. S. Regs., Part II. and the Staff Manual respectively. Title pages will be prepared in manuscript.

Hour, Date, Place	Summary of Events and Information	Remarks and references to Appendices
April 23rd.	A Divisional Conference was held this morning at 10 a.m. It lasted until 12.30.p.m. Brigadier-General Commanding accompanied General Gough Commanding, 5th Division, to the trenches in the afternoon.	
April 24th.	Brigade Major arranged details for gradual relief of line by 1st West Riding Brigade (Infantry). Relief by West Riding Infantry Brigade cancelled.	
April 25th.	Nothing to record.	
April 26th.	In the evening received orders to take over Lines of the BAREILLY Brigade.	
April 27th.	1st Battalion Grenadier Guards and 2nd Battalion Scots Guards took over "G" and "H" Lines of BAREILLY Brigade, now called "D" Section.	
April 28th.	2nd Battalion Border Regiment and half 6th Battalion Gordon Highlanders took over "E" and "F" Lines of the BAREILLY Brigade, now called "C" Section. 2nd Battalion Gordon Highlanders to Billets in LA BASSEE Road and half 6th Battalion Gordon Highlanders in CAMERON LANE. Brigadier-General Commanding and Brigade Major selected FORWARD Report Centre at Farm in M.23.a. (Scots Guards Headquarters). 7th Division less 20th Infantry Brigade moved off. 20th Infantry Brigade came under orders of 8th Division.	
April 29th.	LAVENTIE was shelled twice to-day by the Germans.	
April 30th.	Brigadier-General Commanding and Major Hordern, General Staff, 8th Division, visited the Trenches in the afternoon.	

H.J. Heyworth
B.G... Gen...
Comm'd'g 20th ... Brigade

DIVISIONAL OPERATION ORDERS.

SECRET.   Copy No.

7th Division Operation Order No.1.

by

Major-General H. De la P. Gough, C.B.

Commanding 7th Division.

--------------------- 20th April, 1915.

(Reference map 1/10,000, sheet FAUQUISSART-AUBERS, G.S.G.S.No.2769).

1. INFORMATION.

   The 7th Division will, during the nights 24th/25th and 25th/26th instant, take over the line, now held by the Indian Corps, from the present right of the 7th Division to the road running North of NEUVE CHAPELLE through points (141) and (121). This road is exclusive to the 7th Division.

   The relief is to be completed by 6.a.m. 26th.

2. INTENTION.

   The 22nd Infantry Brigade will carry out this relief under arrangements to be made direct with the MEERUT Division.

3. REPORTS.

   The 22nd Infantry Brigade will inform 7th Division as soon as the relief is completed.

                                                    Lieut-Colonel,
                                           General Staff, 7th. Division.

Issued at 10.a.m. to :-

A.D.C. (for G.O.C.)	Copy No.1.
G.S.O.1.	" " 2.
G.S.O.2. (Office copy).	" " 3.
A.A.& Q.M.G.	" " 4.
R.A.	" " 5.
R.E.	" " 6.
20th Inf. Bde.	" " 7.
21st Inf. Bde.	" " 8.
22nd Inf. Bde.	" " 9.

OPERATION ORDER No. 2.   Copy No. 9

BY

Major-General H. De la P. Gough, C.B.

Commanding 7th. Division.

26th. April, 1915.

1. Under instructions from the 1st Army, the IVth Corps will take over that portion of the Indian Corps trench line from its present junction on the right of "E" lines to the TILLELOY - LA RUSSIE road, exclusive, - points (121) - (142) map 1/10,000.

2. The following reliefs will take place :-
(a). On the night of the 27th/28th instant :-
The 8th Division will take over "F" lines from the 20th Infantry Brigade.
The 1st West Riding Infantry Brigade will take over "E" lines from the 20th Infantry Brigade.
The 20th Infantry Brigade will take over "G" and "H" subsections from the MEERUT Division.

(b). On the night of the 28th/29th instant :-
The 8th Division will take over "E" lines from the 1st West Riding Infantry Brigade.
The 20th Infantry Brigade will take over "E" and "F" Indian subsections from the MEERUT Division.

3. The 20th Infantry Brigade will take one platoon from the West Riding Brigade with each company into the trenches for 24 hours when making these reliefs. These platoons being replaced by others every 24 hours.

4. The G.O.C. 8th Division will arrange for the Artillery support of the new 7th Division front, which will only have the 2nd West Riding Artillery Brigade available for this purpose.

5. The 33rd R.F.A. Brigade will again come under the orders of the 8th Division on the 27th instant at an hour to be notified later.

6. Billeting areas will be communicated separately.

PTO

on 24th instant
7. The troops warned will remain ready to move at 2 hours notice.

                                                       Lieut-Colonel,
                               General Staff, 7th. Division.

Issued at 7.30.p.m. to :-

A.D.C. (for G.O.C.)	Copy No.1.
G.S.O.1.	" 2.
G.S.O.2. (Office Copy.)	" 3.
A.A.& Q.M.G.	" 4.
Divnl.Cavalry.	" 5.
Cyclist Coy.	" 6.
B.G.C.,R.A.	" 7.
C.R.E.	" 8.
20th Infantry Brigade.	" 9.
21st Infantry Brigade.	" 10.
22nd Infantry Brigade.	" 11.
1st W.R.Inf.Brigade.	" 12.
Signals.	" 13.
A.D.M.S.	" 14.
M.M.Gun Battery.	" 15.

Copy. No. 4

7th. Division Operation Order No. 3.

by

Major-General H. De la P. Gough, C.B.

Commanding 7th. Division.

Reference Map 1/100,000.   28th. April, 1915.

Those troops already warned will march to the area PRADELLES, METEREN, FLETRE, via ESTAIRES, NEUF BERQUIN, VIEUX BERQUIN, from which latter place they will be directed to their billeting areas.

Starting point. Road junction ¼ mile North West of A in ESTAIRES.

Troops will march as follows :-

Divisional Cavalry. Divisional Cyclists. Motor Machine Gun Battery.	12.0 noon.
22nd Infantry Brigade. 22nd Field Ambulance.	12.15.p.m.
21st. Infantry Brigade. 21st. Field Ambulance.	1.15.p.m.
Artillery Column (less D.A.C.)	2.15.p.m.
Divisional Train.	3.45.p.m.
Divisional Ammn. Column.	4.30.p.m.

Staff Officers from each Infantry Brigade and from Divisional Artillery will be sent on in advance to meet the A.A.& Q.M.G. at VIEUX BERQUIN Church.

Divisional Head Quarters will be established at PRADELLES, where an office will be opened at 1.30.p.m.

Up to that hour reports will be sent to present Head Quarters.

F. Gathorne-Hardy
Lieut-Colonel,
General Staff, 7th. Division.

Issued at   to :-

A.D.C. (for G.O.C.)	Copy No.1.	A.D.M.S.	Copy No.10.
G.S.O.1.	" 2.	4th Corps.	" 11.
G.S.O.2. (Office copy).	" 3.	8th. Division.	" 12.
A.A.& Q.M.G.	" 4.	Meerut Divn.	" 13.
B.G.C.,R.A.	" 5.		
R.E.	" 6.		
20th. Inf.Brigade.	" 7.		
21st. Inf.Brigade.	" 8.		
22nd Inf. Brigade.	" 9.		

BRIGADE OPERATION ORDERS.

No. 1.

BRIGADE ORDERS
BY
Brigadier-General F.J. Heyworth. D.S.O.
Commanding 20th Infantry Brigade.

War Diary

Reference .:-
Map $\frac{1}{40,000}$. Sheet 36. (Squared)

In the Field.
7th ~~8th~~ April, 1915.

-----ooooo OOOOO ooooo-----

1. The Brigade will be relieved in the Trenches by the 22nd Infantry Brigade ~~to-morrow~~ to-day.

2. Guides (1.N.C.O. per platoon) of the 2nd Battalion Border Regiment, 2nd Battalion Gordon Highlanders and 6th Battalion Gordon Highlanders to conduct the Battalions moving to the Trenches, will meet the leading company of the Battalions of the 22nd Infantry Brigade on the RUE BACQUEROT at 7.15 p.m. as follows.:-

    (a) Guides from 3 Companies 2nd Border Regiment at Cross Roads M.17. to conduct 2nd Queens Regiment.

    (b) Guides from 1 Company 2nd Battalion Border Regiment and 2 Companies 6th Battalion Gordon Highlanders at Cross Roads M.12.c. to conduct 1st Battalion South Staffordshire Regiment.

    (c) Guides from 2nd Battalion Gordon Highlanders at Road Junction M.6.d. 6.5. to conduct 8 Battalion Royal Scots.

3. Periscopes, Very Pistols and Tools on Battalion charge will be withdrawn from the Trenches.

4. The Brigade will move into No. 2 Brigade Area as follows.:-

    (a) The 2nd Battalion Scots Guards and 2nd Battalion Border Regiment will take over the Billets of the 2nd Battalion Warwickshire Regiment and 1st Battalion South Staffordshire Regiment respectively in LAVENTIE.

    (b) The 1st Battalion Grenadier Guards and 2nd Battalion Gordon Highlanders will take over the Billets of the 2nd Battalion Queens Regiment and 8th Battalion Royal Scots respectively in the Factory in ESTAIRES.

(c).

Sheet 2.

(c) The 6th Battalion Gordon Highlanders will receive billetting orders later.

(d) The transport with the exception of that of the 2nd Battalion Scots Guards will remain as at present. Verbal instructions have been issued to the Quartermaster 2nd Scots Guards.

5. The Quartermaster of each Battalion will meet the Quartermasters of the 22nd Infantry Brigade at the Battalion Headquarters of the Units which they relieve at 10 a.m. to-day.

6. The 1st Battalion Grenadier Guards will march to ESTAIRES via LE NOUVEAU MONDE, G 27.c. and will be clear of the level crossing North of LAVENTIE by 5.30 p.m.

The 2nd Battalion Scots Guards will march to their billets in LAVENTIE via Cross Roads RUE DU QUESNES. H.31.c. G.29.d. and G. 34.d. leaving their billets at 7.30 p.m.

The 2nd Battalion Border Regiment as soon as relieved in the Trenches will march to their billets in LAVENTIE via LA FLINQUE and F't D'ESQUIN.

The 2nd Battalion Gordon Highlanders as soon as relieved in the Trenches will march to ESTAIRES via Cross Roads RUE DU BOIS, ROUGE DE BOUT and SAILLY Cross Roads.

7. The 2nd Battalion Scots Guards will relieve the Road Guards (Strength 1.N.C.O. and 3 men) at the Fork road North of LAVENTIE M.4.b. and at Point 300 yards, East of Cross Roads in LAVENTIE M.4.b. at 6 p.m. to-day. These Guards will be found on alternate days by the two Battalions in LAVENTIE and will be mounted at 9 a.m. daily.

MAJOR,
BRIGADE MAJOR.
20TH INFANTRY BRIGADE.

No. 2.

BRIGADE ORDERS
BY
Brigadier-General F.J. Heyworth. D.S.O.
Commanding 20th Infantry Brigade.

Reference Map   In the Field.
$\frac{1}{40,000}$. Sheet. 36.   7th April.1915.

---oooOoOOoooo---

1. TRAINING.

Pending further instructions which will be issued to-morrow, training to-morrow will be carried on as follows.:-

TRAINING AREA "A". FOOTBALL GROUND N.E. of LAVENTIE. M.4.b. will be allotted to the 2nd Battalion Scots Guards in the morning and to 2nd Battalion Border Regiment in the afternoon.

TRAINING AREA "B". Ground marked out with flags or posts, the centre of which is situated East and West by thick rectangular line between G.33 and M.3. North and South by thin rectangular line between the above mentioned square, will be allotted to 2nd Battalion Border Regiment in the morning and to the 6th Battalion Gordon Highlanders in the afternoon.

TRAINING AREA "C". G.26.a., two grass fields South of FERME QUENELLES will be allotted to the 2nd Battalion Gordon Highlanders in the morning and to the 1st Battalion Grenadier Guards in the afternoon.

TRAINING AREA "D". Trench attacking ground between FERME *FERME DE BRETAGNE* and QUENELLE, G.20.d. and G.26.a and b., will be allotted to the 1st Battalion Grenadier Guards in the morning and to the 2nd Battalion Gordon Highlanders in the afternoon. The Battalions not allotted an area either in the morning or afternoon will carry out route marching.

2. WORKING PARTY.

No. 5.

BRIGADE ORDERS

BY

Lieutenant-Colonel L.I. Wood, Commanding
20th Infantry Brigade.

In the Field.
10th April, 1915.

----------ooooo00000ooooo----------

1. GUARD.

The Quarter Guards at 20th Infantry Brigade Head Quarters will be mounted daily at 9 a.m. as follows.:-

April, 11th, 13th, 15th, 17th, 19th, will be found by 2nd Battalion Scots Guards.

April, 12th, 14th, 16th, 18th, 20th, will be found by 2nd Battalion Border Regiment.

2. WORKING PARTY.

With reference to Brigade Order No. 4, paragraph 3, dated 9th April, 1915, the working party therein to be detailed by Officer Commanding 2nd Battalion Scots Guards, will be now detailed by Officer Commanding 6th Battalion Gordon Highlanders.

----------ooooo00000ooooo----------

Major.
Brigade Major.
20th Infantry Brigade.

No. 15.

BRIGADE ORDERS

BY

Brigadier-General F.J. Heyworth. D.S.O.
Commanding 20th Infantry Brigade.

Reference Map
1/20,000.

In the Field.
20th April, 1915.

-----ccoooOOOOOooooo-----

1. The Brigade will relieve the 21st Infantry Brigade in the Trenches at 9 p.m. to-morrow.

2. The Brigade will be disposed as follows.:-
(a) 1st Battalion Grenadier Guards will take over E Lines and part of F.A. Lines up to H in BRITISH. They will also garrison F.1. with 2 N.C.O's and 12 men.
(b) 6th Battalion Gordon Highlanders less two companies thence to end of communication trench in 13.b. They will also garrison Fort F 3. near that point with two N.C.O's and 12 men.
(c) 2nd Battalion Scots Guards will take over the whole of F.b. lines and garrison the two redoubts South of the Communication Trench in 13.b. called SALIENT FORTS No,s 1 and 2, with 1 Officer and 20 men and 1 N.C.O. and 20 men respectively, the Officer being responsible for both forts.

3. A party of 25 Officers and men, Specialists, (Machine Gunners, Signallers, etc,) belonging to the 1/1st West Riding Division T.F. will be attached for instruction to the Battalions in the trenches for 24 hours, and will be placed for instruction with individuals responsible for carrying out the same duties they themselves have to perform, and will be instructed in every detail of this work. This party will arrive at Brigade Headquarters at 6.30 p.m. and will bring their own supplies for 24 hours, a blanket and waterproof sheet. The Brigade Machine Gun Officer will make all arrangements with the 1st Battalion Grenadier Guards..

Sheet 2.

Grenadier Guards, 2nd Battalion Scots Guards and 6th Battalion Gordon Highlanders for apportioning the Specialists to their several duties.

4. "E" Lines and F.A. Lines (No. 1. Subsection) will be under the command of the Officer Commanding 1st Battalion Grenadier Guards.

F.B. Lines (No. 2 Subsection) will be under the command of the Officer Commanding 2nd Battalion Scots Guards.

5. Guides (1.N.C.O. per Platoon) of the 21st Infantry Brigade will conduct the Battalions into the trenches, and meeting the leading companies on the RUE BACQUEROT at 8.30.p.m. as follows.:-

(a) Guides from 3 Companies and 1 Platoon of the 2nd Battalion Bedfordshire Regiment at the Cross Roads M.17. to conduct the 1st Battalion Grenadier Guards.

(b) Guides from 3 Platoons of the 2nd Battalion Bedfordshire Regiment and 1 Company of the 2nd Battalion Yorkshire Regiment at ~~Road junction~~ Cross Roads M.12.c. to conduct the 6th Battalion Gordon Highlanders less two companies.

(c) Guides from the 3 Companies of the 2nd Battalion Yorkshire Regiment at Road Junction M.6.d. 6.5. to conduct the 2nd Battalion Scots Guards.

6. The troops mentioned in para 2 (a) (b) and (c) will remain in the trenches until the night of the 24th April 1915, being relieved on that night by the 2nd Battalion Border Regiment, 2 Companies 6th Gordon Highlanders and 2nd Battalion Gordon Highlanders respectively.

7. Bombs, Periscopes, Very Pistols and Tools on Battalion charge will be taken to the trenches. R.E. Stores in the trenches will be taken over.

8. The Machine guns of the Brigade will relieve those

of......

Sheet 3.

of the 21st Infantry Brigade under the orders of the 20th Infantry Brigade Machine Gun Officer.

9. A Guard on the Depots of Ammunition and Rations in Forts F.2. and F.3. will be detailed by the Officer Commanding 1st Battalion Grenadier Guards and 6th Battalion Gordon Highlanders respectively, who will be responsible for the safe keeping of the stores.

10. Billets will be taken up as follows.:-
   2nd Battalion Border Regiment at FORT D' ESQUIN.
   2nd Battalion Gordon Highlanders at M.6.d. and M.12.b PICANTIN.
   6th Battalion Gordon Highlanders at WENGERIE M.17 and LA FLINQUE M.10.

11. The Quartermasters of the Brigade will meet the Quartermasters of thr 21st Infantry Brigade at the Battalion Headquarters of the units which they relieve at 9.30 a.m. on 21st April, 1915, afterwards shewing Quartermasters of the relieving units their old billets.

12. The transport will remain as at present.

13. The Road Guards at the Fork Road N. of Laventie, M.4.b. and at Pt 300 yards East of Cross Roads in LAVENTIE M.4.b. and the Guards on the Defended Localities No's 10. 11.12.13.14. and 17 in the RUE BACQUEROT now found by the Brigade will be relieved at 6 p.m. by the units of the 21st Infantrys Brigade.

14. Guards (strength 1. N.C.O. and 3 men) will relieve guards of the 21st Infantry Brigade at 6 p.m. to-morrow night as follows.:-
   (a) S.A.A. Store at M.17.d. by the 6th Battalion Gordon Highlanders.
   (b) R.E. Store at M.12.c. by the 2nd Battalion Border Regiment.
   (c) Road Picquet in M.4.c. LAVENTIE by the 2nd Battalion Border Regiment.

15. March Table.

(See sheet 4.)

Sheet 4.

Unit.	Starting Point.	Route.	Place of arrival
1st Battalion Grenadier Guards.	Billets. 7.45 p.m.	G,32,b, G.32.d. LAVENTIE. Ft D'ESQUIN. M.10.d. LA FLINQUE.M.17.a.	Cross Roads M.17.a.
6th Battalion Gordon Highlanders. less two Companies.	Billets. 7.45 p.m.	LE DRUMEZ. M.9.a. RUE DE PARADIS LAVENTIE. Ft D'ESQUIN.	Cross Roads. M.12.c.
2nd Battalion Scots Guards.	Billets. 8 p.m.	M.5.a. M.6.c.	M.6.d. 6.5.

16. 2nd Battalion Gordon Highlanders will exchange Billets with the Royal Scots Fusiliers reaching their new billets in M.6.d. and M.12.b. PICANTIN by 7.p.m.

IX. The 2nd Battalion Border Regiment will exchange billet with the 4th Battalion Cameron Highlanders reaching their new billets at FORT D'ESQUIN by 6 p.m.

The 2 Companies 6th Battalion Gordon Highlanders will exchange billets with 2nd Battalion Wiltshire Regiment reaching their Billets at WENGERIE M.17.a. and LA FLINQUE. M.10.a. at 6 p.m.

17. Beginning from the night of the 22nd April, 1915, a platoon from the 1/1st West Riding Infantry Brigade will be detailed for each successive 24 hours to every company in the Trenches, i.e., 10 platoons for 10 companies.

These platoons will reach ~~Battalion~~ Brigade Headquarters at 4 p.m. daily and will be directed to report to the Headquarters of the Battalion to which they will be attached forthwith. Officer's Commanding will send a N.C.O. to Brigade Headquarters at that hour for the purpose of guiding these platoons.

18. Brigade Headquarters will remain as at present at the
level

Sheet 5.

level Crossing LAVENTIE. The Brigadier-General Commanding 21st Infantry Brigade will be in command of the Lines until 7 a.m. 22nd April, 1915, and reports will be sent to him up to that hour.

[signature]

Major.
Brigade Major.
20th Infantry Brigade.

BRIGADE ORDERS No.18.
BY
Brigadier-General F.J. Heyworth. D.S.O.
Commanding 20th Infantry Brigade.

In the Field.
23rd April, 1915.

----

1. Brigade Order No. 15, para 17, dated 20th April, 1915, is cancelled.

2. The 1st Battalion Grenadier Guards, 2nd Battalion Scots Guards and 2 Companies of the 6th Battalion Gordon Highlanders will be relieved in their present positions in the trenches at 9 p.m. to-morrow night by the 2nd Battalion Border Regiment, 2nd Battalion Gordon Highlanders and 2 Companies 6th Battalion Gordon Highlanders respectively. The Officer Commanding 1st Battalion Grenadier Guards, 2nd Battalion Scots Guards, and 6th Battalion Gordon Highlanders will send guides (1 N.C.O. per Platoon) to meet the relieving companies at RUE BACQUEROT at 8.30 p.m. as follows.:-

(a) Guides from 4 Companies 1st Battalion Grenadier Guards at Cross Roads M.17. to conduct the 2nd Battalion Border Regiment.

(b) Guides from 2 Companies 6th Battalion Gordon Highlanders at Cross Roads M.12.c. to conduct the 2 relieving Companies of the 6th Battalion Gordon Highlanders.

(c) Guides from 4 Companies 2nd Battalion Scots Guards at Road Junction M.6.d.6.5. to conduct the 2nd Battalion Gordon Highlanders.

N.B.

(1). The Officer Commanding 2nd Battalion Gordon Highlanders will inform the Officer Commanding 2nd Battalion Scots Guards whether it is his intention to place 3 or 4 companies in the front line, if the former, the 1 company 2nd Battalion Gordon Highlanders is to be conducted to its
billets....

billets or dug outs by guides of the 2nd Battalion
Scots Guards.

(2) Reference Brigade Order No. 15 para 2., dated 20th
April, 1915, the following should be added to end of
paragraph.:- "The Officer Commanding 2nd Battalion Scots
Guards will also garrison Fort F.5. with 2 N.C.O's and
12 men".

3. (1) By 6 a.m. on the morning of the 28th inst the line
now held by the 20th Infantry Brigade will be occupied
by 1 and a half Battalions of the 21st Infantry Brigade
and 1 Battalion of the 1st West Riding Infantry Brigade.

(2) On the night of the 24/25th April, (To-morrow) the
2nd Battalion Border Regiment when relieving the 1st
Battalion Granadier Guards will take in with it 1 Platoon
of each Company of the 1st West Riding Brigade, leaving
1 Platoon of each company out of the trenches.
Billets for these Platoons will be notified later.

(3) Similarly on each of the nights 25/26th, 26/27th,
27/28th, one platoon of each Company 1st West Riding
Infantry Brigade will be substituted for 1 Platoon of
each Company of the 2nd Battalion Border Regiment, so that
by the morning of the 28th inst, the 2nd Battalion Border
Regiment will be entirely relieved by a Battalion of
the 1st West Riding Infantry Brigade.

(4) Officer Commanding 2nd Battalion Border Regiment will
make arrangements direct with the G.O.C. 1st West Riding
Brigade for guides to meet the relieving platoons on each
of the above mentioned nights at 9 p.m. except on the
night 24/25th April, when the platoons of the 1st West
Riding Brigade will report to the Officer Commanding 2nd
Battalion Border Regiment at 7.30 p.m.

(5) On the night of the 27/28th the 2nd Battalion Gordon
Highlanders and the 6th Battalion Gordon Highlanders
will be relieved by 1 and a half Battalions of the 21st

Brigade...

21st Infantry Brigade under instructions to be issued later.

4. Billets for to-morrow night will be notified later.

5. The relieving Battalions will take their own Machine Guns into the trenches, relieving those of the outgoing Battalions. They will ascertain the occupied emplacements by daylight. 1 Machine Gun of the 2nd Battalion Border Regiment will be relieved in the trenches on the night of the 24/25th by 1 Machine Gun of the 1st West Riding Brigade and similarly another Machine Gun will be relieved on the night of 25/26th.

6. Guards (Strength 1 N.C.O. and 3 men) will be relieved at 6 p.m. to-morrow as follows:-
  (a) S.A.A. Store at M.17.d. by the 5th Battalion Gordon Highlanders.
  (b) R.E. Store at M.12.c. by the 1st Battalion Grenadier Guards.
  (c) Road Picquet in M.4.c. LAVENTIE by the 1st Battalion Grenadier Guards.

7. Guards on the Depots of Ammunition and Rations in Forts F.2. and F.3. will be detailed by the Officer Commanding 2nd Battalion Border Regiment and 5th Battalion Gordon Highlanders respectively, who will be responsible for the safe keeping of the stores.

8. The Command of Sections, Battalions and companies will remain in the hands of the Officers of the 20th Infantry Brigade until the relief is completed, irrespective of rank.

9. No trouble must be spared to acquaint all ranks of the 1st West Riding Brigade with every detail of trench life, lines of approach, positions of defended points, hostile positions, etc.

10. CHURCH SERVICE.
  Church of England. Service will be held in the Field of the Grenade Company opposite Brigade Headquarters,

for........

for Brigade Headquarters Staff and 20th Infantry Brigade Grenade Company, at 9.30 a.m.

<u>Roman Catholic</u> Service will be held at the La Patronage, LAVENTIE, at 8.45 a.m.

<u>Presbyterian Church Service</u> will be held under arrangements made by the Officer's Commanding 2nd Battalion Scots Guards and 6th Battalion Gordon Highlanders

11. <u>FIELD GENERAL COURT-MARTIAL.</u>

The trial of No. 5809 Sergeant Malcolm MacDonald and No. 10048 Sergeant John Hardie, 2nd Battalion Gordon Highlanders, will take place at the Court-Martial Room, LA GORGUE, at 9.30 a.m. to-morrow, 24th instant.

The Officer Commanding 2nd Battalion Gordon Highlanders will arrange for the attendance of the necessary evidence.

The Officer Commanding 2nd Battalion Gordon Highlanders will detail a Captain to act as Member of the above Court.

The Officer Commanding 2nd Battalion Scots Guards will detail a Subaltern to act as Member of the above Court.

-----ooooo00000ooooo-----

Major.
Brigade Major.
20th Infantry Brigade.

No. 22.

BRIGADE ORDERS
BY

Brigadier-General F.J. Heyworth. D.S.O.
Commanding 20th Infantry Brigade.

Reference
FAUQUISSART - AUBERS
Sheet 1/10,000.

In the Field.
27th April, 1915.

-----ooooo0OOOOO0ooooo-----

1. The Brigade will take over "G" and "H" Subsections of the BAREILLY Brigade Lines to-night.

2. The Brigade will be relieved in the 7th Division lines to-night as follows.:-

    (a) "E" Lines by the 1/6th West Yorkshire Regiment.

    (b) "F" Lines by the 25th Infantry Brigade.

3. The Brigade will be disposed of as follows.:-

    (a) 2nd Battalion Scots Guards will take over "H" Subsection lines from the 4th Battalion Black Watch less 2 Companies, and 2 Companies 58th Rifles from the right of "E" Lines from the "2" of 24 to the South side of the "U" in the British Line in M.29.b.

    The Officer Commanding 2nd Battalion Scots Guards will also detail 3 N.C.O's and 25 men to garrison Forts C.4. and C.5 respectively.

    N.B. The line joining up the S.E. Points of the "U" shown on the map has been reclaimed, the old line being used as a support trench.

    Guides to meet the 2nd Battalion Scots Guards will be at the Southern Roads Junction at M.22.b. at 8.30 p.m.

    4 Platoons 1/8th West Yorkshire Regiment will accompany the 2nd Battalion Scots Guards, one platoon to be attached to each Company, these will report to the Officer Commanding 2nd Battalion Scots Guards at RED HOUSE at M.6.d. at 6 p.m.

    (b) The 1st Battalion Grenadier Guards will take over "G" subsection lines from the 41st Dogras from the right of the 2nd Battalion Scots Guards to the "T" of BRITISH.

The

Sheet 2.

The Officer Commanding 1st Battalion Grenadier Guards will also detail one Officer and 50 men to each of the Forts C.2. and C.3.

Guides to meet the 1st Battalion Grenadier Guards will be at "G" Subsection Headquarters, RUE BACQUEROT, M.22.c.9.10. at 8.30 p.m.

N.B. White Guides will be provided.

Four Platoons of the 1/7th West Yorkshire Regiment will report to the 1st Battalion Grenadier Guards at Battalion Headquarters, LAVENTIE, in M.10.b. at 6.p.m. These will accompany the 1st Battalion Grenadier Guards to the trenches, in the proportion of one platoon to each Company.

The Officer Commanding 1st Battalion Grenadier Guards will be in Command of "G" and "H" Subsections.

4. The Defended Localities in the RUE BACQUEROT will be relieved as follows.:-

Nos. 10. 11. 12. 13. by the West Riding Brigade.

Nos. 14 and 17. by the 1st London Regiment.

5. The 2nd Battalion Gordon Highlanders and the 6th Battalion Gordon Highlanders will be relieved in the trenches to-night by the 25th Infantry Brigade.

Guides (1 N.C.O. per platoon) from the 2nd Battalion Gordon Highlanders will meet the relieving Companies at Road Junction M.6.d.3.5. at 8 p.m.

Guides from the 6th Battalion Gordon Highlanders will meet the relieving Companies at Cross Roads M.12.c. at 8pm.

6. The 2nd Battalion Border Regiment will be relieved in the trenches by the 1/6th West Yorkshire Regiment to-night. Guides (1 N.C.O. per Platoon) from the 2nd Battalion Border Regiment will meet the relieving Companies at Cross Roads M.17.d. at 8.30 p.m.

7. BRIGADE RESERVE

(a) The 2nd Battalion Border Regiment will take up the

present.....

Sheet.3.

present Billets of the 1st Battalion Grenadier Guards at M.10.b.

(b) The 2nd Battalion Gordon Highlanders will take up the present Billets of the 2nd Battalion Scots Guards at M.6.d.

(c) The 6th Battalion Gordon Highlanders will take up the Billets in CAMERON LANE in M.21.b.

8. BATTALION HEADQUARTERS IN THE TRENCHES.

"H" Subsection at Farm 150 yards West of the B. of BACQUEROT M.23.a.

"G" Subsection about 400 yards W of Southern Road Junction in M.22.b.

9. AID POSTS. are situated at Battalion Headquarters of "G" and "H" Subsections.

10. RATIONS. for "G" and "H" Subsections can be taken down the tramway line.

11. The 1st Battalion Grenadier Guards and the 2nd Battalion Scots Guards will take the bombs sent down to-day into the trenches. The 2nd Battalion Border Regiment and 6th Battalion Gordon Highlanders will retain the bombs they have and take them into the trenches to-morrow.

12. Machine Guns will be taken into the Trenches under arrangements made by the Brigade Machine Gun Officer. Machine Guns are to march in front of the leading companies

13. The 1st Line Transport can accompany the 1st Battalion Grenadier Guards and the 2nd Battalion Scots Guards to their Section Headquarters.

14. ROUTE to Battalion Headquarters of Subsections.
1st Battalion Grenadier Guards will march via LA FLINQUE, Cross Roads, M.9.d. and CAMERON LANE.
2nd Battalion Scots Guards will march along the RUE BACQUEROT.

15. Two Control Posts (Strength 1 N.C.O. and 3 men) will

be ......

Sheet 4.

be detailed by the Officer Commanding 6th Battalion Gordon Highlanders at ROUGE CROIX and at PONT DU HEM. They will be mounted at 9 a.m. to-morrow.

16. The Officer Commanding 1st Battalion Grenadier Guards and 2nd Battalion Scots Guards will take over the supply Bi-carbonate of Soda now in the trenches.

17. The 1st Battalion Grenadier Guards and 2nd Battalion Scots Guards will receive from the units in "G" and "H" Subsections, all Trench Stores, Implements, and equipment, also surplus S.A.A. and Units regimental S.A.A. Reserve.

18. The Brigadier-General Commanding 20th Infantry Brigade will take over the Command of "G" and "H" Subsections at 10 p.m. on the night of the 28/29th April. Up till that hour the Brigadier-General Commanding BAREILLY Brigade will be in Command and will receive all reports.

The Brigadier-General Commanding 20th Infantry Brigade will retain Command of "E" and "F" Lines until 10 p.m. tommorrow night, at which hour he will hand over to the Brigadier-General Commanding 25th Infantry Brigade.

All Reports will be sent as usual to the present Brigade Headquarters which are at the Fork Road West of LAVENTIE LEVEL Crossing in M.34.c.

-----ooooo00000ooooo-----

Major.
Brigade Major.
20th Infantry Brigade.

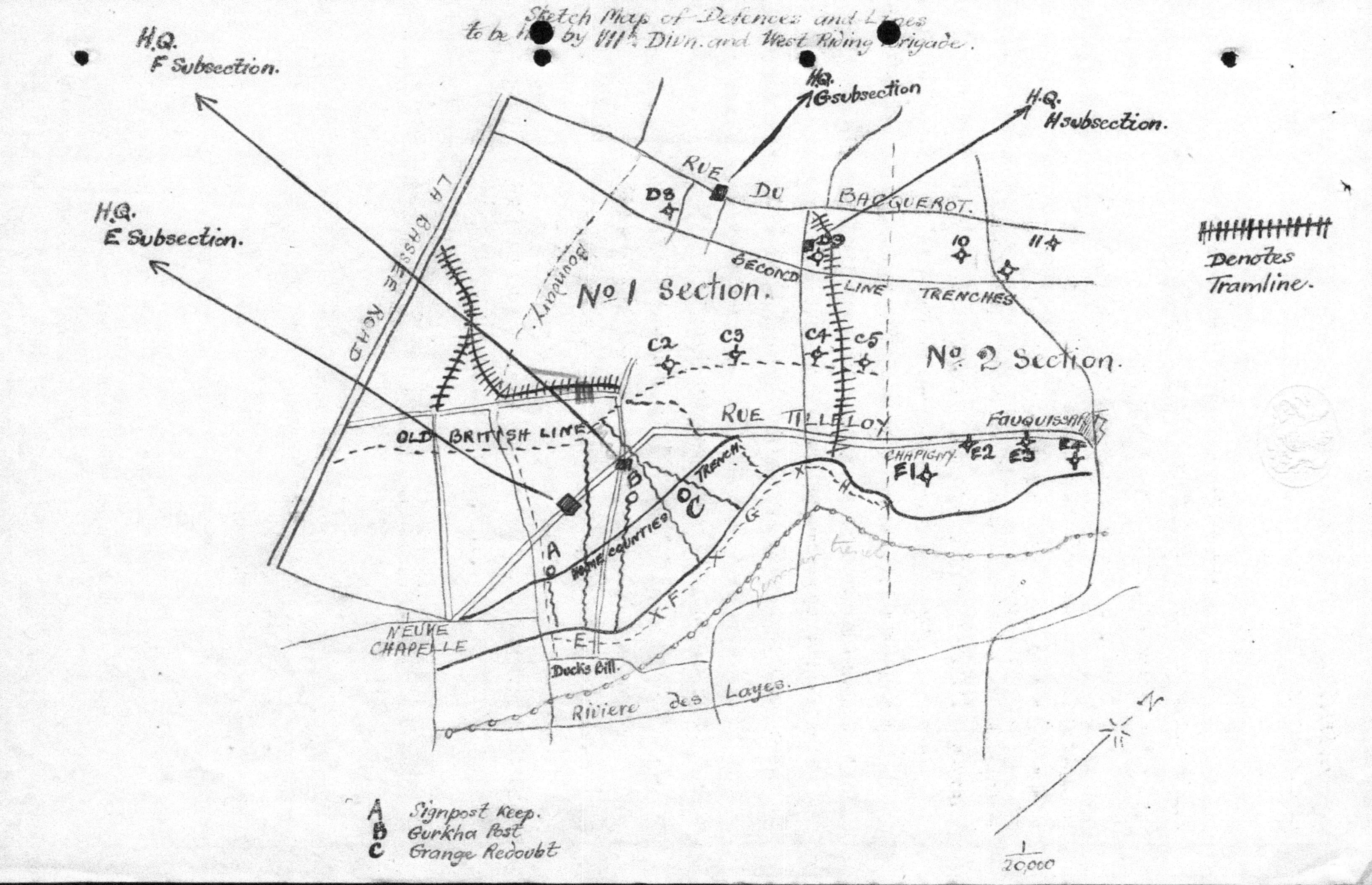

Sketch Map of Defences and Lines
to be held by VIIth Divn. and West Riding Brigade.
H.Q. F Subsection.
H.Q. E Subsection.
H.Q. G subsection
H.Q. H subsection.
RUE DU BACQUEROT.
D8
D9
10
11
SECOND LINE TRENCHES
No 1 Section.
No 2 Section.
Boundary
LA BASSEE ROAD
C2
C3
C4
C5
RUE TILLELOY
FAUQUISSART
CHAPIGNY
E1
E2
E3
E4
OLD BRITISH LINE
TRENCH
HOME COUNTIES
A
B
C
E
F
G
H
NEUVE CHAPELLE
Ducks Bill.
Riviere des Layes.
Denotes Tramline.
N
A Signpost Keep.
B Gurkha Post
C Grange Redoubt
1/20,000

No. 22.

BRIGADE ORDERS
BY
Brigadier-General F.J. Heyworth. D.S.O.
Commanding 20th Infantry Brigade.

Reference Map
FAUQUISSART - AUBERS
Sheet 1/10,000.

In the Field.
26th April, 1915.

------ooooOOOOoooo------

1. The Brigade will take over "E" and "F" Right Subsections of the BAREILLY BRIGADE Lines to-night.

2. From this date "E" and "F" Subsections of the Trenches will in future be known as "C" Section. "G" and "H" Subsections will in future be known as "D" Section.

3. (a) 2 Companies 6th Battalion Gordon Highlanders will take over the left half of "C" Section (the old "F" Subsection) from the right of the 1st Battalion Grenadier Guards as far as the S of BRITISH.

    Guides to meet the 6th Battalion Gordon Highlanders will be at the TRAM TERMINUS in the LA BASSEE Road. M.27.d. at 8.30 p.m. Guides will be British.

    The 6th Battalion Gordon Highlanders will march by via the ROUGE CROIX to TRAMWAY TERMINUS in the LA BASSEE Road.

    (b) 2 Platoons of the West Riding Brigade will accompany the 6th Battalion Gordon Highlanders, two platoons of the latter not being withdrawn.

    The detachment of the West Riding Brigade will report to the Officer Commanding 6th Battalion Gordon Highlanders in CAMERON LANE. M.15.c. and d. and M.21.b. at 6 p.m. to-night.

    (c) The 2nd Battalion Border Regiment will take over the right half of "C" Section (the old "E" Subsection) from the S of BRITISH to the road inclusive by the N of LINE.

    Guides to meet the 2nd Battalion Border Regiment will meet at the TRAM TERMINUS in the LA BASSEE Road. M.27.d. at 9.30 p.m.

Sheet 2.

ROUTE.

2nd Battalion Border Regiment will march via LA FLINQUE, M.15. PONT DU HEM, ROUGE CROIX to TRAM TERMINUS on the LA BASSEE ROAD.

4 Platoons of the West Riding Brigade will accompany the 2nd Battalion Border Regiment in the proportion of 1 platoon to each Company for instructional purposes.

These platoons will report to the Officer Commanding 2nd Battalion Border Regiment in LAVENTIE in M.10.b. at 6.30 p.m. to-night. Four Platoons of the Border Regiment will not go into the trenches.

4. BRIGADE RESERVE.

(a) The 2nd Battalion Gordon Highlanders will move their Billets from the neighbourhood of PICANTIN to the LA BASSEE Road M.8, and take over the Billets of the 125th Rifles at 6 p.m.

(b) 2 Companies 6th Battalion Gordon Highlanders will remain in CAMERON LANE.

(c) The four platoons, 2nd Battalion Border Regiment will be billetted in CAMERON LANE, arriving there not earlier than 8.30 p.m.

5. (a) 4 Platoons of the West Riding Brigade will relieve to-night 4 Platoons of the 1/8th West Yorkshire Regiment now attached to the 2nd Battalion Scots Guards.

Guides of the 2nd Battalion Scots Guards will meet these platoons at Scots Guards Battalion Headquarters, FARM South of Road Junction in M.23.a. at 7.45 p.m.

(b) 4 Platoons of the West Riding Brigade will relieve to-night the 4 platoons of the 1/7th West Yorkshire Regiment now attached to the 1st Battalion Grenadier Guards.

Guides of the 1st Battalion Grenadier Guards will meet these platoons at the RUINED Farm, North of the RUE DE BACQUEROT North of the R in the RUE de BACQUEROT, Headquarters 1st Grenadier Guards at 8.15 p.m. to-night.

Sheet 3.

to-night.

6. AID POSTS. will be as follows:-

"E" Lines at M.29.

"F" Lines at Subsection Headquarters (6th Battalion Gordon Highlanders.)

7. WATER CARTS.

Water Carts for "C" Section ("E" and "F" Subsection) can march to PONT LOGY, thence along the TILLELOY ROAD to point SOUTH of the old "E" Subsection Headquarters, (2nd Battalion Border Regiment) behind the hedge.

8. 1st Line Transport of the 2nd Battalion Border Regiment and the 6th Battalion Gordon Highlanders will march via LA FLINQUE, M.15. POND DU HEM, to ROUGE CROIX, not going further than the last named place.

9. Rations for "C" Lines will be taken along the Tramway Line on to the LA BASSEE Road.

10. The Officers Commanding 2nd Battalion Border Regiment and 6th Battalion Gordon Highlanders will take over all trench Stores, Implements, etc., also surplus S.A.A. and Units Regimental S.A.A. Reserve.

11. MACHINE GUNS.
(a) The Officer's Commanding 1st Battalion Grenadier Guards and the 2nd Battalion Scots Guards will leave three Machine Guns in the trenches, the remaining gun to be placed in reserve at Battalion Headquarters.

(b) The Officer Commanding 6th Battalion Gordon Highlanders will take 2 Guns to the trenches.

(c) The Officer Commanding 2nd Battalion Border Regiment will have to take all their Machine Guns to the trenches.

(d) The Guns of the 2nd Battalion Gordon Highlanders and 2 Guns of the 6th Battalion Gordon Highlanders will remain with their units.

Machine Guns will march at the head of the leading Companies.

12.....

Sheet. 4.

12. The Brigade Ammunition Reserve is situated on the LA BASSEE Road at the BAREILLY INFANTRY BRIGADE Headquarters in Square M.27.b.

13. The Brigadier-General Commanding 20th Infantry Brigade will assume Command of "C" and "D" Sections as soon as the relief is completed.

Brigade Headquarters will remain as at present.

-----ooooOOOOoooo-----

Major.
Brigade Major.
20th Infantry Brigade.

No. 23.

BRIGADE ORDERS
BY
Brigadier-General F.J. Heyworth. D.S.O.
Commanding 20th Infantry Brigade.

In the Field.
29th April, 1915.

-----ooooo OOOOO ooooo-----

1. The 14 Platoons of the West Riding Infantry Brigade attached to the Brigade will be withdrawn to-night.

2. 2 Platoons of the West Riding Infantry Brigade will relieve the 2 Platoons of the same Brigade with the 6th Battalion Gordon Highlanders.to-night.

   Guides (1. N.C.O. per Platoon) of the 6th Battalion Gordon Highlanders will meet the above party at M.27.d. at TRAM TERMINUS on the LA BASSEE Road at 7.45 p.m. to-night.

3. 2 Platoons of the West Riding Infantry Brigade will relieve the 2 Platoons of the same Brigade attached to the 2nd Battalion Border Regiment.

   Guides (1.N.C.O. per Platoon) of the 2nd Battalion Border Regiment will meet these platoons at M.27.d. TRAM TERMINUS on the LA BASSEE Road at 8.15 p.m. to-night.

4. The remaining 2 Platoons of the West Riding Infantry Brigade attached to the 2nd Battalion Border Regiment will be relieved by 2 Platoons 2nd Battalion Border Regiment to-night under arrangements to be made by the Officer Commanding 2nd Battalion Border Regiment.

5. No Territorial Force Troops will be attached to the 1st Battalion Grenadier Guards and 2nd Battalion Scots Guards to-night.

-----ooooo OOOOO ooooo-----

Major.
Brigade Major.
20th Infantry Brigade.

No. 23.

BRIGADE ORDERS

BY

Brigadier-General F.J. Heyworth. D.S.O.
Commanding 20th Infantry Brigade.

In the Field.
29th April, 1915.

-----oooooOOOOOooooo------

1. The 14 Platoons of the West Riding Infantry Brigade attached to the Brigade will be withdrawn to-night.

2. 2 Platoons of the West Riding Infantry Brigade will relieve the 2 Platoons of the same Brigade with the 6th Battalion Gordon Highlanders to-night.

Guides (1 N.C.O. per Platoon) of the 6th Battalion Gordon Highlanders will meet the above party at M.27.d. at TRAM TERMINUS on the LA BASSEE Road at 7.45 p.m. to-night.

3. 2 Platoons of the West Riding Infantry Brigade will relieve the 2 Platoons of the same Brigade attached to the 2nd Battalion Border Regiment.

Guides (1. N.C.O. per Platoon) of the 2nd Battalion Border Regiment will meet these platoons at M.27.d. TRAM TERMINUS on the LA BASSEE Road at 8.15 p.m. tonight.

4. The remaining 2 platoons of the West Riding Infantry Brigade attached to the 2nd Battalion Border Regiment will be relieved by 2 Platoons of the 2nd Battalion Border Regiment to-night under arrangements to be made by the Officer Commanding 2nd Battalion Border Regiment.

5. No Territorial Force Troops will be attached to the 1st Battalion Grenadier Guards and 2nd Battalion Scots Guards to-night.

-----oooooOOOOOooooo------

Major.
Brigade Major.
20th Infantry Brigade.

No. 24.

BRIGADE ORDERS
BY

Brigadier-General F.J. Heyworth. D.S,O.
Commanding 20th Infantry Brigade.

In the Field.
30th April, 1915.

-----ooooo@@@@ooooo-----

N I L.

-----ooooo@@@@ooooo-----

[signature] Major.
Brigade Major.
20th Infantry Brigade.

No. 25.

BRIGADE ORDERS
BY

Brigadier-General F.J. Heyworth. D.S.O.
Commanding 20th Infantry Brigade.

In the Field.
1st May, 1915.

-----ooooo::::::ooooo-----

1. **RELIEFS.**

The 1st Battalion Grenadier Guards will be relieved in the trenches to-night by the 2nd Battalion Gordon Highlanders, under arrangements made by the Officer's Commanding concerned.

The 1st Battalion Grenadier Guards will take over the billets of the 2nd Battalion Gordon Highlanders in the LA BASSEE Road.

The Officer Commanding 6th Battalion Gordon Highlanders will withdraw one company from the trenches replacing it with his two companies now in Divisional Reserve.

-----ooooo::::::ooooo-----

Major.
Brigade Major.
20th Infantry Brigade.

No. 27.

BRIGADE ORDERS

BY

Brigadier-General F.J. Heyworth. D.S.O.
Commanding 20th Infantry Brigade.

In the Field.
4th May, 1915.

----oooo@@@@oooo----

NIL.

----oooo@@@@oooo----

Major.
Brigade Major.
20th Infantry Brigade.

APPENDICES.

M.G./81.

G.S.,

With reference to my visits to the French Armies, I am now in possession of the details of their new Machine Gun Organization.

All machine guns are taken away from the battalion commander and incorporated into a company, under the command of a captain. Attached herewith schedule showing constitution of a Company.

I had the opportunity of discussing this organization with officers of all ranks from the army commanders down to the lieutenants in charge of sections, and they are all much in favour of the system.

The chief advantages, according to them, are as follows :-
- (i). Uniform system of training.
- (ii). Co-ordinated action.
- (iii). Less chance of conflicting orders.
- (iv). The Brigadier knows how his guns are being used and where he can lay his hand on a unit capable of great fire effect on a small front.
- (v). The guns are handled by an officer, experienced in the particular arm, who has been trained for his specific work.
- (vi). Guns can be used wherever required and not where they happen to be, as was the case formerly.

These arguments in favour of machine gun companies apply with equal force to our own army and, perhaps even more so, as the French machine gun instruction is more universal than ours and their officers are more highly trained.

3-4-15.
Sd. C.D.Baker Carr, Major,
Commandant, Machine Gun School.

Present organization.

of a machine gun company for a regiment of infantry.

8 Guns.
----

1 Captain.
2 Lieutenants.
7 Sergeants.
14 Corporals.
119 men.

16 Draught horses.
36 pack mules.

4 wagons.

30,000 rounds of ammunition per gun is carried.

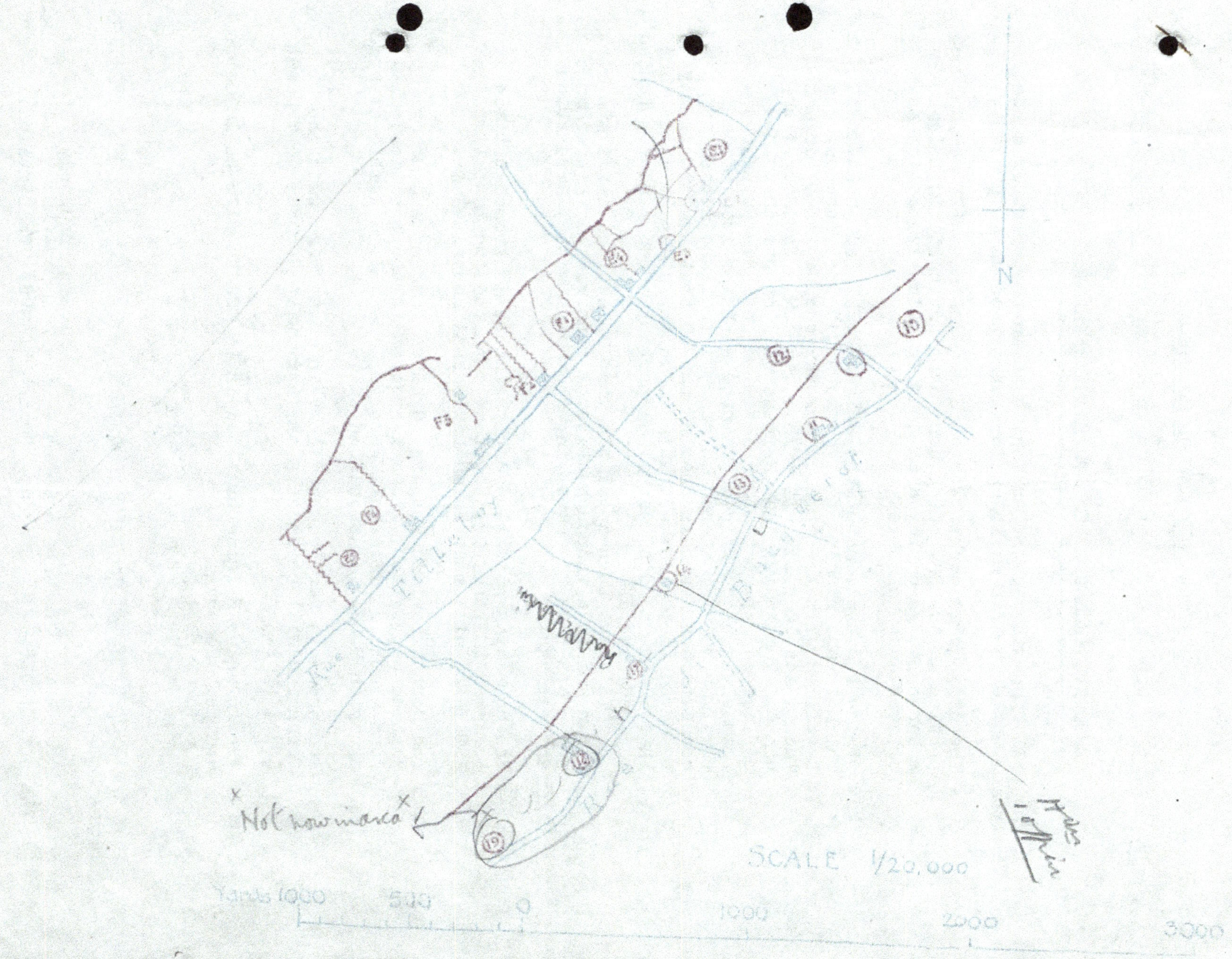
N
Not now inaccô
SCALE 1/20,000
Yards 1000 500 0 1000 2000 3000

CIRCULAR MEMORANDUM No. 16.

CONFIDENTIAL (To be substituted for Circular Memorandum No 14. d/24-3-15).

DEFENSIVE ARRANGEMENTS FOR PRESENT PHASE.

The following will be the arrangements in the event of a hostile attack while the 7th Division is distributed as at present.

(a). The Brigade in occupation of E and F lines will retain such portion as the Brigadier considers advisable in Brigade reserve, to be employed in counter offensive action as circumstances dictate.

(b). Of the 3 Battalions of the Brigade billeted in LAVENTIE, which is not finding the garrison for the trenches, one battalion will be detailed for the occupation of defended localities 10 - 11 - 12 - 13 - 14 - 17. The Brigadier General Commanding that Brigade will ensure that the officers of the battalion detailed for this duty make themselves thoroughly acquainted with the localities they may be called upon to occupy; that the method of occupation of each is thought out so that the troops may be moved in to them without confusion by day or night; and that the methods of mutual support by cross fire is studied and understood.
   He will also be responsible that these localities are kept clean and in a thorough state of repair, and that arrangements are made for supplying them with water, ammunition and rations.

(c). The remaining battalions of the above-mentioned Brigade billeted in LAVENTIE, together with the two battalions in ESTAIRES, will be held in Divisional Reserve.

(d). The Northumberland Hussars, Cyclist Company and Motor Machine Gun Battery (less 1 section in the trenches) will form a Mobile Divisional Reserve, and will assemble at road junction G.27.c. when called out.

(e). Arrangements for the Artillery in connection with the foregoing will be made by the Brigadier-General Commanding Royal Artillery.

(f). The Infantry Brigade billeted in LA GORGUE will be in Corps and Army Reserve.

F. Gathorne Hardy, Lt-Col:
7th April, 1915.   General Staff, 7th Division.

PROGRAMME OF TRAINING.

Issued are No. 8/4/15

During the time the Brigade is out of the trenches the Brigadier General Commanding wishes the following to be carried out.:-

(1) Route Marching, attention being paid to march discipline.

(2)
a. Attack of an enemy's trench.
b. Formation of bombing parties.
c. Parties to block trenches.
d. Working parties practising reversing the parapet immediately the trench is gained.
e. Special parties to be told off to make good the flanks
f. Continuous practice in bringing machine guns up quickly and in getting them into action.

(3) To find out and practice the best means of keeping up communication by day, both to the rear and to the flanks, assuming that no movement above ground is possible. The 7th Division state that the Indian Division has been able to communicate by day with electric torches. This method is to be given a good trial. The Brigadier would be glad if Battalion Commanders would suggest some other methods, communication by day being all important. Communication by means of orderlies is more than likely to fail owing to possible casualties, and it is therefore imperative that some reliable means of communication shall be devised.

(4)
a. Musketry.
b. Bayonet Exercises.
c. Physical Drill.
d. Setting up drill.

(5) Companies are to be practised in crossing wire by means of rabbit netting vide circular letter No. 20/27D of 7th April, 1915.

(6) Companies are to be practised in jumping ditches and other obstacles.

(7) Each Battalion will form a "Corps of Snipers" consisting of 16 - 20 picked shots under two specially selected N.C.O's. This Corps will be trained and will operate as a separate unit. In the trenches, their sole duties

duties will be to keep down the enemy's snipers. During an action the "Snipers Corps" will probably be best utilized on both flanks of their Battalion and will endeavour to locate stalk down and silence hostile machine guns or pick off snipers hidden in houses, etc., who may be causing loss to our troops. These men must be trained in making good snipers loopholes, and in taking advantage of every kind of cover such a hollow trees, haystacks, shell holes, etc., for the purposes of sniping.

Brigade Headquarters.
8th April, 1915.

Major.
Brigade Major.
20th Infantry Brigade.

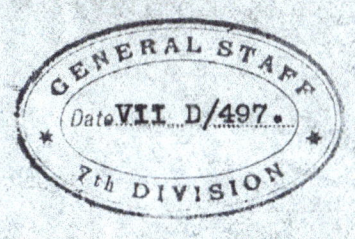

20th Infantry Brigade.
~~21st Infantry Brigade.~~
~~22nd Infantry Brigade.~~

    Will you please express your views on the subject dealt with in attached Memorandum and forward to this office with least possible delay.

Div. H.Q.
8th April, 1915.

for. Lieut-Colonel,
General Staff, 7th Division.

IVth Corps. 556 (G)
VIID/497.

Headquarters,
7th Division.
================

Will you please submit your views, as early as possible, on the attached proposals for the organization of a Brigade Machine Gun Company.

                              Sd.   P.Game, Major
                                      for Brigadier-General,
8th April,1915.   General Staff, IVth Corps.

Formation of a Machine Gun Company in an Infantry Brigade.

1. A proposal has been put forward that each Infantry Brigade should form a machine gun company, by taking from units those additional guns which have been allotted to them owing to the increase in War Establishments. These guns and personnel would be formed into a company under an officer and act directly under the orders of the Brigade Commander.

2. The arguments put forward in favour of the proposal are :-

(a). There would be greater uniformity in training and consequently better tactical handling, as officers and men would be greater experts in machine gun tactics.

(b) There would be better co-operation between machine guns and the guns could be more easily found when wanted.

(c). Reliefs could be easily arranged.

(d). The company would form a mobile reserve in the hands of the Brigade Commander.

(e). There would be less chance of confusion of orders as the company commander would receive them direct from the Brigadier.

(f). The Germans have this organization and are better machine gunners than we are.

As regards (d) and (e) it should be noted that our present system allows of guns being brigaded when desired by the Brigadier, under a special officer.

3. On the other hand -

(a) The proposal involves the addition of 5 officers in a brigade and good regimental officers are scarce. The present brigade machine gun officer is excluded in the W.E. of the battalion from which he is taken. It also involves the provision of extra N.C.O's.

(b) It adds another unit to be administered by the brigade, and it has been represented that the present brigade staffs find difficulty in dealing with their enlarged brigades.

(c) Alterations in our existing organization when we expect to be fighting are difficult to carry out.

(d). There will be two systems of handling machine guns i.e. those with units and those under Brigade Commanders.

(e). There will be difficulty in administration i.e., provision of clothing and equipment, rations, etc., when 4, 5, or 6 different units are involved.

(f) /

(f). There will be difficulty in replacing casualties in the company.

As regards (e) and (f), the Germans have 1 Machine Gun Company per Regiment i.e., the 13th Company, and administration is carried out by the Regimental Staff. This could not be done under our organization.

4. A suggested establishment for the Company is attached, Personnel in excess of that laid down in War Establishment is underlined in Red.

5. A copy of a report by the Commandant Machine Gun School who has recently visited the French Armies is attached.

6. The question is whether the drawbacks enumerated will be more than compensated for by increased efficiency in the Field.

BRIGADE MACHINE GUN COMPANY.

WAR ESTABLISHMENT.

Personnel.	Horses.	Bicycles.
<u>Headquarters.</u> 1 Captain. 8 other ranks.	1 Riding. 2 Hy Draught.	2.
*<u>Each Section.</u> ⁰ 1 Subaltern. 18 other ranks.	4 draught.	1.

* The number of sections in a company varies, and is equivalent to the number of battalions in a brigade.

⁰ 1 Sub.", 1 Serj', 1 Cyclist, 1 Batman surplus to W.E.

TRANSPORT.

	Vehicles.	Drivers.	Horses. Draught.	Hy Draught.	Total.
<u>Headquarters.</u> Wagon G.S., for supplies, tools &c.	1	1	-	2	2
<u>Each Section.</u> Wagons, 1 bd, G.S. for 2 M.G. tripods and ammunition.	1	1	2	-	2
Carts, S.A.A.	1	1	2	-	2

Subject:- Communication.

Headquarters. 1st Bn Grenadier Guards

20/287

The Brigadier-General Commanding has decided that the following system is to come into force from Wednesday 14th instant.:-

1. All Battalion Signalling Communication and as well the Signallers belonging to the Battalions of the Brigade will be placed under the control of the Brigade Signalling Officer for operations and training.

2. The N.C.O's and men will be responsible to the Brigade Signalling Officer for the charge and care of the instruments.

3. Officers Commanding Battalions will furnish a nominal roll of al the Signallers of their Battalions.
They will be billetted and rationed as a separate detachment for operations and training, but for the purposes and discipline and pay will remain on the roll of their companies.

4. The Brigade Signalling Officer will detail men required for daily duty and he is also responsible for their relief but at all times Officer's Commanding will have the first call on their senior Signalling N.C.O.

5. The Brigade Signalling Officer will be responsible for laying and maintaining all lines right up to the trenches.

6. The hours of relief will be arranged so as not to coincide with the relief of the troops in the trenches, in order to ensure that telephone communication may be at its best during these hours.

7. It will be also the concern of the Brigade Signalling Officer to train additional men as signallers in order that casualties may be speedily replaced.

                         Major.
                         Brigade Major.
9th April, 1915.   20th Infantry Brigade.

20th. Infantry Brigade.
~~21st. Infantry Brigade.~~
~~22nd. Infantry Brigade.~~

It has been suggested that in view of the difficulty of transmitting messages during operations and the present scarcity of signallers, all Officers should be instructed in a simple code, to include some ten or twelve of the most probable situations; these messages being sent by waving a circular disc.

The messages decided on might include such situations as :-
"Our artillery firing short".
"Am enfiladed by a machine gun",
etc.

Will you please consider whether this suggestion is of any practical value and if the answers are in the affirmative the scheme will be further elaborated.

F. Gathorne Hardy
Lieut-Colonel,

Div.H.Q.
9th. April, 1915.
General Staff, 7th.Division.

2

All 5 Battalions

Please forward a reply as quickly as possible with any suggestions you may wish to make.

9/April/15

Headquaters.

7th Division.

With reference to your 7/D/497 dated 8th April 1915, I forward herewith my remarks.:-

1. I am in favour of the proposal to form a Brigade Machine Gun Company in each Infantry Brigade, but the organisation suggested in the above quoted letter does not appear to be sound because.

(1) The existence of the Battalion Machine Guns as distinct from the Brigade Machine Guns would possibly result in loss of fire effect.

(2) At this stage of the war it will be difficult to maintain the establishment of both separate units in Officers, N.C.O's, and men.

(3) In order to obtain the best material from Battalions it would have to be distinctly stated whether the Brigade Company or Battalion Machine Gun Sections are to have the first call on N.C.O's and men as they become trained, otherwise Officer's Commanding will naturally look upon the Battalion Machine Guns as their first concern.

(4) The arguments used in favour of the proposal are to a great extent those advocated for another system, i.e. the French system.

(5) Possible divergencies of views in the system of training.

2. I respectfully suggest however that all Machine Guns (4 per Battalion) should be brigaded into the Brigade Machine Gun Company and placed for operations in the hands of the Brigadier.

In this manner many of the objections would disappear.

(1) There would be one command only.

(2) There

(2) There would be a saving in the numbers of Officers required, because if all the guns were handed over, the existing Machine Gun Officers would accompany them and the additional ones would not be required by the Battalions.

(3) In case of Battalions moving to the assault it would be possible for an Officer Commanding to be given the four guns of his own Battalion, whilst the Brigadier retained intact the guns of the Battalions in Brigade Reserve for any specific role.

(4) The equalizing of the personnel of machine guns, supposing one portion to have suffered more severely than another, would be facilitated.

(5) Increased efficiency in the field would be obtained without splitting up Regimental Units.

3. I strongly recommend that if a change is to be made, the French system should be adopted or the Battalion Commander be left with his four machine guns.

LWood

Brigade Headquarters.
10th April, 1915.

Lieutenant-Colonel.
for Brigadier-General.
Commanding 20th Infantry Brigade

Headquarters.

VIIth Division.

With reference to your VII/D/500, dated 9th April, 1915, I have to report as follows.:-

The suggestion to institute a simple code of signals for use during operations appears to be feasible, but it will be necessary to reduce the number of messages to a minimum, as the difficulty does not lie so much in their despatch as in the difficulty in men when under fire being able to see them sufficiently well in order to read them without error.

Another dificulty presents itself in the fact that to attract the attention of troops in rear is not an easy matter

A solution of the latter and incidentally one which might prove of great value in getting over the present difficulty of transmitting messages is suggested as follows

PROJECTING WRITTEN MESSAGES FROM A VERY PISTOL.

1. To prepare the pistol, withdraw the cardboard disc the wad and metal cannister from the cartridge. The cannister is half emptied of the powder which normally causes the flare. A plug of mud about ½ inch thick is then placed against the powder in the cannister which is then ready to hold a written message. A flap of/strong adhesive plaster sealing it.

TO FIRE A MESSAGE.

2. Roll up the message, place it in the cannister, seal the mouth of it with the adhesive plaster which is already attached.

Place cannister in cartridge with the message at the front end.

Insert wad and disc and ram home. The cartridge is now fired in the normal way.

3..........

3. During the latter part of its flight the cannister flares brightly and can be easily seen in the strongest sunlight.

The flames cease as it reaches the ground. Its course and the place where it pitches is thus very easily seen.

The remains of the cannister, the back of which is burnt are picked up, the message is taken out and can be re-fired in the same way for a further distance.

4. <u>Range</u> from 100 to 150 yards, varying in the quality of the cartridge. With a double charge, 150 yards is easily obtainable.

5. <u>Accuracy of aim</u> depends on practice, but it should be possible to train men and fire within 6 yards of any given point.

6. I watched experiments this morning and am of opinion that with practice and with a more suitable holder for the message with a slightly heavier charge, and with a rudimentary sight ensuring consistent elevation, this method might become very accurate and speedy.

In otherwords the system should be elaborated and improved, in order that an issue of a standard cartridge may be made.

A message fired 150 yards was replaced in another pistol and fired again a similar distance. The quickest rate to receive a message at 300 yards was 1 minute 10 seconds.

The lightness and portability of the pistol is in its favour.

The suggestion is put forward by Captain G.C. Moss Grenadier Guards, temporarily in command of the 6th Battalion Gordon Highlanders.

Brigade Headquarters.
12th April, 1915.

JWood
Lieutenant-Colonel.
for Brigadier-General.
Commanding 20th Infantry Brigade.

Headquarters.
VIIth Division.

With reference to your VII/D/500, dated 9th April, 1915, I have to report as follows.:-

The suggestion to institute a simple code of signals for use during operations appears to be feasible, but it will be necessary to reduce the number of messages to a minimum, as the difficulty does not lie so much in their despatch as in the difficulty for men when under fire being able to see them sufficiently well in order to read them without error.

Another dificulty presents itself in the fact that to attract the attention of troops in rear is not an easy matter

A solution of the latter and incidentally one which might prove of great value in getting over the present difficulty of transmitting messages is suggested as follows

PROJECTING WRITTEN MESSAGES FROM A VERY PISTOL.

1. To prepare the pistol, withdraw the cardboard disc the wad and metal cannister from the cartridge. The cannister is half emptied of the powder which normally causes the flare. A plug of mud about ½ inch thick is then placed against the powder in the cannister which is then ready to hold a written message. A flap of strong adhesive plaster sealing it.

TO FIRE A MESSAGE.

2. Roll up the message, place it in the cannister, seal the mouth of it with the adhesive plaster which is already attached.

Place cannister in cartridge with the message at the front end.

Insert wad and disc and ram home. The cartridge is now fired in the normal way.

3.........

3. During its flight the cannister flares brightly and can be easily seen in the strongest sunlight.

The flames cease ~~just before~~ as it reaches the ground. Its course and the place where it pitches is thus very easily seen.

The remains of the cannister, the back of which is burnt are picked up, the message is taken out and can be re-fired in the same way for a further distance.

4. <u>Range</u> from 100 to 150 yards, varying in the quality of the cartridge. With a double charge, 150 yards is easily obtainable.

5. <u>Accuracy of aim</u> depends on practice, but it should be possible to train men and fire within 6 yards of any given point.

6. I watched experiments this morning and am of opinion that with practice and with a more suitable holder for the message with a slightly heavier charge, and with a rudimentary sight ensuring consistent elevation, this method might become very accurate and speedy.

In otherwords the system should be elaborated and improved, in order that an issue of a standard cartridge may be made.

A message fired 150 yards was replaced in another pistol and fired again a similar distance. The quickest rate to receive a message at 300 yards was 1 minute 10 seconds.

The lightness and portability of the pistol is in its favour.

The suggestion is put forward by Captain G.C. Moss Grenadier Guards, temporarily in command of the 6th Battalion Gordon Highlanders.

Brigade Headquarters.
12th April, 1915.

Ellwood
Lieutenant-Colonel.
for Brigadier-General.
Commanding 20th Infantry Brigade.

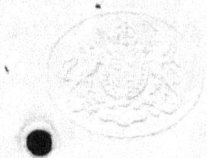

To H.Q. 20th Brigade.
From O.C. 6th Gordon Highlanders
11-4-15.

PROJECTING WRITTEN MESSAGES FROM A "VERY" PISTOL

1.) In continuation of my report of yesterday I can now state the results of further experiments

2.) The best results are obtained by withdrawing the card board disc – the wad – and the metal cannister from the cartridge. The cannister is half emptied of the powder which normally caused the blue flare.
A plug of mud about ¼" thick is then placed against the powder in the cannister which is then ready for holding a written message, a flap of adhesive plaster sealing it.

omit ~~A stock of cartridges so treated should be carried with the wads and cardboard discs separately.~~

3.) To fire a message
Roll up the message place it in cannister. Seal the mouth of it with the adhesive plaster which is already attached.
Place cannister in cartridge with the message at the front end.
Insert wad and disc and ram home.
The cartridge is now fired in the normal way

4.) During its flight the canister flares brightly and can easily be seen in the strongest sunlight
The flames cease just before it reaches the ground
Its course and the place where it pitches is thus very easily seen.
The remains of the canister, the back of which is burst, are picked up; the message is taken out and can be refired in the same way for a further distance.

5.) The consistency of range is good and it can be gauged as about 175 yards as a rule.

omit 6.) Accuracy of aim during the experiments today carried by 2 Lt. Sellar of this Bn. the messages fell as a rule within 6 yards of the intended recipient at a range of 175 yards.

7.) Experiments were made in throwing messages for long distances.
An intermediate man was placed at 170 yards. He was armed with a pistol.
4 messages were fired at him.
The furthest from him fell within 8 yards.
The messages were taken by him, placed in fresh canisters and refired a further distance of 160 yards.
The messages were here taken out of the canister by another man. The messages were readable.
Times were taken from the moment that the message was written to the moment when it was opened ready to read at the further point.
The quickest rate was 1 min. 10 sec
The longest rate was 2 min —
An orderly took to run the same distance 1 min 20 sec.

8.) It is believed that with practice this manner of throwing messages might be reduced to a matter of great accuracy and speed

9.) The use of a more suitable holder for the messages. A slightly heavier charge, and a rudimentary sight to ensure a consistent elevation would greatly improve the system.

10.) The lightness and portability of the VERY PISTOL and ammunition are in its favour.
The novelty of the system would probably render it unlikely that the enemy would realize that a system of written and not visual signalling was being adopted.

G. C. G. Moss
Capt
Grenadier Guards
Commanding
6th Bn Gordon Highlanders

SKETCH ATTACHED

Reference 7th Div. No 7/D/500.

To H.Q. 70th Brigade.

I think that the suggested method of signalling might prove of great value as did the now discarded signals "I am short of ammunition" etc.

The great difficulty in such cases is usually experienced in attracting the attention of troops in rear.

G. C. S. Moss
Capt.
commanding
6th Bn. Gordon Highlanders

INSTRUCTION FOR ESCORT OF BOMBERS.

The Brigadier wishes all men to be trained in assisting Bombers who, when clearing a trench are working from traverse to traverse, and counter-bombing against an enemy attempting to do this.

It is essential that one or two men with bayonets should always assist bombers during the operations, thus giving the bombers greater confidence. Their duties will be as follows.:-

1. To cover and protect bombers from any rush on the part of the enemy.
2. To rush forward ahead of the bombers as soon as the bomb has been thrown and capture that position of the trench - by bayoneting any of the enemy who are still found there.

This procedure should be adopted from one traverse to another.

All men detailed for escort to bombers or men who happen to find themselves in a trench where our bombers are clearing out the enemy, should be trained to know instinctively what to do so as to be able to act without hesitation or delay.

The following plan is illustrated as a guide.

[Diagram: trench plan with annotations — "Bayonet men", "Direction of attack", "Enemy", "Bomber", "N.C.O.", "Bomber"]

Brigade Headquarters.
12th April, 1915.

Major.
Brigade Major.
20th Infantry Brigade.

Officer Commanding.
   1st Battalion Grenadier Guards.
   2nd Battalion Scots Guards.
   2nd Battalion Gordon Highlanders.

      With reference to Divisional Order No. 189, para 2., giving the percentages of men inoculated in the 7th Division, the Brigadier directs me to say that while the precentages of two Battalions in the Brigade are all that can be desired, he trusts that you will take steps to put this matter on a more satisfactory footing. It need hardly be pointed out that the personal influence of Company officers should be sufficient to persuade men who are still reluctant to be inoculated though at the same time it should be explained to them that

      (1) Statistics in past wars as well as the present prove beyond doubt the efficacy of the treatment, the result of which they can see for themselves.

      (2) Men who refuse to be treated become a danger to their own comrades by the possibility of spreading the disease.

      (3) Every effort should be made in all possible ways to prevent any outbreak during the forthcoming summer in order to maintain the present high efficiency of units.

      The Brigadier therefore hopes to see a very great improvement in this matter.

      It will be noted that only a proportion of men should be treated at the same time so as not to lower the fighting effectives of a Battn. in case of need. There is ample time however for a large number of men to be in inoculated before the Brigade returns to the trenches on April 21st.

Bde Hqrs.
14/4/15.

                                              Major.
                                              Bde Major
                                              20th Infantry Bde.

Headquarters.
    7th Division.

With reference to your letter No. 504/G, dated 10th April, 1915, I have to report as follows.:-

1.   Four Battalions have no information on the subject.

2.   Officer Commanding 2nd Battalion Scots Guards reports that Lieutenant Swinton, 2nd Battalion Scots Guards picked up a charger of German Cartridges in one of the enemy's trenches during the NEUVE CHAPELLE operations. These cartridges had a red edging round the cap and bore the date 1/15. It was thought that the red edging only indicated the different date, and the officer did not keep the charger. Other cartridges picked up by the Battalion were of the ordinary pattern and were dated 12/14 and 1/15, but a charger of the old pattern cartridges (round nosed) dated 5/13 was also picked up.

                        J.Wood.

Brigade Headquarters.   Lieutenant-Colonel.
                                   for Brigadier-General.
15th April, 1915.   20th Infantry Brigade.

General Staff 7th Div.504/G.

7th Division.

Forwarded. Please ascertain is there is any information available of this subject.

From samples of ammunition captured during the recent fighting at NEUVE CHAPELLE, it is probable that such bullets were being used by the Germans. It is believed that the cartridges can be identified by a red edging just round the cap on the base of the cartridge case, instead of a black edging as in the ordinary German cartridge cases

The bullet is about 1/8th of an inch longer than the ordinary German bullet and has a tapered base. The extra length of bullet, however, would probably not be evident in the cartridge, the portion of it protuding beyond the case being of the ordinary length and shape.

H.Q. IVth Corps.   (Sd) H.W. STENHOUSE. Capt. for Br.Gnl
10th April, 1915.   General Staff, IVth Corps.

--- 4 ---

20th Infantry Brigade.

Have you any information on this subject, please.

Div. H.Q.   (Sd) W.Ryan Captain for Lieut-Colonel.
10th April, 1915.   General Staff, 7th Division.

--- 5 ---

Headquarters.

Please say.

Brigade Headquarters.   Major.
                                       Brigade Major.
11th April. 1915.   20th Infantry Brigade.

C O P Y.

121/Stores/953 (F.W.4c.)

War Office, London. S.W.
31st March, 1915.

Sir,

With reference to your letter "No.1606" dated 16th March, 1915, I am commanded by the Army Council to inform you that care-ful examination of the first two plates, makes it quite clear that each of them was perforated by a single bullet, and both of them are indisputably proof at even the shortest range, against the ordinary German 7.9.m/m rifle firing a 154 grain steel covered bullet with solid lead core with a muzzle velocity of 2900 f.s.

Information has reached the Army Council that pointed bullets with tapered bases and a composite core, rear half lead, front half iron or steel, have been used by the Germans, and they will be glad of any information that may be available on this point.

So far as the Army Council are aware, the only nation using such a tapered base bullet, with a core of coloured lead, is Switzerland. It would seem likely, therefore, that the Germans are using such a bullet with a tungsten steel fore-part to the core, and a very high velocity such as 3,200 feet per second in order to penetrate our plates and shields.

The third perforated plate has been subjected to the following tests:-

(1) 5 shots close together at 30 yards range from .276" rifle — No effect.

(2) 5 shots close together from the German rifle. — Third shot caused a slight bulge at the back. Fourth shot produced a slight crack. Fifth shot penetrated flaking off a piece of the back.

(3) 12 rounds from the German rifle - six of them on to an area which could be covered by a shilling. — The twelfth shot penetrated where 5 had already struck.

(4)./

(4) One round with a special load from)
    the German rifle, giving a striking)
    velocity of 3,300 f.s. - i.e. an   ) This penetrated
    excess of 12 per cent above the   )
    normal, or 25 per cent greater   )   easily.
    striking energy.   )

The Army Council find it impossible to believe that the penetration of these plates has been caused by an ordinary German bullet, or from several shots from a Maxim grouped together, there being no signs of the inevitable stray shots, and they will be glad therefore of any information that can be supplied to them, as requested in paragraph 3.

    I am, Sir.
     Your obedient Servant.

       (Sd) J.B. CUPITT.

To/
The Field Marshal.
 Commanding-in-Chief.
  British Army in the Field.

3.

7th. Division.

Forwarded. Please ascertain if there is any information available on this subject.

From samples of ammunition captured during the recent fighting at NEUVE CHAPELLE, it is probable that such bullets were being used by the Germans. It is believed that the cartridges can be identified by a red edging just round the cap on the base of the cartridge case, instead of a black edging as in the ordinary German cartridge cases.

The bullet is about 1/8th of an inch longer than the ordinary German bullet and has a tapered base. The extra length of bullet, however, would probably not be evident in the cartridge, the portion of it protruding beyond the case being of the ordinary length and shape.

H.Q., IVth Corps,   (Sd) H.W.STENHOUSE, Capt. for Br.Genl:
10th. April, 1915.   General Staff, IVth Corps.

4.

20th Infantry Brigade.
21st Infantry Brigade.
22nd Infantry Brigade.
B.G.C., R.A.
D.A.D.O.S.

Have you any information on this subject please.

Div.H.Q.   for Lieut.Colonel,
10th. April, 1915.   General Staff, 7th. Division.

C O P Y.

Q.M.G., G.H.Q. No. Q/1606.
IVth Corps No. 491.

1st. Army.
_____

     With reference to the attached copy of War Office letter No.121/Stores/955 (F.W.4c) dated 31st March 1915, will you please say if you have any information regarding the pointed bullet said to be used by the enemy.

G.H.Q.   (Sd) H.de C.MARTELLI, Major,
7.4.15.   for Quartermaster General.

2.

Head Quarters,
     4th. Corps.
_____

                                     No.Q.1029.   8/4/15.

     Forwarded, with request that any information available on this subject may be forwarded as soon as possible.

Headquarters,   (Sd) H.C.HOLMAN, Lieut.Col:
1st. Army.   A & Q . M . G.

General Staff 7th Div. 506/G.
G.S. H.Q. 4th Corps. 561/G.

General Officer Commanding.
7th Division.

At the inspection of the grenadier company of the 20th Brigade on the 12th instant, the Corps Commander was well satisfied with the standard of efficiency that had been attained.

Some of the detachments were, of course, more efficient than others but it is evident that much time and trouble has been devoted to the training of the company in their important duties. In some cases there was room for improvement in the accuracy with which the bombs were thrown and the actual drill of the parties, which in the case of the Grenadier Guards was excellent, requires to be more practised by some of the other units. The work of the two bayonet men who lead the party is almost as important to success as that of the actual bomb throwers and too much attention cannot be paid to their drill and instruction.

In view of the very gallant action of this company at the battle of NEUVE CHAPELLE and the heavy losses that they sustained there, the question of replacing casualties is most important and in rear of each party which is working its way along a trench there should always be a second party of trained men ready to fill up the gaps that may occur in the ranks of the leading party as well as to carry a reserve of grenades to replace those which have been expended.

The Corps Commander was very well satisfied with the turnout and smartness of the Company and with the high standard of discipline which is evidently maintained.

H.Q. 4th Corps.   (Sd) A.G. Dallas. Brigadier-General.
14th April, 1915.   General Staff, 4th Corps.

C O P Y.

121/Stores/955. (F.W.40).

War Office, London, S.W.
31st. March, 1915.

Sir,

With reference to your letter "No.1606" dated 16th March,1915.

I am commanded by the Army Council to inform you that careful examination of the first two plates, makes it quite clear that each of them was perforated by a single bullet, and both of them are indisputably proof at even the shortest range, against the ordinary German 7.9 m/m rifle firing a 154 grain steel covered bullet with solid lead core with a muzzle velocity of 2900 f.s.

Information has reached the Army Council that pointed bullets with tapered bases and a composite core, rear half lead, front half iron or steel, have been used by the Germans, and they will be glad of any information that may be available on this point.

So far as the Army Council are aware, the only nation using such a tapered base bullet, with a core of coloured lead, is Switzerland. It would seem likely, therefore, that the Germans are using such a bullet with a tungsten steel fore-part to the core, and a very high velocity such as 3,200 feet per second in order to penetrate our plates and shields.

The third perforated plate has been subjected to the following tests:-

(1) 5 shots close together at 30 yards range from .276" rifle — No effect.

(2) 5 shots close together from the German rifle. — Third shot caused a slight bulge at the back. Fourth shot produced a slight crack. Fifth shot penetrated flaking off a piece of the back.

(3) 12 rounds from the German rifle - six of them on to an area which could be covered by a shilling. — The twelfth shot penetrated where five had already struck.

(4)./

(4) One round with a special load from)
 the German rifle, giving a striking)
 velocity of 3,300 f.s. - i.e. an) This penetrated
 excess of 12 per cent above the) easily.
 normal, or 25 per cent greater)
 striking energy.)

The Army Council find it impossible to believe that the penetration of these plates has been caused by an ordinary German bullet, or from several shots from a Maxim grouped together, there being no signs of the inevitable stray shots, and they will be glad therefore of any information that can be supplied to them, as requested in paragraph 3.

        I am,
           Sir,
              Your obedient Servant,

                  (Sd) J.B.CUBITT.

To/
The Field Marshal,
    Commanding-in-Chief,
        British Army in the Field.

Officer's Commanding,

    1st Battalion Grenadier Guards.
    2nd Battalion Scots Guards.
    2nd Battalion Border Regiment.
    2nd Battalion Gordon Highlanders.
    6th Battalion Gordon Highlanders.

    Please peruse the attached letter, which is to be passed quickly, initialled and finally returned to this office.

    From the 17th April, 1915, each Battalion having the use of Training Area "B" in the morning will notify Lieutenant Brownlee, No. 1. Trench Battery.

        C/o 105th Battery R.F.A.

        Square M.5.b.

of the time of reaching the Training Area in order that the Battery may practice to attack with Infantry.

                Staff Captain.
                20th Infantry Brigade.

Brigade Headquarters.
15th April, 1915.

20th Infantry Brigade.

No.1 Trench mortar battery (now in LAVENTIE) will be attached to the 20th Infantry Brigade until further orders, for training in combination with infantry.

A copy of a 1st Army letter is attached, and particular attention is called to the proviso that arrangements are to be made to enable this battery to accompany the infantry in an advance.

It is understood that various forms of transport are now being experimented with by the Officer Commanding No.1 trench battery.

Sandilands Major
for. Lieut-Colonel,

Div.H.Q.
15th. April, 1915.
General Staff, 7th.Division.

1st Army G.S.137 (G).

4th Corps.
----

1. Nos. 1 and 2 Trench Batteries (1½" mortars) and No.3 Trench Battery (4" mortars) have been issued to Corps, and it is hoped that more batteries will shortly be formed and issued as soon as the mortars and personnel become available at the Mortar School, St.VENANT.

2. Corps Commanders will take steps to have these batteries thoroughly trained not only in actual trench warfare but also offensively in co-operation with infantry in attack.

3. The mortar offers an efficient means of attacking houses and defended localities, and if properly handled in an advance will materially assist the infantry, more especially when the latter are unable to obtain effective artillery support.

4. At the present moment there is a shortage of ammunition for the mortars, but it is hoped that this will shortly be rectified. In the meantime, the opportunity exists for systematic training of these batteries in co-operation with infantry.

5. The question of mobility of the batteries arises.

It would seem that so long as the mortars and sufficient ammunition can be carried forward rapidly with the infantry for a mile or so, that is probably all that will be required. The mobility of the batteries with a view to a sustained advance involving considerable marches need not be considered.

6. No means of transport has been provided, but it is a comparatively simple matter to extemporize such transport as would be necessary for the purposes indicated above. For instance, hand carts could be obtained locally for the carriage of the mortars, or wooden stretchers suitably constructed to carry the ammunition.

7./

2.

7. Please report in due course what steps are being taken in training the batteries, and providing them with the requisite facilities to enable them to accompany the infantry in an advance.

                                                  (Sd) R. Butler, Brigadier-General,
8th April, 1915.   General Staff, 1st Army.

20th Brigade No. 20/271.

Subject.:- Use of Rabbit Wire Netting for Crossing Wire entanglements.

Headquarters.
   7th Division.

With reference to your 7/D/478, dated 5th April, 1915, reports vary greatly.

All reports state that the netting enables troops to cross both high and low entanglements. Two Commanding Officer's recommend that rolls of netting should be carried by the tropps.

One Commanding Officer suggests that the length ahould be reduced to 15 or 20 feet, in order to reduce the weight and enable the wire to be thrown with greater accuracy.

However efficacious this means of crossing wire may be, I am of opinion that owing to its weight, size, and the number of men which would necessarily have to be employed in carrying the rolls (in order to be of any value) this method is not superior to the use of wire cutters.

Wood

Brigade Headquarters.
16th April, 1915.

Lieutenant Colonel.
for Brigadier-General.
20th Infantry Brigade.

G.O.C., 7th Division.

Six copies of the attached description of a method of crossing wire entanglements, devised by the Canadian Division, are forwarded for your information.

The Lieutenant-General Commanding wishes experiments carried out on these lines and the men practised in the use of wire netting for this purpose. He wishes a report, with any remarks you may have to offer, in due course.

Copies of any instructions which may be issued to the troops regarding this method of crossing wire entanglements are not to be taken into the trenches.

H.Q.4th Corps,   Sgd.   A.G.DALLAS, Brigadier-General,
5th April,1915.   General Staff, IVth Corps.

(2).

20th Infantry Brigade.

For trial and report.

                                        Ian Stewart Major
Div. H.Q.   Lieut-Colonel,
5-4-15.   General Staff, 7th Division.

3

To 5 Bn

1. On trial & report please.
2. Rabbit wire has been demanded fr t CRE.
3. Attention is drawn to Para 3 of min 1.

                                        Major
                                        B.M.
7th April 1915.   20th Inf Bde

Use of Rabbit Wire in crossing wire entanglements.

System.

The system of crossing wire entanglements by means of rabbit wire is as follows:-

Rolls of wire netting are thrown across the obstacle and form a species of bridge over which the men following can cross. Experiments go to show that it is quite easy for men to cross in this way. The wire netting forms a convenient bridge over the space between the strands, on which the men can place their feet.

To obtain the best result it is advisable that the wire should not be cut at all. It does not matter whether the wire is taut or slack.

Size of rolls.

The length of netting will vary according to the width of obstacle to be crossed, and is limited by the amount one man can conveniently carry. 30' has been found by experiment to be the maximun an average man can carry & throw into position. This length would enable a depth of 8 yards to 9 yards to be bridged. Each length or roll has a wooden post or stay at each end to which the wire is fastened. The wire is then rolled tight thus placing one stay in the centre and one at the outside. The most suitable netting is the standard size of 2'6" or 3' wide, with a 1" mesh and made of No.16 or 18 wire.

Method of use.

On reaching the obstacle, the man carrying the roll holds it with both hands - with one hand he holds the outer stay & with the other, with a motion somewhat similar to "putting the shot" or "bowling" heaves the roll over the obstacle. By holding the outer stay the roll is thus caused to

unwind/

unwind as it flies through the air. The actual throwing requires a certain amount of practice in order to ensure its unfolding completely and reaching the other side.

The wire must be thrown in between the posts. Once it has fallen on to the entanglement it will not be possible in the heat of action to alter its position owing to the barbs on the entanglement.

Men must, therefore, be well practised in order that they can ensure throwing it accurately at the first attempt.

Types of entanglement to be crossed.

This method of crossing wire has been found most successful with the apron fence double and single, and with the chevaux de frise (the most common form used by the Germans) double and single.

With the aeroplane type of wire entanglement it has not proved successful owing to the projecting posts causing the wire to hang perpendicularly and their failing to provide a slope up which the troops can run.

From what I saw to-day with the Canadian Division, I consider this form of crossing wire entanglement, with the exception noted above, a most satisfactory method.

Its chief use appears to me to be the crossing of secondary lines of entanglements behind the first line of trenches which may be encountered by the further advance, and against which an accurate artillery fire cannot be brought to bear.

It would also be most useful in crossing the first line, should the artillery fail to cut this.

Subject:- Use of rabbit netting for crossing wire entanglements.

20/271

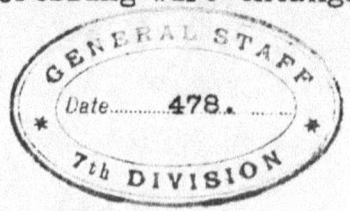

20th Infantry Brigade.

Can you now furnish the report called for in this office minute No VII D/478 dated 5th instant?

Div. H.Q.
16-4-15.

for Lieut-Colonel,
General Staff, 7th Division.

Officer Commanding,
All Battalions.

20/328

With reference to the Circular letter passed to you on the 15th April, 1915, on the subject of Trench Mortars. No. 1. Trench Mortar Battery has now been attached to the 20th Infantry Brigade, and may permanently become a unit belonging to the Brigade during the present phase of operations.

The provisional establishment of the Battery consists of 4 Guns, 1 Officer, 1 Sergeant, 4 Corporals, 12 men, 1 Batman. Probably 5 additional men will be attached.

In addition to its being thoroughly trained in trench warfare, its role will be to act offensively with Infantry in the attack.

This will entail the closest co-operation between the Battery and the Infantry.

At times when no effective artillery support can be obtained for the Infantry, and where by reason of a defended house of locality or a Battery of Machine Guns, an advance has been temporarily checked, the mortar guns if properly handled, may prove of material support.

Owing to its limited range, (a 18 lb shell ranges 326 yards, a 33 lb shell ranges 207 yards), it will be therefore necessary for the Battery to follow up the Infantry during the first phase of an attack as closely as possible.

Its means of transport is to carry the gun on one sleigh, its ammunition on another.

In order that the gun may prove tactically effective, the Brigadier wishes all Company Commanders who are daily detailed to train with the Battery not only to

co-operate with

co-operate with Lieutenant Brownlee in producing situations which may occur during an Infantry attack, but also to give the Battery the benefit of their experience as regards use of ground and cover, in order that the guns may be brought up unseen as far as is possible. The Infantry should at all times be ready to assist if necessary in the haulage of the guns.

The best method of co-operation is therefore to be thought out.

Major.

Brigade Headquarters.　　　　　　　Brigade Major.
18th April, 1915.　　　　　　　　　20th Infantry Brigade.

Officer Commanding,

Battalions.

INSPECTION.

At the Inspection of the Brigade to-morrow, 19th April, 1915, the following signals will be used by the Brigade Commander. The executive word of command being in all cases given by Officers Commanding Units.

On arrival of the Field Marshal Commanding-in-Chief on the Ground, a long drawn whistle will be the signal for the Brigade to come to attention and slope. A second long drawn whistle will then be given as the signal for the Brigade to present arms. A third long drawn whistle will afterwards be given as a signal for all units to come to the slope, order arms, and stand at ease, with the exception of the 1st Battalion Grenadier Guards, who will remain at the slope.

As the Field Marshal approaches each succeeding unit, the Battalion Commander will call his Battalion to attention and slope, on completion of the Battalion Inspection, he will order arms and stand at ease unless otherwise ordered.

As the Field Marshal finally leaves the Inspection ground, the whistle will again be blown as a signal to come to attention and slope, a further whistle being blown as a signal to present arms, a final whistle will be blown as a signal to slope, order arms and stand at ease.

1st whistle.	Attention and slope arms.
2nd Whistle.	General Salute - Present Arms.
3rd Whistle.	Slope Arms, order arms and stand at ease, except 1st Battalion Grenadier Guards, who will remain at the slope.
4th Whistle.	Attention and slope arms.
5th Whistle.	General Salute - Present Arms.
6th Whistle.	Slope arms, order arms and stand at ease.

2. All Officers will take post in front of their companies during the inspection.

3. All troops will be in marching order.

A rehearsal of the above will take place on the Ground as soon as the Brigade is formed up.

April 18/15

Major.
Brigade Major.
20th Infantry Brigade.

H.Q.4th Corps No.553 (G).

To 20th Bde
for information

Head Quarters,

7th. Division.

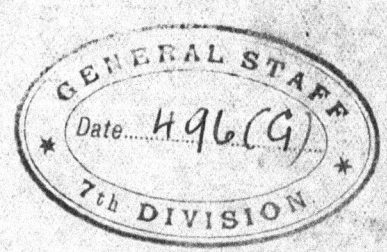

The attached programme of inspections by the Field Marshal Commanding-in-Chief, received from Army Head Quarters this morning, is forwarded for your information.

Battalions should be drawn up in three sides of a square in such a manner that, if possible, the Commander-in-Chief can address them down-wind and from a slightly elevated position.

(Sd) A.G.DALLAS, Brigadier-General,

13th. April, 1915.   General Staff, IVth. Corps.

Programme of Inspections by Commander-in-Chief.

Date.	Formation to be inspected.	Place.	Time.	C-in-C to be met at.
Monday, 19th April.	20th Infantry Bde.	Square G.26.b. south of Fme DE LA BRETAGNE.	2.30.p.m.	Eastern exit from ESTAIRES square G.25.a.c.
Wednesday, 21st April.	22nd Infantry Bde.	Square G.26.b. South of Fme DE LA BRETAGNE.	3.30.p.m.	An officer of the IVth Corps will be at BAC ST.MAUR at 2.30.p.m. ready to guide the C-in-C to Fme DE LA BRETAGNE.

Headquarters.

---

1.   With reference to my B.M. 71. dated 9th April, 1915, regarding the Inspection of the Brigade by the Commander-in-Chief on Monday, April, 19th, near LA GORGUE at 2.30 p.m., will you kindly inform me as early as possible the number of yards frontage required by the Battalion under your Command when formed up in mass forming 3 sides of a square with two companies in the centre and one company on each flank.

Distance in yards required from "A" to "B".

2.   Adjutants, Sergeant-Majors, and left markers of each company will meet the Brigade Major at 2.30 p.m. on Saturday, April 17th on the ground, Square G.26.b. South of FERME de la BRETAGNE.

                                    Major.
Brigade Headquarters.   Brigade Major.
15th April, 1915.   20th Infantry Brigade.

Hd.Qrs.4th.Corps No.553 (G).

7th. Division.
───────────

In continuation of IVth Corps No.553 (G) dated 8th. instant, and the Field-Marshal Commanding-in-Chief's forthcoming inspection of brigades of the 7th and 8th Divisions, an amended programme is forwarded herewith.

Please acknowledge by telegram and confirm the arrangements made by telephone.

H.Q.IVth Corps,　　　　　　(Sd) A.G.DALLAS, Brigadier-General,
10th. April, 1915.　　　　　　　General Staff, IVth Corps.

2.

20th Infantry Brigade.
~~21st Infantry Brigade.~~
~~22nd Infantry Brigade.~~
────────────────────

For your information.

Div.H.Q.　　　　　　　　　　　　Ian Stewart Major
10th. April, 1915.　　　　　　　for Lieut.Colonel,
　　　　　　　　　　　　　　　General Staff, 7th. Division.

INSPECTION OF INFANTRY BRIGADES OF THE IVth CORPS
BY THE FIELD-MARSHAL COMMANDING-IN-CHIEF.

APRIL.

Monday, 12th.
    23rd Brigade.   ...   BAC ST. MAUR at 2.30.p.m.
    21st Brigade.   ...   LA GORGUE at 4.p.m.

Saturday, 17th.
    25th Brigade.   ...   BAC ST. MAUR at 2.30.p.m.

Monday, 19th.
    20th Brigade.   ...   near LA GORGUE at 2.30.p.m.

Wednesday, 21st.
    24th Brigade.   ...   BAC ST. MAUR at 2.30.p.m.
    22nd Brigade.   ...   near LA GORGUE at 4.p.m.

SECRET.

20th. Infantry Brigade.
~~21st. Infantry Brigade.~~
~~22nd. Infantry Brigade.~~

The attached Memorandum, 7th.Division No.Op/1/32 is forwarded for your information.

Div.Hd.Qrs.
20th. April, 1915.

Lieut-Colonel,
General Staff, 7th. Division.

2

Hᵈqʳˢ 1st Bn Grenadier Guards *Charles Corkran*
  "   2nd Bn Scots Guards *A B F Later*
  "   2nd Bn Border Regt *Cmt*
  "   2nd Bn Gordon Highlanders *A Wood*
  "   6th Bn Gordon Highlanders *S.J.R.*

Please note, circulate, pass quickly
& finally return

Ernest Austen
Major
Brig.-Major
20th Infantry Brigade

21/4/15

S E C R E T.

Headquarters, Meerut Divn.
19th April, 1915.

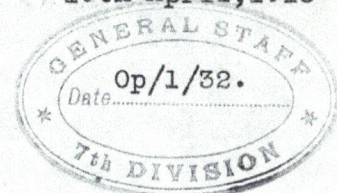

Op/1/32.

7th Division.

Memorandum.

      In order to mark advanced troops' furthest limits during an action, distinguishing flags - 3' x 3' on 9' or 10' poles, have been made up for the Meerut Divn,
These are red and black divided diagonally, and with a white diagonal cross.

                              Sd/ C. Norie, Colonel,
                                     General Staff,
                         Meerut Division.

Copy for information to :-

    Indian Corps.
    Dehra Dun Bde.
    Garhwal Bde.
    Bareilly Bde.

SECRET.

20TH INFANTRY BRIGADE.
7TH DIVISION.

      A draft copy of Operation Orders and a draft copy of Infantry Instructions is forwarded herewith, which should be carefully studied before the Conference to be held at 10-0 a.m. on Friday next.

      The contents of this paper should be known only to those whom it is absolutely necessary to acquaint with the details.

F. Gathorne Hardy

7th Div H.Q.
April 21st 1915.

Lt. Colonel.
General Staff. 7th Div.

DRAFT.   SECRET.

No orders or sketches, giving information to the enemy, are to be taken into the Field.

References are to Maps (Reduction) AUBERS and BAS MAISNIL FROMELLES, 1/10,000 and to the 1/40,000 map.

----

1.   INFORMATION.
     (a) General.

     (b) Local.

2. INTENTION.

The first army will operate so as to break through the enemy's line and gain the LA BASSEE - LILLE road between LA BASSEE and FOURNES; and then advance on DON.

The 1st Corps and INdian Corps will operate south of the BOIS DE BIEZ, the Indian Corps on the left of this attack will eventually join hands withthe 4th Corps in the neighbourhood of LA CLIQUETERIE FARM.

The 4th Corps will break the enemy's line about ROUGE BANCS, from a defensive flank in the vicinity of LA CORDONNERIE FARM and FROMELLES and turn the AUBERS defences from the north east. The subsequent advance will be directed on LA CLIQUETERIE FARM, with a view to effecting a junction with the Indian Corps.

The task allotted to the 4th Corps will be carried out by the 7th Division (less two battalions) and the 8th Division, the defensive line being taken over by the West Riding Division, reinforced by two battalions of the 7th Division.

The 8th Division will :-

(i). Break the line on the front (351) - ROUGES BANCS - (828)

(ii). Extend to (349) - DELEVAL FARM on the right (and if possible the salient at (371) and to LA BIETTE - (832) on the left.

(iii). Capture FROMELLES.

As soon as the second task of the 8th Division has been accomplished the 7th Division will advance through the right of the gap made by the 8th Division and move on LECLERQ FARM (709) with a view to attacking AUBERS from the north-east.

3. General Plan.

To carry out its task the 7th Division will be formed up in dug-outs as follows :-

Advanced Guard.

Commander. Brigadier General S.T.B.Lawford, C.B.

22nd Infantry Brigade.)
54th Field Coy. R.E.) In square N.2.a.

3 Troops Northumberland Hussars in square G.23.c.

2 R.H.A. guns, who will be in action in square   until required by Advanced Guard Commander.

Supporting Column.

Commander. Brigadier General F.J.Heyworth, D.S.O.

20th Infantry Brigade.)
55th Field Coy. R.E.) In square N.1.b & d.

Reserve.

Commander.

21st Infantry Brigade,)
(less two battalions).) In square G.36.b.
Highland Field Coy.R.E.)

As the 8th Division vacate their dug-outs in the RUE DU BOIS and RUE PETILLON, these will be occupied by the Advanced Guard of the 7th Division.

When the 8th Division has occupied the line Fe DELEVAL - (349)- LA BIETTE - (832), the Advanced Guard will commence its advance on to the line (292) - (709) - (710) simultaneously with the advance of the 8th Division on FROMELLES, detaching one battalion to occupy the RUE DELEVAL from (300) to (292). Immediately the line (292) - (709) - (710) is occupied, (700), (698), (712), (758) should also be seized, this line prepared to resist attack from the S.E. and preparations made for attacking AUBERS from the north east.

The Support and Reserve Columns will be moved forward as required under Divisional orders.

The/

The present line will be held by the 1st West Riding Infantry Brigade, reinforced by two battalions of the 21st Brigade, the whole under the command of

The reserve battalion of this force should be in M.10.a.

4. **Artillery**.

The artillery of the Corps, and the attached artillery, will, under the orders of the Brigadier-General Commanding Royal Artillery, 8th Division, be at the disposal of the 8th Division until their second objective has been reached. Subsequent to that it will assist the advance of the 7th Division on AUBERS and the 8th Division on FROMELLES, as shown in the attached artillery table.

Should any of the 13 or 18 pounders belonging to the seventh Division be moved forward to support that Division, they will then pass under the command of the G.O.C.7th Division.

5. The Mobile Machine Gun Section will be in position in square G.29.b.

6. Time Table.

The date and hour for the commencement of the operations will be notified later, but the following time table will hold good :-

By 4.a.m. everyone is to be in position, and everything to be quiet and normal.

0.0. Artillery bombardment commences.
0.40. Infantry advance of 8th Division commences.

7. <u>March table.</u>   *N. Brigade*

Troops will move to their assembly positions according to the attached march tables.

Roads must be cleared as rapidly as possible for the passage of the troops.

8. Dress and Equipment.

Troops will not wear packs or great coats. They will carry not less than 200 rounds of ammunition.

Every man will carry one day's preserved rations besides the remainder of the current day's issue.

9. Depots.

Depots of food, ammunition, and engineer material will be formed as follows :-

Rations.

8,000 rations in a farm just East of the cross roads in M.17.c.

4,000 rations earthworks F 2, and F 3 (half in each).

Small Arm Ammunition.

200,000 rounds in E 4.

1,300,000 rounds in M.17.c.2.1.

400,000 rounds in dug-outs 100 yards N. of the road junction RUE MASSELOT - RUE TILLELOY.

200,000 rounds in each of F 2 and F 3.

Water.

Four water carts will be   after dark.

Engineer material.

10. Transport.

All 1st line transport not absolutely necessary will be kept N. of LAVENTIE Station.

22nd Brigade in G.34.a.

20th Brigade in G.33.d.

21st Brigade in G.33.b.

1st West Riding Brigade in G.33.a.

Small Arm Ammunition carts will be formed up as follows:-

22nd Brigade.)
20th Brigade.)   in G.30.c.
21st Brigade.)

1st West Riding Brigade as required by their G.O.C.

Brigade Ammunition Columns.

14th H.A.Brigade Ammunition Column in
    Supplies S.A.A. to 20th Infantry Brigade.

22nd F.A.Brigade Ammunition Column in
    Supplies S.A.A. to 21st Infantry Brigade.

35th F.A.Brigade Ammunition Column in
    Supplies S.A.A. to 22nd Infantry Brigade.

2nd West Riding Ammunition Column

11. Maps.

The maps to be used are AUBERS (reduction) and BAS MASNIL and FROMELLES. (1/10,000).

All officers and senior N.C.O's must be in possession of these maps and carry them in the field.

All reports are to be made with reference to this map.

For places off this map the 1/40,000 map is to be used.

12. <u>Medical.</u>

Advanced dressing stations will be established at

13. <u>Prisoners.</u>

A prisoner of war collecting station will be established at LAVENTIE Station.

14. <u>Road traffic.</u>

A map showing road control is attached.

15. <u>Headquarters.</u>

Divisional Headquarters will be in a house on the RUE DU QUESNES in H.31.d.

S E C R E T.

Special Instructions for the Infantry.

The general idea of this operation is that the 8th Division should make a gap and subsequently enlarge it. and that then the 7th Division should move rapidly through the gap and advance on LE CLERCQ Fe and AUBERS while the 8th Division attack FROMELLES.

The underlying principle of this movement is that the advance should be rapid and that every tactical feature - even if it be in front of the given objective - that can be taken, should be at once seized and placed in a state of defence.

Rapidity will be gained and loss of life avoided. if these points can be determined in advance.

The advance will not commence until the 8th Division have occupied the line Fe DELEVAL - 349 - LA BIETTE - 832.

The 8th Division may also capture the cluster of houses at 295; if not, this will be the first tactical point in the way of the 7th Division.

Subsequent to this the first objective will be LE CLERCQ Fe and the line of trenches in its vicinity for the capture of which the whole Division will be employed if necessary.

Further moves must depend on the dispositions of the enemy. but the principle should be to gain ground in the direction of LE PLOUICH and LA CLIQUETERIE. rather than to lose time and suffer heavy loss in an attack on AUBERS which must fall if the other operations of the 1st Army are successful.

At the same time the approaches to AUBERS should be reconnoitred with a view to its attack and any houses which can be occupied seized without delay.

In fact the guiding principle is to seize every point to the south and south east which can be occupied.

This move should be carried out by the Advance Guard, who will be reinforced by the Divisional Squadron. 2 guns and the Mobile Machine Gun Section. if the roads become in any way possible.

Under cover of this advance. the Supporting Column will be pushed forward to assist the advanced guard if necessary. to complete the occupation of AUBERS, and to push on towards LA CLIQUETERIE.

To assist officers in finding their direction during this advance a table showing the compass direction of various points is attached.

It should be noted that the bearings are magnetic, calculated with the variation of 13 56" degrees.

It is impossible to accurately time table this move but the following time table has been given to the artillery and, if possible, should be adhered to by the infantry.

0.0. to 0.15.	Wire cutting.
0.10 to 0.40.	Bombardment of enemy's trenches.
0.40.	Infantry of 8th Division attack.
0.50.	Secondary attack of 8th Division on 372 launched.
1.25.	Leading troops of 7th Division advance.
1.50.	Leading troops of 7th Division reach 295.
2.	Leading troops of 7th Division reach 291- 292 - 760.
2-10	Leading troops of 7th Division reach 709-710.

During this advance the Infantry will be closely supported by and covered by barrages of artillery, and the heavy artillery will be bombarding all the points of tactical strength.

Secret

20th. Infantry Brigade.
21st. Infantry Brigade.
22nd. Infantry Brigade.
1st. West Riding Brigade.

Attached instructions are forwarded for your guidance. Detailed arrangements as regards the relief should be made direct between Brigadiers concerned.

Div.Hd.Qrs.
22nd. April, 1915.

Lieut-Colonel,
General Staff, 7th. Division.

SECRET.

Instructions as to the relief of the 22nd and 20th Infantry Brigades by the 1st West Riding and 21st Infantry Brigades during the period night 24th/25th - 27th/28th April.

----

1. By 8.a.m. on the morning of the 28th instant, the line which is now held by the BAREILLY Brigade, as well as that now held by the 20th. Infantry Brigade will be occupied by the 1st West Riding Brigade and two battalions of the 21st. Infantry Brigade.

2. This line will be divided into two sections.
The right, or BAREILLY section, will be held by three battalions of the 1st West Riding Brigade, and half a battalion of the 21st. Infantry Brigade, under the command of G.O.C. 1st West Riding Brigade. The left, or 20th Brigade section, will be held by one battalion of the 1st West Riding Brigade on the right, and one and a half battalions of the 21st Infantry Brigade, the whole under the command of G.O.C. 21st Infantry Brigade.

3. (a). BAREILLY Front.
On the night 24th/25th April the 22nd Infantry Brigade will take over part of the line with the 2/Queens and 1/S.Stafford Regiments. One platoon in each company of those battalions will be found by the 1st West Riding Brigade and will go into the trenches with them.
This move should clear the RUE DU BACQUEROT by 9.30.p.m. for the movement of other troops.
On the night 25th/26th April the remainder of the BAREILLY front will be taken over by the 2/Warwicks and 2 companies 1/R.W.Fusiliers. On this night 2 platoons per company of the 2/Warwicks will be found by the 1st West Riding Brigade, which will also put in a second platoon in each company of the 2/Queens and 1/S.Staffords.
Thus during the night 25th/26th each company of the 2/Queens, 1/South Staffords, 2/Warwicks will consist of two regular platoons and 2 platoons of the 1st West Riding Brigade.
On the night 26th/27th April a third platoon of the 1st West Riding Brigade will be substituted for a regular platoon in each company of the Queens, 1/S.Staffords and 2/Warwicks.
On the night 27th/28th April the remaining regular platoons of the 2/Queens, 1/S.Staffords and 2/R.Warwicks will be relieved by platoons of the 1st West Riding Brigade..
On the same night the 2 companies 1/R.W.Fusiliers will be replaced by ½ battalion from the 21st Brigade.

(b). 20th Brigade Front.
On the night 24th/25th April the 2/Border Regiment relieves the 2/Scots Guards and will take in with it 1 platoon from 1st West Riding Brigade with each company.
Similarly on each of the nights 25th/26th, 26th/27th, 27th/28th - 1 platoon 1st West Riding Brigade will be substituted for 1 regular platoon in each company, so that by the morning of the 28th instant the 2/Border Regiment will be entirely relieved by a battalion of the 1st West Riding Brigade.
On the night 27th/28th - the remaining 1½ battalions of the 20th. Brigade will be relieved by 1½ battalions of 21st Brigade, the half battalion being of the same regiment as that placed on the left of the BAREILLY front.

P.T.O.

4. The Command of sections, battalions and companies will remain in the hands of the officers of the 20th and 22nd Infantry Brigades until the relief is completed, irrespective of rank.

5. The 21st Infantry Brigade will form the reserve to both sections, and one and a half battalions of this brigade will be billeted about L'EPINETTE and PONT DU HEM.
Officers must ascertain the best routes of approach to the BAREILLY front.

6. No trouble must be spared to acquaint all ranks of the 1st West Riding Brigade with every detail of trench life, lines of approach, positions of defended points, hostile positions, etc.

Div. Hd. Qrs.

22nd. April, 1915.

F. GATHORNE HARDY, Lieut-Colonel

General Staff, 7th. Division.

To G.O.C. 20th Brigade
From O.C. 6th Gordon High[landers]
10-4-15

I send herewith a description of experiments made in the throwing of written messages; to be forwarded if G.O.C. deems expedient.

The D.A.Q.M.G. could, perhaps, give information as to whether the "Very" pistol would stand an increased charge, as if it would message might be thrown for some 300 – 400 yards

G. [signature]
commanding
6th Bn Gordon Highlanders

85

To G.O.C 20th Guards Brigade
From O.C 6th 8th Gordon Highlanders
10th April 1915

EXPERIMENT IN COMMUNICATION IN THE FIELD

1.) In accordance with the Divl. order to establish and contrive devices for the passing of messages under fire,
   I ordered experiments to be carried out with a VERY PISTOL

2.) Written messages can be thrown from these pistols up to a distance of about 200 yards in moderate weather

3.) Accuracy as to "line" and "range" is fairly good and consistent With practice a message could be thrown by a pistol to within about 10 yards of a given spot whence it would have to be retrieved by the man waiting for it

This distance (200 yards) is about that between successive lines in the attack.

4) <u>Methods of loading</u>

Before starting the cardboard disc and the wad are withdrawn by a cork screw and the the canister containing the blue flare powder is emptied out of it.

The back of the now empty canister is filled with mud or clay to obtain the necessary weight. Several cartridges should be prepared in this way and carried for use.

To Five

Place written message in canmister. Replace cannister in cartridge – re-insert wad and card board disc and ram them home.
Then fire pistol in ordenary way
A ribbon tail can be used for visibility

Time required

With cartridges ready for use as described the charging of them with the message and loading of the pistol should be performed in 20 seconds.

G. C. G. Moss
Capt
Grenadier Guards
Commanding 6th Bn Gordon Highlrs

XX'th Brigade

In reference to 7th Div No 7/0/500
I think the suggestion is practical
and might be of value.
The difficulty of communication
however has not been found
so much in the scarcity of
officers or men able to send
messages, as in the impossibility
of men exposing themselves
sufficiently to ~~send~~ enable
the messages to be read.
A system of transmitting messages
by means of discs is being
tried in this Battn, the discs
being of blue cardboard with
white bands across them.

10-4-15   EC Warner Capt
             A/Adj 2nd Scot ffs

Headquarters
20th Infantry Brigade.

Reference your no. 20/288 of 9/4/15.
I consider that the suggestion is quite practical, and likely to be of great use. I suggest that Officers must clearly understand that no messages should be passed outside the unit except through the Officer Commanding that unit.

Also that two messages informing the Artillery to fire more to the right and more to the left be included.

J. Hamilton Maj.
5/Gordon Highlanders.

10/4/15.

Quarters
20th Brigade

ORDERLY ROOM No. B/55 2nd Bn THE BORDER REGIMENT

Reference your letter
No. 20/288 I beg to report that I consider that signal communication by a simple code as suggested in 7th Division letter No. 7/D/500 might be useful in certain situations but on the other hand it might be very liable to be misread which would be more dangerous than having no code at all.

11th April 1915

L Wood
Lieut. Colonel,
Commanding 2nd Bn The Border Regt.

Headquarters
20th Brigade -

I certainly think something can be done on these lines, but suggest that messages be confined to information as to actual position of companies & as to touch with neighbouring troops

E.g. Coy No 4. at N14
In touch with No 1 at O14

Chichester
a/st for Lieut Col
Commdg 1st Battalion Grenadier Guards

13/4/15

Diagram A.
Showing gradual relief of 1 Battalion
W. Riding by 1 Battalion W.R. Bde.

```
         1 Coy.    1 Coy.    1 Coy.    1 Coy.
24/25    ─────────────────────────────────────
25/26    ─────────────────────────────────────
26/27    ─────────────────────────────────────
27/28    ─────────────────────────────────────
                        } 1 Bn.
```

— 1 Platoon 7th D.W. Bn.
— 1 Platoon West Riding Bn.

Diagram B.
Showing gradual introduction of whole of West Riding Brigade into the Defensive line.

BAREILLY BRIGADE

```
          7th Dn.   ½ Bn.   1 Bn.    ½ Bn.   1 Bn.   1 Bn.    1 Bn.
          1 Bn.    ½ Bn.   1 Bn.    ½ Bn.   1 Bn.   1 Bn.    1 Bn.
         2nd Goorkas  1/6 Gurkhas Indians  4 R.W.F. R.W.R. S.Staffs Puseas
24/25    ───────────────────────────────────────────────────────────────
25/26    ───────────────────────────────────────────────────────────────
26/27    ───────────────────────────────────────────────────────────────
                           2 W.R.
27/28    ───────────────────────────────────────────────────────────────
          2nd D.O.F
```

— 4 Platoons 7th D.W. Bn.
— 4 Platoons W.R. Bn.

SECRET   No: 7.D.A./C/521

ORGANISATION OF ARTILLERY FOR DEFENCE
7th DIVISION

General Staff — Date: 0p/65 — 7th Division

1. From 6 a.m. 25th April, the artillery then at the disposal of G.O.C. 7th Division for defence will be grouped and addressed as under with regard to all matters relating to defence.

R.A. RIGHT GROUP.   N° 1 Section. Infantry.

    Commander - Lt. Col. G.H.W. Nicholson,
                Commanding 35th Brigade, R.F.A.
    "U" Battery, R.H.A.
    12th & 25th Batteries, R.F.A. each less 1 section.
    2nd West Riding Brigade, R.F.A.(T.F.).

R.A. LEFT GROUP.   N° 2 Section. Infantry.

    Commander - Lt. Col. E.W. Alexander, V.C.,
                Commanding 22nd Brigade, R.F.A.
    14th Brigade, R.H.A.
    22nd Brigade, R.F.A.

2. This office Secret No: 7.D.A./C/516, dated 22/4/15 is cancelled.

24th April, 1915.
                                        Major, R.A.
                   Brigade Major, 7th Divisional Artillery.

SECRET.

No. 7.D.A./C/520.

Copy No. 9

INSTRUCTIONS FOR THE ARTILLERY SUPPORT OF THE DEFENCE.

1. This office No.7.D.A./C/515, dated 22/4/15, is cancelled.

2. The 22nd Brigade, R.F.A., assisted by 14th Brigade, R.H.A. will continue to support the left half of the line held by 7th Division as follows :-

   (a) Till 6 a.m. 25th April from a point opposite the junction of the RUE MASSELOT with the RUE TILLELOY, as at present.

   (b) From 6 a.m. 25th April onwards, from Point 274 to the left of 7th Division in N.8.c.

   O.C. 22nd Brigade, R.F.A. will direct O.C. 14th Brigade, R.H.A. as to what front he requires his two batteries to cover.

3. At 6 a.m. on 25th April, O.C. 35th Brigade, R.F.A. will take over from O.C. 9th Brigade, R.F.A.(MEERUT) Division the responsibility for covering the line held by the BAREILLY BRIGADE from the road at M.35.d.4.8. to CHAPIGNY. He will establish communication with B.G.C. BAREILLY Brigade at M.14.b.9.1.
   He will also be responsible for covering the right of the 7th Division from CHAPIGNY to Point 274.
   For these purposes he will have at his disposal :-
   28th Battery, R.F.A.(9th Brigade, R.F.A.).
   "U", 12th & 25th Batteries, each less 1 Section.
   2nd West Riding Brigade, R.F.A.

4. At 10 p.m. on 25th April -

   (a) The 28th Battery, R.F.A. will be withdrawn.

   (b) B.G.C. 22nd Infantry Brigade assumes ~~responsibility for~~ command of the line Road at M.35.d.4.8. - CHAPIGNY.

   (c) O.C. 35th Brigade will assume responsibility for supporting the right of the 7th Division from Road at M.35.d.4.8. - Point 274, having at his disposal :-
   "U", 12th & 25th Batteries, each less 1 Section.
   2nd West Riding Brigade, R.F.A.

5. O.C. 35th Brigade, R.F.A. will, from 6 a.m. on 25th April, direct O.C. 2nd West Riding Brigade, R.F.A. as to what front he requires his batteries to cover.

6. O.C. 4th Brigade, R.F.A. (MEERUT Division) is arranging to establish telephonic communication between his 44th Battery M.26.a.8.9. and the 6th West Riding Battery M.21.a.5.3.

7. In the event of emergency, the 57th Howitzer Battery at M.21.c.9.4. can be called upon to assist by fire.
   O.C. 2nd West Riding Brigade will arrange to establish telephonic communication with this Battery.

24th April, 1915.

Major, R.A.,
Brigade Major, 7 AC

Officer Commanding.
   All Battalions.

In consequence of the inability of getting in touch at once with Headquarters of Battalions last night about the time Battalions were relieving each other in the Trenches, the following procedure will be adhered to in future as long as the Brigade is not on the march.

1. Headquarters of Battalions, to which reports can be sent either by wire or by messenger, will never be closed, for example, if a Battalion is being relieved in the Trenches at 9 p.m., the Officer Commanding will inform Brigade Headquarters the time at which his Head Quarters will close in the Trenches, notifying at the same time the locality of his new Headquarters. These will be opened at the same time as the old Headquarters are closed.

2. Officers Commanding will be responsible that he, his Adjutant or a responsible Officer are always at Battalion Headquarters in case it is necessary to communicate with them in a hurry. In order to carry out the instructions of para 1. above, an officer will be ~~directed~~ _deputed_ to go forward to the new Headquarters in time to reach there before the old Headquarters are closed.

M.
Major.

Brigade Headquarters.   Brigade Major.
25th April, 1915.   20th Infantry Brigade.

To From

HEADQUARTERS,
20th INFANTRY BRIGADE.

Genl Hezworth

London Kindly arrange orders (1 pr platoon)
to take the 1st Bn Irish Rifles into the left
of F. lines, left at the road junction N.6.
d.5.5. at 8.30 pm.

Similarly orders for 2 Co 1st London Reg to
be cross roads N. 12. C. 2.3 at 8.30 pm.

Therefore have the 1st Bn Irish Rifles showed
into the portion of the line from N. 8 to
N. 13 & the 1st London continues to E
lines.

The C.O. & Co. Comdrs will be at Som

Hd Qrs LAVENTIE at 3 pm today. Will
you very kindly let them have orders to take

been out this Tuesday –
So sorry not to find you in –

Yrs sincerely
Anthony Eden –

Confidential

20TH INFANTRY BRIGADE.

The following is a summary of the arrangements made verbally with the Staff of the 8th Division, regarding the relief of 'E' and 'F' lines by the 25th Infantry Brigade:-

1. (a) On the 27th instant, the relieving troops will rendezvous at 8-30 pm at the road junction M.6.d.central. The 20th Brigade will have guides at this place and hour to conduct the units of the 8th Division (Royal Irish Rifles and ½ Battalion 1st London Regiment) into the trenches.

    (b) On the 28th instant, the relieving troops of the 8th Division (One Battalion) will rendezvous at the road junction M.5.d. at 8-0 pm, at which place and hour the 20th Brigade will supply guides as above.

2. The B.G.C. 20th Brigade will retain command of 'E' and 'F' lines until 10-0 pm, 28th instant, at which hour he will hand over to the B.G.C. 25th Infantry Brigade.

3. Reserves of S.A.A. in the trenches together with R.E. Stores such as Sand bags, Wire etc., will be left for the 8th Division. All other trench equipment, e.g. Periscopes, Very's Lights etc., will be taken out.

4. Question of the removal of the contents of Forward Depots of Supplies, Ammunition, and R.E. Stores will be settled later.

5. Working Parties for the 173rd Mining Company, R.E. will be found by troops of the 7th Division until 4 a.m. 28th inch after which hour the responsibility for the operations of this Company will devolve on the 8th Division.

7th Div. H.Q.,
April 27th 1915.

for Lt. Colonel.
General Staff, 7th Div.

Confidential

20TH INFANTRY BRIGADE.
21ST INFANTRY BRIGADE.
22ND INFANTRY BRIGADE.
1ST WEST RIDING BRIGADE.
B. G. C. R. A.

In continuation of previous correspondence, the Indian line which we are about to take over will in future be described as follows:-

'E' and 'F' sub-sections ~~called No 1. section on our map~~ will in future be known as 'C' section.

'G' and 'H' sub-sections ~~called No 2. section on our map~~ will in future be known as 'D' section.

The following permanent garrisons will be required for the various fortified posts and will be found from the troops holding the line:-

D.R. and D.S. One Company in each, a portion of whom may be billetted in the farms in the immediate vicinity.

C. 2. 3. & 5. 30 men.

C. 4. 15 men.

A large amount of work is still required to put these fortified posts into a suitable state, and this work should at once be taken in hand by troops holding them, a great deal of it could be done in the daytime. The necessary stores should be drawn from the R.E.

Care in working at post P/5. should be taken to avoid observation, as it is used by several batteries of Artillery as an Observation Station.

The O.C. 20th Brigade should establish and Advanced Report Centre in the neighbourhood of the RUE DE BACQUEROT, which should be at once occupied in case of alarm, and will be available for future Brigadiers on taking over the line.

7th Div H.Q.,
April 27th 1915.

Lt. Colonel.

20th Infantry Brigade.
~~21st Infantry Brigade.~~
22nd Infantry Brigade.
B.G.C., R.A.

The following points came to the notice of the Divisional Commander during the march today. It is of the utmost importance that the vitality of the men should be preserved for fighting, and it is only by attention to all details that good results can be attained.

1. One Brigade marched in file. This is no doubt conducive to the comfort of the men, which consideration the Divisional Commander will always bear in mind, but as all staff calculations are based on the Infantry being in fours, this practice must not continue without a distinct Divisional order. Today the troops in rear were in consequence put to great inconvenience.

2. There was a great number of men falling out during the march and apparently no adequate Brigade arrangements to deal with this. In future each Battalion should have a senior N.C.O. behind and each Brigade 1 officer to collect stragglers and bring them on together at the pace of the slowest.

3. The pack is made so that it can be easily thrown off at a halt and officers must see that at every 10 minutes or longer halt the men remove their packs.

4. Sufficient care was not taken to ensure that the hourly halts should take place simultaneously all down the column. The Standing Order on this subject is to be brought to the notice of all ranks, and strictly complied with, namely, that the column halts at 10 minutes to the hour and march off again at the hour, irrespective of the time at which the march commences.

5. Many/

5. Many men were carrying 220 rounds of ammunition and the majority carried more than the 120 which experience has proved to be the maximum that can be carried on the march, though it may often be necessary to serve out extra rounds before going into action.

F. Galhoone Hardy
Lieut-Colonel,

Div.Hd.Qrs.
28th. April, 1915.
General Staff, 7th. Division.

2/Bns   20/399

In necessary action when the Bttn is on the march.

29/4/15

BM/20/400

Officer Commanding
    All Battalions.
----

1.   The attached paper handed over by the BAREILLY
BRIGADE is forwarded for information and necessary action
as regards the works in the lines at present held by the
20th Infantry Brigade.

2.   Written in pencil are remarks made by the
Brigade Major when handing over.

        Their accuracy is not vouched for.

                                            M

                                            Major.
Brigade Headquarters.   Brigade Major.
29th April, 1915.   20th Infantry Brigade.

NB.

(a) There are a good number of "aeroplanes"
in front of the Home Counties Trench, these can
be removed to the front line & replaced
by ordinary wire.

(b) Under the "aeroplanes" in M 23 a near the
Sewbrigade HQrs, the RE are making
them in Sinkhole Post M 29 c a at
CHAPIGNY

WORKS BEING DONE.

"E" Subsection.

(a) New Communication trench in Right flank from support line to firing line. FINISHED

(b) Construction of Traverses and Parados of Advanced Posts. FINISHED

(c) Construction of bomb-proofs in firing line.

(d) Improvement of Parados in Firing Line.

"F" Subsection.

(a) Putting left communication trench into a proper state of fitness for use. FINISHED

(b) Construction of bomb-proofs in firing line and strengthening of wire.

(c) Improvement of parapets of support trenches and construction of bomb-proofs.

"G" Subsection.

(a) Making parapet bullet-proof and/adding loopholes. Strengthening wire. FINISHED

(b) Construction of Parados of Firing Line.

(c) Construction of Bomb-proof of firing line.

(d) Opening up Right Communication trench (passes via MOATED GRANGE.) FINISHED

"H" Subsection.

(a) Completion of new breastwork across Reentrant. Making parapet bullet-proof, wiring the front. Construction of parados, traverses and firing step. Over half of this is ready now and ¾ should be finished by to-morrow night. REQUIRES COMPLETION

(b) Heightening parados of left section. FINISHED

(c) Adding loopholes. FINISHED

(d) Improvement of communication trench. The above are in hand at present. NOT FINISHED

When these are completed the next works to be taken in hand are :-

hand are.:-

"E" Subsection.

(a) Construction of support trenches across SUNKEN road. FINISHED

(b) Improvement of HOME COUNTIES Breastwork, loopholes, firing step, and parados and bomb-proofs to be added. BEGUN

"F" Subsection.

(a) Support trench to be made, continuation up to Right Communication Trench of Section on left. BEGUN

(b) Work on HOME COUNTIES breastwork continued towards MOATED GRANGE, and to be made into a really good fire trench with Traverses, Parados, loopholes and bomb-proofs added. BEGUN

"G" Subsection.

(a) Construction of support lines closer up to firing line.

(b) Improvement of old British Line breastwork into a proper defensible position and to be provided with traverses, parados, Loopholes and Bomb-proofs.

(c) Drainage of ditches behind the firing line. DIFFICULT

"H" Subsection.

(a) Construction of a second communication trench leading up to left of subsection.

(b) Construction of proper supporting trenches behind centre and left.

-----ooooooOOOOOooooo-----

SUBJECT.

General instruction for writing of books

Contents.	Date.

www.ingramcontent.com/pod-product-compliance
Lightning Source LLC
Chambersburg PA
CBHW081434300426
44108CB00016BA/2364